Do You Speak

Mode

Airplane ?

the
story
of
aeromodeling
in
America

BROWN JR. MODEL D, 1938

by Dave Thornburg

dedication

*Over the years, some 10 to 12 million Americans have
participated in the hobby-sport-science that is
aeromodeling.*
*Senators and astronauts and movie stars, captains of
industry and everyday people have all come together
at flying field and hobby shop and club meeting
to speak the curious language of modeling—to share
with one another the purely personal thrill that comes
from creating things that fly.*
No one has ever captured that thrill in words.
*But one man, in fifty years of writing, has come closer
than anyone else.*
Bill Winter, this book's for you.

contents

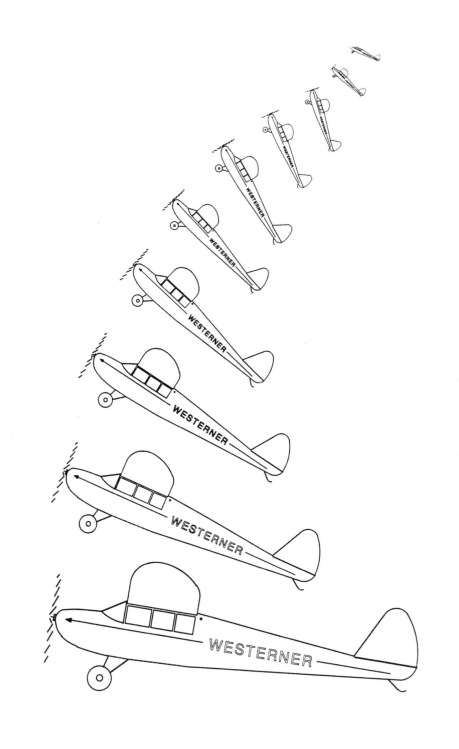

Chapter One

THE DREAM OF FLIGHT

There is no one to whom the romance of aviation makes more of an appeal than it does to the boy between seven and fifteen years of age, and these boys are building model aircraft by the millions.
—Scientific American, *October 1930*

The white Ford station wagon pulls onto the field and swings around, nose to the wind, lining up beside half a dozen other assorted vehicles. When the driver's door opens a man in his early fifties emerges—a big man in sunglasses, surprisingly tall and broad-shouldered. He takes a perfunctory swipe at a mass of thick brown hair and slaps on a faded blue cloth hat.

"Hey! Buzz," somebody says by way of greeting. Three or four other voices echo the phrase.

"Gentlemen!" the tall man responds, walking around to the back of the wagon and dropping the tailgate. Inside, standing on a pair of immense black sponge-rubber wheels, is the bright orange fuselage of a 150% scale E.J. Weathers' *Westerner*. The model's wing panels, each nearly six feet in length, lounge against the wheel wells, presenting their massive root ribs to the morning sun. This is the Westerner's debut at the flying field, and a loose circle of modelers forms around the open tailgate.

Labor of Love

"How many square inches that sucker got?" somebody asks, and Buzz answers without hesitation: "Two thousand one hundred and sixty." Fifteen square feet of wing.

So much for the "big man, small airplane" myth.

A sleek cabin design from 1937, the Westerner is covered in a filmy negligee of transparent orange Monokote—forty-three linear feet of it, all told—to show off a bone structure that is, by just about anyone's standards, immaculate. Fuselage longerons sweep backward toward the tail with a mathematical symmetry. Wing ribs grip the main spar with vise-like perfection, and soft wingtip balsa manages somehow to blend into harder trailing edge stock without so much as a color change. *Labor of love* is the phrase that springs to mind. Clearly the big Westerner is the work of a seasoned modeler—a craftsman—a person who builds flying machines primarily for the love of building, and not simply out of an urge to get something in the air next weekend.

The man is C.S. "Buzz" Averill, a deep-voiced, six-foot-three master plumber, boss of a twenty-man shop in Albuquerque, New Mexico that he calls, with characteristic directness, Averill Plumbing and Heating. Buzz Averill is one of that vanishing breed of Americans who, half a century after the fact, still lives in the city of his birth. From this rough, informal flying field northeast of town, a good pair of binoculars might pick out, in the gray-green valley below, the dark shape of Albuquerque High, where Buzz graduated in 1955.

Part of what keeps him here is the city's unique geography and weather: three hundred days of sunshine, average wind velocities under nine mph, and a thousand square miles of flat, treeless *mesa* (the local term for desert) within easy driving range. Dry heat in the summer, dry cold in the winter. Except for a few weeks of blowing dust in the spring, this long, populous valley that lies in the morning shadow of the southern Rockies is something of a modeler's paradise. And Buzz Averill, as the big *Westerner* testifies, is a lifetime modeler.

Lifers

There are, in America, fewer than a hundred thousand such people left: people for whom the building and flying of miniature aircraft is a passion, an obsession, a source of energy and enthusiasm virtually inseparable from their life force—people who are hooked by this unique hobby/sport not for a year or a decade, but forever. Lifers.

Paradoxically, the number of lifetime modelers continues to shrink even as their hobby itself grows. Of the thousands of beginners who take up aeromodeling each year—buy the kits and the hardware and the fuels and glues necessary to get that first model into the air—most lose interest and drift away within 24 to 30 months. The rest may last a few years . . . five, ten . . . before other interests seduce them away. The half-finished models in basements, the boxes of engines and radios that float like driftwood through the flea markets all testify to the high turnover within the hobby.

But throughout this turnover, lifers like Buzz Averill carry on—the solid core of a hobby/sport that, back in the thirties and forties, numbered its adherents in the millions. Scattered thinly across America, these lifers are the local experts, the 'old timers' whose opinions are sought whenever anyone starts thinking about modifying a kit or an engine, designing something original, straying from the well-worn path that aeromodeling has become in its eighty-year history.

Even though they are the backbone of the hobby, most of America's lifers keep a low profile. Half a dozen monthly magazines cover the U.S. modeling scene, and yet comparatively few of the nation's lifetime modelers ever appear in these magazines, either in name or picture. Not many seem to crave hero status. No more than a thousand are national-level competitors, willing to trek endlessly back and forth across a 3000-mile-wide flying field in pursuit of a gilded trophy and a weekend of camaraderie and fame.

Almost a Fanatic

Lifetime modeler Harold 'Pappy' deBolt long ago recognized the high cost of competitive modeling. "To become an expert," he observed in 1950, "you must be almost a fanatic, to put in the hours required to learn the ropes and keep on top." At the time of this statement, deBolt had already made it to the top of two separate

3

modeling fields, freeflight and controlline, and was just starting up the radio control ladder.

Few of America's lifers share deBolt's competitive drive. The vast majority of them, if asked, would describe themselves modestly—and accurately—as *sport fliers*.

Urge to Create

One hallmark of a lifer is the urge to create original designs. Almost every long-term modeler has designed at least a few ships 'from scratch,' driven by what Larry Scarinzi once described as "the pleasure of following my own ideas through . . . to see if it works and hope that it's a little different than any other guy has." But unlike Scarinzi, whose U-Control designs appeared for years in *Flying Models* and *Model Airplane News,* comparatively few lifers ever seem to get around to publishing their creations in the mags.

Publishing means writing the mandatory step-by-step construction article that begins with the 'perfect weather, perfect flight' vignette and ends—almost inevitably—with the eighty-year-old admonishment to test fly over tall grass.

Publishing means taking a dozen or more building photos, and coming up with clever captions for each of them—knowing full well that, even if the article sells, only two or three of these shots are likely to make it into print.

But worst of all, publishing means *building a second model exactly like the first.* For all but the most fanatical of modelers, this is asking too much. They'd much rather put that energy into the next project. And no real modeler is ever without a next project. He carries it about in his head even as he's buying supplies to build the current one.

Endless Fascination

America's lifetime modelers. Take away their hobby, take away their endless fascination with things that fly, and you take away the raw material of their daydreams, their chief creative outlet, and much of their motivation for getting out of bed in the morning.

Like Buzz Averill, most of these hundred-thousand or so lifers fell in love with flying machines between the ages of seven and fifteen, exactly as the *Scientific American* quote at the beginning of this chapter suggests. And like Buzz, most of them are now well into middle age. Today, newcomers to the hobby are almost invariably adults. There is no rising generation of *air minded youth*—the phrase itself is from the thirties—to take the place of these lifers once they're gone. Buzz and his contemporaries are the last remnants . . . the victims, in a sense . . . of America's three-decade-long love affair with the air.

They are the sons, not of Wilbur and Orville directly, but of an obscure young barnstormer from Minnesota, a baby-faced twenty-six-year-old who became an overnight hero by crossing the Atlantic Ocean by air—something dozens of people had done before him.

Lindbergh-crazy, Aviation-mad

The young barnstormer was Charles Lindbergh, of course, and when he touched down at Le Bourget in the *Spirit of St. Louis* on that chill May night in 1927, he touched something deep and untapped in the human psyche. The Lone Eagle's flight across the North Atlantic—one man against an empty sea and sky—set off a worldwide celebration that was virtually unprecedented in history.

In the weeks following, Europeans and Americans alike went Lindbergh-crazy, aviation-mad. Magazines and newspapers carried 'Lindy' news and little else. Gadget makers flooded three continents with souvenirs of the flight—everything from cast-iron monoplane models to commemorative ashtrays—and the public gobbled them up. People who had never gone near an airport and never intended to, still identified somehow with this shy young conqueror of the air. Everyone, it seemed, felt some of the Lindbergh magic.

The sociologists of the time, looking down on this madness from their ivory towers, shook their heads in amazement. Where did all this energy, all this adulation spring from? How could a skinny young man in a tube-and-fabric monoplane become such an overnight celebrity? Why should a single aerial stunt turn a complete unknown into *the most widely recognized name in human history?* Sixty-five years later, historians still puzzle over the intensity of the Lindbergh phenomenon. Nothing quite like it has ever happened before or since.

Number One in the Air

The epicenter of the world's Lindy madness was in the United States itself. Here was a quiet young man from Minnesota—no daredevil ace from the Great War, merely a shy college dropout with only four or five years' flying experience—who had somehow managed, in one daring leap, to make America number one in the air again. In just thirty-three hours, the *Spirit of St. Louis* and its pilot had recaptured the country's long-lost aviation crown, returned the United States (in its own eyes, at least) to the forefront of aerial progress.

Before Lindbergh, America had never really taken the airplane to its heart. Following the Wright brothers' initial successes of 1903-8, it was European fliers and European manufacturers who took the lead in aeronautics. For nearly two decades, the machines that dominated the skies bore French or English, German or Italian names. To the 1914-18 war, the war that lifted aeronautics out of its bamboo cradle and set it firmly in the vanguard of twentieth-century science, the United States of America contributed a single, outdated engine, the Liberty, and only one notable aircraft, Glenn Curtiss's big, lumbering Jenny—a trainer.

Up for Adoption

It was as if America, having given birth to the airplane, had decided to put it up for adoption. After a brief flurry of interest in flying machines around 1910, the nation's attention quickly turned elsewhere. Automobiles and phonographs, radios and refrigerators, toasters and fans and curling irons—a whole host of consumer goods that wouldn't become common in England and Europe until well after the Second World War—diverted the country's interest from the airplane during the teens and twenties. In our headlong rush to fill our lives with gadgetry, to build roads and dams and power lines and bank accounts, to move our population from farm to city, from the nineteenth century to the twentieth, the Wright brothers' immense accomplishments at Kitty Hawk and Dayton were

6

largely ignored. The possibilities of human flight had somehow failed to capture the American imagination.

Until the evening of May 21, 1927.

When the first reports of "Lucky" Lindy's success poured in by telegraph from Paris, the news fell upon a nation that was already half intoxicated with its own good fortune. The bitter recession of the early twenties was only a memory. The stock market was once again in a full-power climb, ceiling and visibility unlimited. Everybody and his bootlegger was driving a shiny new Ford, and a stocky, six-foot-two New York Yankees outfielder named George Herman Ruth was just warming up for what would prove to be a record-shattering sixty-run season.

America was on a roll in May of '27, and anything seemed possible. All that was missing was a focus for this wild optimism—a lightning rod to polarize all this random energy. Charles Lindbergh became that rod.

The Thirty-year Dream

Preflight publicity had been intense, and every American who owned a radio that spring followed Lindbergh's flight. The prize for success was a whopping $25,000—something like half a million today. Two larger and better-equipped airplanes, Byrd's *America* and Chamberlain's *Columbia*, were poised to make the same attempt, should Lindbergh fail.

When the little Ryan finally popped out of the clouds over Paris, Americans who had waited anxiously for over thirty hours went mad with relief and joy. A wave of air-mania swept the country like a flu virus. The flight of the *Spirit of St. Louis* launched a brand-new American dream, the dream of the coming "air age."

At first vague in outline, the air-age dream soon solidified into one of the most powerful and pervasive communal myths in all of American history. After Lindbergh, the exploits of a dozen other headline-making pilots of the summer of '27 transformed the sky above into a new frontier. Almost overnight the air became a new West to conquer, a mysterious and exciting new ocean on which everyone might someday sail as heroically as the Lone Eagle had.

And, because ignorance is bliss, it seemed only natural to Americans that this new frontier should belong exclusively to American daring, American know-how, American back-yard genius.

A Secular Religion

For the next three decades the country's opinion shapers—journalists and politicians, entertainers and admen and song writers and preachers—seldom took their eyes from this promising new frontier. Aviation, as Joseph Corn points out in his wonderful little 1983 book *The Winged Gospel,* was elevated during this period into a kind of secular religion. Lindbergh's flight kicked off a thirty-year barrage of pro-aviation propaganda, a blitzkreig of fact and fiction that was partly spontaneous and partly contrived. Its purpose was to condition the sons and daughters of a horse-and-buggy culture to think of flying as not only safe and natural, but inevitable . . . unstoppable . . . God's will for America . . . the wave of the future.

And America's sons and daughters took all this marvelous ballyhoo to heart.

During the years following Lindbergh's success, if you had asked any representative group of American citizens to complete this sentence in twenty-five words or less:

America's future . . .

you would have gotten a surprising percentage of four-word replies:

. . . is in the air.

From the late twenties, throughout the Great Depression, through World War II and right up to the evening of 4 October 1957, most of the American public believed unskeptically in the rosy future and the endless opportunities of this 'field of tomorrow', American aviation. An entire generation grew up under this creed.

Children of the Dream

The small group of model airplane enthusiasts who crowd the tailgate of Buzz Averill's station wagon, anxious for a look at his *Westerner*, his brand-new old-fashioned flying machine, bear mute testimony to the power of this thirty-year myth. Parents and grandparents now, they are the living legacy of the American Air Age—the children of the dream.

That the public at large no longer shares their dream, no longer looks up when a plane flies over, must feel to many of them like a sort of betrayal. When they were young, the world pointed them toward a bright and magical future in the air—pointed them skyward and gave them an encouraging shove. But just as they were getting up to flying speed, that magical future suddenly faded and the world changed its course. Like those young soldiers who marched off to Vietnam as heroes and returned to a nation embarrassed by their presence, the children of the Air Age carry a vague sense of having been cheated . . . let down . . . betrayed, somehow. And not by any one person, but by history itself.

Wings for Everyone

While it lasted, the Air Age dream was a comforting dream, one that dovetailed almost perfectly with the optimism and isolationism of those three decades between 1927 and 1957. First and foremost, it took for granted American superiority in all things aeronautical. Ignoring Italy's flying boats, ignoring Spain's autogyros, ignoring Canada's transports and England's marvelous engine development—ignoring, for a time, even Hitler's entire *Luffwaffe*—America managed to focus its myopic attention on purely national heroes. Flyers like Chamberlain and Byrd, like Roscoe Turner, Wiley Post, Amelia Earhart and Jimmy Doolittle, dominated our headlines and our daydreams.

But hero worship was only one aspect of the dream. The real essence of the Air Age was its ardent belief in America's flying future—a certainty that the day would come when *every suburban garage would contain both an automobile and a flying machine.*

At least once a year, one of the 'pops' (*Popular Science, Popular Mechanics, Popular Aviation*) would run a cover story featuring some sort of folding autogyro, inflatable helicopter, winged car, or backpack rocket—some simple and inexpensive family flyer that seemed to be just over the consumer horizon and

9

rising fast. And people of the thirties and forties—even people with little or no interest in aviation—believed that it was so.

In a *Saturday Evening Post* survey taken in the spring of 1945, just as WW II was winding down, 32% of that magazine's vast audience reported that they fully expected to own an airplane after the war ended. Not one in a hundred of these respondents held a pilot's license, of course, but this seemed no barrier. Didn't every week bring another news story about some advance in technology that promised to make flying as simple as driving? The *Ercoupe*, the Waterman *Arrowbile*, the Bensen *Autogiro*, the Custer *Channel Wing*—these and a hundred other spinproof, stallproof, foolproof flying machines made headlines and raised expectations almost daily throughout the air age.

Meanwhile, every crossroads village in the country scrambled to build itself a dirt-strip airport. Nobody wanted to be left behind when those millions of postwar lightplanes came winging down from America's bountiful skies. To read the upbeat aviation columns in the newspapers of the day was to be convinced that the law of gravity itself was just about to be suspended—maybe even repealed outright—for every man, woman and child in these United States.

No Closer

But the years passed, and somehow the day of the family flying machine never got any closer. Beyond a certain point, flying failed to get much cheaper—or safer, or more practical. By the mid-fifties the air-age fervor had begun to subside. It was becoming obvious that, while Americans might well have a chicken in every pot, they were probably never destined to have a lightplane in every garage.

And so the sweet dream of an aerial future began to fade. But it was a hardy dream, deep-rooted and appealing, and it wasn't shattered completely until that cool October evening in 1957 when word came filtering in from Europe that Russia had just launched into low orbit the 184-pound aluminum medicine ball that they nicknamed *Sputnik*, a Russian word that translates precisely into the infamous McCarthy-era phrase "fellow-traveler."

Beep-beep-beep

The eerie beeping of Sputnik I was the signal from on high that America's air age was officially over—over before it had really begun. The little Russian satellite, a mere glowing pinpoint slipping meteor-like across the night sky, reminded us with every orbit that the nation's future was now no longer in the air, but somewhere far above it.

Aviation—that magic word!—disappeared from headlines. The tomorrow game had suddenly taken a quantum leap upwards into a totally different sphere, and if America wished to play, it would have to begin by playing catch-up to the USSR—not in the clouds but high above them now, in cold and lifeless Space. All across the country aeronautical engineering departments sent to the printers for new letterhead, becoming overnight departments of "aerospace" engineering.

Aviation had suddenly become a museum term.

Changed Forever

And yet, even though the abrupt arrival of the space age left much of the air-age dream unfulfilled, its thirty-year propaganda barrage had changed America forever. By 1957, travel by air was fast becoming as unremarkable as train travel had been in Lindbergh's day. By 1957, few Americans still exhibited that fear of flying that had kept their grandparents earth-bound. Fewer and fewer people boasted of never having been off the ground, and almost no one under forty would have refused, if offered, a free air ticket to just about anywhere on earth.

This universal acceptance of flying is due almost entirely to the propaganda of the air age dream—the preachments of the winged gospel.

But the unlimited enthusiasm and public support for aviation that characterized the thirty-year air age was gone forever. By the end of the fifties, parents no longer urged their children to join the Air Force, or to study aero engineering, or to take courses to prepare themselves for some glorious career in the skies. The spotlight of public attention, focused for so long on the flashing wings of the flying machine, had finally moved on.

11

Still, not every American has been able to shake off the sweet dream of flight. Its roots go deep into the human psyche—deeper than Da Vinci, deeper even than the mythical Icarus with his waxen wings.

So deep is the dream that merely strapping your body into a silver airliner, or even a wire-and-dacron hang glider, may not totally fulfill it. Thousand-hour pilots continue to report, sometimes a bit sheepishly, how they jumped off a hill last night in their sleep—jumped off a hill, and spread their arms . . . and soared.

Flying in the Mind

Probably no one in history has testified more eloquently to the elusiveness of the dream of flight than Orville Wright himself. Recalling, some twenty-five years later, the experience of that damp December morning on Kill Devil Hill, Orville declared that neither he nor his brother had been especially surprised or elated at having finally flown. They had, after all, done their homework. They'd built toward the moment step by careful step, and backed each step with empirical testing in the very best scientific manner. And so those first tentative flights at Kitty Hawk, although satisfying on one level, were also somehow a bit hollow—a bit disappointing—a bit of an anticlimax. "In fact," Orville confessed, *"I had got more kick out of flying before I had ever been in the air— while lying in bed thinking of how exciting it would be."*

This frank admission of the power of the dream by one of the fathers of human flight—this acknowledgement that flying in the air can never quite match flying in the mind—is not to be dismissed lightly. It is a principle that lies at the very heart of the model airplane hobby, if not at the heart of all human creativity: *no reality ever quite lives up to human anticipation.*

If you doubt this principle, ask any modeler whether he's perfectly satisfied with the models he now owns—even the one he just finished.

12

Dreaming of the Next One

Ask Buzz Averill, as he begins to prepare the big *Westerner* for its maiden flight. Grabbing the prop by its hub, he hauls the monster fuselage out of the station wagon to a chorus of oohs and aahs from the circle of onlookers. Like a slow freight emerging from a tunnel, the Westerner just keeps coming and coming. Finally the tailfeathers appear, and Buzz scoops a hand under the plane's sleek belly, swinging it around and setting it lightly (it is light, for an object so large) onto the gravel-strewn field. Immediately people kneel to peer in the cabin windows, to run their fingers along the invisible seams of the glossy Monokote covering.

"I brought home balsa by the pickup-load for that mother," Buzz remarks. "About two hundred and fifty dollars worth, all told. Stan at the hobby shop got this permanent two-meter grin! For weeks he kept telling everybody, 'Boy, you oughta see Buzz's Westerner. *You oughta build one of those!'* I doubled his balsa business for a month or so there."

"Ready to start on the second one?" somebody asks.

Buzz acknowledges the joke with a grunt. "It's a neat airplane," he says, "but two of 'em wouldn't be twice as neat." He pauses. "I've been looking at a set of plans for a plane called *Miss Arpiem.* Cabin model, 64-inch span, vee dihedral just like this one. Kinda looks like a rounded-off *Buzzard Bombshell*, only with a *Brigadier* wing." His voice fades a click or two and his eyes focus somewhere in the middle distance. "You ought to see it," he says. "It's one of those models that *just needs building* . . . ."

To anyone listening carefully, the fate of the Westerner seems plain. A half dozen flights, maybe less, and it will wind up hanging from the ceiling down in Stan and Helen Johnson's hobby shop. Buzz is almost through with it already. To those of us in the semicircle, the Westerner seems like a dream come true— flawless, beyond price. But Buzz is already looking right through it, toward the next model, the next project. Something just a little closer to his heart's desire. Something just a little closer to the dream.

13

The Historical Present

Cranking fuel into the Westerner's tank, Buzz parries a remark on the unusual way the rounded balsa cowl fairs back into the flat fuselage sides through a series of short, tapered gussets.

"That's typical of how Joe Weathers designs," he says with obvious pride. "If you look at some of his other cabin jobs—like the *Mystery Man,* the one that started the drop-off landing gear controversy—you'll see the same thing. Weathers has some really nifty ideas about construction."

Buzz talks of Joe Weathers, a man he never met, a man who's been dead for more than seven years, as if they were next-door neighbors, as if Joe were still busy designing models. All his verbs come out in what English teachers call the historical present: Joe Weathers *designs*, Weathers *has*. The drop-off landing gear controversy that he mentions so casually occurred during F.D.R.'s second administration, when Buzz Averill was two years old.

Historical present might be the best description for the entire world of aeromodeling. While a few modelers strive to recreate current aircraft—new helicopters, or the military's latest jet fighters—the vast majority, as measured by kit sales, are drawn to semi-scale cabin designs not unlike the Weathers Westerner. One of the most popular models in America today is Sig Manufacturing Company's *Kadet*—a high-wing, box-fuselage cabin model that, except for its tricycle landing gear, wouldn't have looked out of place in the Great Depression.

Tied to the Past

Part of what keeps modeling tied to the past is its powerplants. Since the late thirties, the most popular power source for models has been the single-cylinder, two-cycle gasoline engine. Such engines function best when harnessed to conventional propellers— and it is that big wooden airscrew up front that locks the hobby firmly into the pre-Sputnik era.

Most modelers still prefer it that way. Commercially produced 'jet' engines—everything from three-pound, ear-bursting ramjets to half-ounce solid fuel rocket motors—have been waved under the model builder's nose since the end of World War II, but

99% still choose to build prop jobs. The increasingly effecient fanjets of the past few years may eventually alter this picture, but probably not before most of the air-age generation, today's lifers, pass from the modeling scene.

And even then, to judge from the history of the hobby, the propeller is not likely to disappear. Few things do, in the world of model aircraft. Gas engines were supposed to supplant rubber power in the thirties—but the twisted rubber band is still very much with us. U-Control began "killing" freeflight just after the war—but freeflight is still around. Twenty years ago R/C started to ride roughshod over every other branch of the hobby—but today most of those other branches are alive and well, still represented in the official rulebooks, still flown each year at the various national championships and at hundreds of local meets in every part of the country.

Like so many other art forms, aeromodeling continually forges ahead by reabsorbing and recycling its own past. Buzz's big Westerner is a prime example. Covered in modern mylar, powered with a Japanese four-stroke engine, and carrying for ballast a state-of-the-art microprocessor radio and three servos, the Westerner, with its rounded wingtips and its thick, undercambered airfoil, is a kind of ideal blend of the old and the new, the nostalgic and the practical.

I watch Buzz slipping the Westerner's wing panels in place as the crowd edges back respectfully. Twelve feet of model airplane! Like everyone else, I find myself entranced by the flowing grace of the big machine, and I glance around at the semi-circle of other faces, other addicts of the air. Every face registers the same look, the same far-off glint in every eye.

What Men Are These?

Looking at this ring of rapt faces I think, *What is it that attracts a person to this sport? Why are we so fascinated by these curious and useless and anachronistic devices, these fragile sculptures of wood and plastic that ride the invisible air?*

The earliest model aircraft—beginning about a hundred and fifty years ago—were purely experimental, a method of testing

15

aerodynamic theories without risk to life, limb, or pocketbook. Crude, heavy devices of wire and wood and muslin, they paved the way for man-carrying machines in much the same way that nineteenth-century bicycles paved the way (quite literally) for the automobile. The model airplane . . . and this was probably its greatest single contribution to history . . . demonstrated empirically what so many scientists of the time were inclined to doubt: that *machinery* could be made to fly. Successful models proved that man-made devices were indeed capable of rising into the air under their own power, of balancing on the wind without capsizing, of paddling themselves about the sky like aerial steamboats.

Today, no one doubts this proposition. Today no one needs to be convinced that a curved plate, when held at a low angle to a stream of air, generates lift. Mechanical flight has ceased to be the miracle it once was. A few cranks may still argue that America's moon landings of the seventies were faked at some secret location on the Arizona desert, but no one seriously doubts man's ability to heave almost anything into the air and make it hang there suspended for indefinite periods of time.

Art Form

Model airplanes today—with the exception of a handful of wind-tunnel models and another handful of radio controlled flying testbeds sponsored by the aircraft industry and carrying six-figure pricetags—don't have a whole lot left to prove. Like black-and-white photography, aeromodeling has moved from the experimental stage through the tool-of-science stage into its mature (and perhaps final) stage, as a creative popular art form. The people who pursue the hobby today are a species of folk artist, working in an esoteric and as-yet-unrecognized tradition.

Case in point: Buzz Averill's twelve-foot Westerner. So nearly transparent in its Monokote skin that it casts on the dry earth beneath it a faintly orange shadow. So huge and graceful and birdlike. So massive, and so yet sensitive to every gust of passing air. An even prettier plane, I can't help thinking, than the *Pacificoaster*—another Joe Weathers design from the early days,

16

and one that's always been close to my own heart. Both are models in the Rearwin *Speedster* tradition: high wings, see-through cabins, curves and ellipses and smoothly faired lines everywhere.

What is it that makes a Rearwin prettier than a Cub? Both designers were working to similar parameters, but Rearwin seemed to have an eye for line, Taylor for function. Beauty, of course, *non est disputandum*, as the dead Romans say. That same E.J. Weathers who did the Westerner and the Pacificoaster also created *Tubby*, a kind of caricature of the potbellied old Aeronca C-3, a lightplane that only an expectant mother could love.

These are the things the mind ponders as Buzz chokes and flips, flips and chokes the Westerner's big four-stroke engine.

A Bird in the Hand

With both hands on autopilot (in a lifetime of modeling, Buzz has started thousands of engines) he is busy apologizing to the gods for having put Monokote on an 'old-timer' design. He'd intended to use a type of Coverite that duplicates gas-model silkspan, the heavy tissue that was popular in the late thirties. But when he tried to order the Coverite, he found that the manufacturer had dropped that type in favor of what he sneeringly refers to as "a slick, shiny stuff that looks like you bought it in a dime store."

"I called all over the country looking for the old-style Coverite," Buzz grumbles, "but nobody had any left. I should have gone ahead and silked it, but by then I was so disgusted I just wanted to be *done*."

None of this alleged impatience shows in the Westerner's flawless finish, of course, and I can't help wondering how much of Buzz's anger at the Coverite people is really just a displaced disappointment in the model itself—in its failure to live up to the dream. There it sits, big as life, but still not quite as big (or beautiful, or perfect) as it was in his mind before he began to build it. Reality is the enemy of our dreams. The more real a work of art becomes, the less ideal it is—and the more it falls short of our hopes and expectations. In the artist's world, a bird in the hand can't hold a candle to the one in the bush . . . .

17

The four-stroke fires once, twice, and is off and running, kicking out a stream of fine dust behind it, making the Westerner's huge tailfeathers twitch and leap anxiously, as if eager to be airborne. Buzz reaches for the transmitter, cuts the the roar to a soft idle. Then, in a ritual as old as R/C itself, he stands up, walks around behind the plane and throws a leg over the rear of the fuselage just in front of the stab, straddling it to anchor the model while he runs through various power settings and checks all the controls once more—something he's almost certain to have done half a dozen times at home, during the bench-flying we all go through as our models take shape.

Satisfied, he steps back and advances the throttle, and the big plane begins to roll forward clumsily over the rough ground. He taxis it out onto the dirt road, glances around automatically for clearance (he's a full-scale pilot with both power and soaring tickets) then opens the throttle. Dust flies, the tail lifts immediately, and the Westerner is suddenly rolling forward on two wheels . . . then one . . . then the other . . . then none at all.

One click, and one more, of right rudder trim. Now the big plane is climbing out smoothly, flawlessly, at a realistically low angle—exactly like the 1930s lightplane it's meant to resemble. Another phrase comes to mind, another cliché of the hobby: "She flew right off the board." In the long tradition of aeromodeling, that's the proper way to report it.

A far less eventful liftoff, no doubt, than the prototype Westerner made back in 1937. The original was a free flight, eight feet of paper-covered hope turned loose upon the world behind a throaty Ohlsson .60. Free flight: the launch-and-pray branch of the hobby. Engine cutoff timers were already common on the west coast by 1937, so the original Westerner was probably test-flown on a ten or twenty-second run. But a lot of bad things can happen to an eight-foot, five-pound model in ten seconds.

None of these things happen to Buzz's plane, of course. He has in his hands a silver box made by Ace R/C—a five hundred dollar electronic training leash, ready to correct instantly any flaw in the trim, should any flaw show up. The model continues its gentle climbout, the big four-stroke mumbling like a tamed lion, like a far-off electric lawnmower. Half a minute into the flight, the engine is almost inaudible—and so is Buzz Averill's breathing. First flights, thanks to radio control, are not the heartstoppers they used to be. A quote from another lifetime modeler and full-scale pilot, the late Walt Mooney of San Diego, flashes through my head:

"The government has about killed all the excitement, and [full scale] flying is safer for it, but duller too."

The Sound of an Open-throated .60

I find myself faintly disappointed by the quietness of the Westerner. And so I think next of Carl Goldberg—the man whose pylon free flights almost singlehandedly ended the reign of realistic cabin models like the Westerner.

After gas engines became popular in the mid-thirties, it didn't take models long to become too efficient, too adept at disappearing into the clouds. Rulemakers countered by shortening the engine runs. As early as 1941 Goldberg began pleading for the use of dethermalizers instead of shorter runs to stop these flyaways. His arguments were reasonable, but he didn't base them on reason. He based them on the sound of an open-throated .60, screaming skyward.

Stop cutting the length of engine runs, he begged, *or we'll all get bored to death.* It was the unfettered roar of the engine, Goldberg maintained, that provided most of the thrill of free flight. (Just five years earlier, this same Goldberg had been national indoor champion, flying three-gram rubber-powered microfilm models with a propeller rpm somewhere under sixty . . . .)

At a couple of hundred feet of altitude (more or less; the Westerner is so big that no one is quite sure how to judge its height or distance) Buzz throttles back and tries a few gentle turns. The plane pirouettes easily on a wing, everything happening as if in slow motion, as if underwater.

19

"Will she loop?" somebody asks, and Buzz puts the nose down obligingly to build up speed. (Both front and rear wing spars are shear-webbed, I had noticed—something the original eight-foot Westerner almost certainly lacked. Although Weathers may have done it on his own 12-foot version, which he built and flew with a single-channel radio in 1946.) Up and over she goes, with grace.

As the plane levels out again, Buzz turns to the person nearest him. "Here!" he says gruffly, handing over the transmitter, "fly this damn thing!" The box is passed among three or four people, and each one gets the same slow grin as he tweaks the stick and the big model dances amiably to his bidding. Place your right thumb over the golf-tee-shaped stick. Move it just a fraction and the control surfaces, high in the air, move just a fraction. Breathe on the throttle and the whisper of the engine changes just perceptibly.

No ailerons, no flaps—the Westerner is a simple three-channel—and yet the link between pilot and craft seems flawless, seems almost dreamlike in its perfection. Twelve feet of airplane doing precisely what the pilot wills, from takeoff to the long, floating, two-point landing that culminates in a rollout right up to Buzz's feet, the prop still ticking over quietly.

Dream Fulfilled

The maiden flight of the *Westerner*: a dream fulfilled. Buzz makes it look so simple, so effortless. And in a way, it is. But a flight like this represents not only the skill and expertise of a master craftsman and a lifetime modeler. It represents, as well, the culmination of eight decades of aeromodeling progress—sporadic and often chaotic progress, most of it amateur, and most of it occurring within the life span of the group of men standing here on the field.

The full story of these eight decades would fill an encyclopedia, and probably bore us all into an early grave. What follows, then, is a kind of 'pop' history, a thumbnail sketch, of modeling in America—the highlights and low spots, the people and things and events that I have found interesting or surprising or funny.

20

The real importance of the sport, of course, will always be personal to each of us: the marvelous models we've created, the crazy things that have happened to us and to our OFBs (ol' flying buddies) over the years. What I hope to do in the following pages is give us all a context to put our own stories into—give us a sense of the long tradition we're operating within. History can tell us who we are, and a little bit about the bigger picture we're all part of. It can provide a kind of sketch of the stage where we act out our dreams.

If that seems worthwhile to you, read on.

WESTERNER

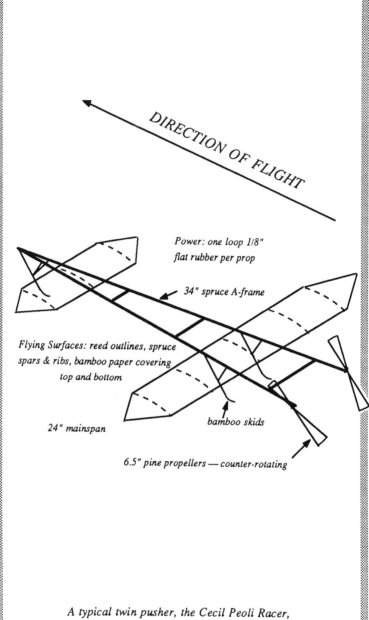

DIRECTION OF FLIGHT

Power: one loop 1/8"
flat rubber per prop

34" spruce A-frame

Flying Surfaces: reed outlines, spruce
spars & ribs, bamboo paper covering
top and bottom

24" mainspan

bamboo skids

6.5" pine propellers — counter-rotating

A typical twin pusher, the Cecil Peoli Racer,
kitted by Ideal Models from 1911 to 1930

Chapter Two

FLYING MACHINES

The Pre-Lindbergh Era: 1907-27

*Among these young men there may be geniuses who may evolve
new and better types of aircraft, or features which will improve
the existing types . . . .*
—*Aerial Age,* August 30, 1915

*Balsa is the best wood to use for the fuselage. It is easy to shape,
strong, and only half as heavy as cork. If you prefer, however, you
can use any straight-grained soft wood, such as white pine or
basswood, although these are heavier and will cut down the time
your ship will stay in the air.*
—Merrill Hamberg, *Beginning to Fly,* 1928

For some delicate cutting, a razor blade is preferable to a pen knife . . .
—*Popular Aviation,* September 1927

To say that American aeromodeling began with Lindbergh's
flight to Paris is like saying there was no touch football before
JFK, no cancer before John Wayne. Lindy's flight—and the whole
marvelous 'aviation summer' of 1927—simply brought into focus a
scattered and haphazard grassroots modeling movement that was
already at least twenty years old.

Some of the earliest organized model building and flying in the
U.S. took place in New York City, starting around 1907-8. And
why not? New York was the site of dozens of "aerial expositions,"
as the full-scale flying (or sometimes just hopping and shaking)

demos of the day were called. And it was exposure to big ships that made people want to create little ones. The pugnacious Charlie Grant, editor of *Model Airplane News* from 1932 to 1943, saw his first exposition at Mt. Morris Park on Madison Avenue, in 1908, and took home from it a ready-built, rubber-powered flying model—which, like most flying models of 1908, didn't.

Science vs. Sport

As modelers, we like to tell each other that little airplanes preceded big ones—preceded them and laid much of the scientific groundwork for them. And this is so. Down through the centuries, the most important aeronautical thinkers and tinkerers (da Vinci, Cayley, Stringfellow, Chanute, Langley) all turned to models to test their theories. It kept them from breaking their bank accounts, not to mention their necks. Wilbur Wright, recalling a 1901 visit to Octave Chanute's apartment in Chicago, said he could barely see the old man's ceiling for all the models hanging from it.

But models-for-science is not the same thing as models-for-fun, and aeromodeling in America, as elsewhere, has always been primarily for fun. That's too bad, in some instances. If the Wrights, for example, had tested their designs in model form first, like old O.G. Corben did his *Aces*, they might have discovered the pitch problems in their 1912 rear-stabilizer *Model B* without killing anybody. (Although being modelers first didn't seem to help the Granville Brothers, of *GeeBee* fame, who still managed to design some pretty scary flying machines.)

Twin Pushers

The really memorable models of the pre-World War I period you could count on one hand. They were all rubber-powered, of course. Compressed air was around, and clock springs, and even the occasional five-pound air-cooled gasoline engine. Ray Arden, who perfected the glow plug in the forties, nearly decapitated a young New York woman in a local park with one of his experimental gas jobs—in either 1904, 1907, or 1909, depending on whose story you choose. Afterward he married the lass, probably to avoid a lawsuit. Modelers today look for subtler ways of introducing their brides to the hobby.

But Arden's "gassie" was an aberration, an experiment clearly not worth repeating. (A repeat might have led to bigamy charges, anyway.) The pre- World War I models that worked, the ones that didn't dash themselves headlong into strange women, were not gas powered. They were almost all propelled by twisted rubber bands.

The most popular design of the era was the "twin pusher," a creation of the English automotive engineer F.W. Lanchester, back in the 1890's. Twin pushers had two separate fuselage sticks joined at the front in an "A" shape, and separated at the rear just enough to keep the props from walloping each other.

No Names

Twin pushers weren't thought of as works of art, so they didn't have names like models do today. Fortunately, their designers did—and that's how we can distinguish between the 1909 "Percy Pierce," said by many to be America's first successful twin pusher design, and the little pointy-winged "Cecil Peoli" of 1911, immortalized the following year in an Ideal Model Aeroplane and Supply kit that was still on the market when Lindbergh hit the headlines in '27.

Before WW I, most full-scale machines were pushers rather than tractors, so it isn't surprising that most models were, too. Pushers made sense: when you had to carve your own props out of a packing crate, using a dull jack-knife, you preferred not to break one in every crash.

But why twins? Who would want to carve *two* props when a single one would do?

Old Devil Torque

Anyone who didn't want to deal with torque, that's who. The props on a twin pusher were counter-rotating, canceling out each other's torque. Provided, of course, that you carved them identically (only backwards: one left, one right) and then wound them identically (only backwards: one left, one right.) And provided you matched the rubber motors, so one prop didn't overpower the other.

Torque affects virtually everything that takes to the air by propeller. But it's always been a special headache to rubber fliers because of the rubber model's radical power curve, which starts off at max and then tapers away to *nada* as the rubber unwinds. Torque was particularly hard on the pioneers, who had a dozen other (and equally invisible) forces to deal with, and almost no theory to help them.

In aerodynamics, theory is what makes the invisible plain. Trying to fly an airplane without theory is like getting into a fistfight with a poltergeist.

But in the days of the twin pusher, theory was scarce. So if you could eliminate one of the invisible evils—torque—by carving a second prop and building a second motor stick, you did it. Today we'd simply add some right thrust and be done with it, but in 1910 thrust-line adjustments were still ten years in the future. And as for opposite rudder, forget it—twin pushers seldom had rudders. Or *any* kind of vertical surface, for that matter. About all they had was a big wing in the back and a small wing in the front. The earliest ones lacked even dihedral. (Dihedral, proposed by Cayley around 1800, was still somewhat suspect. It was dihedral, after all, that got Wilbur and his brother in trouble in the crosswinds at Kitty Hawk.)

Big wing in the back and small wing in the front: what we now call the 'canard' or 'tail-first' layout. This was another idea that seemed to make sense at the time. Canard layouts had been the key to the Wright's success, from their earliest gliders until the advent, in late 1910, of the "headless" and pitch-sensitive Model B.

Today most folk tend to feel that, in miniature at least, canards never seem to quite hold their own with conventional big-wing-first designs. The stab in a tail-firster has to carry too much of the plane's weight, and small wings just aren't as efficient as large wings.

But all this would have sounded like necromancy in 1910.

26

Racers and Flyers

Twin pushers, in those days, were called "racers," to distinguish them from flying scale models, called simply "flyers." It was the first of many schisms in the brand-new religion of aeromodeling. Either you were a flyer man, and you looked down your nose at those grossly unrealistic racers, or else you were a racer man, and considered scale models a great waste of time.

Flyers and racers. Both of these terms seem, from today's perspective, hopelessly optimistic. Generally speaking, racers didn't race and flyers didn't fly. Peoli coaxed a straight-line distance of almost 1700 feet out of his little 24" racer in 1911, and this was good enough for people to claim it as a "world" record for rubber models. Good enough, in fact, to justify kitting the design essentially unchanged for the next two decades.

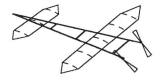

Vacuum

Making fun of the pioneer period is easy. But just try putting your head back into 1910 for a moment, and consider the vacuum these people were operating in.

Penaud, the Frenchman, had flown a small rubber model about 150 feet in 1871. Twenty-five years later, in 1896, Langley's steam-powered *Aerodrome #5* staggered three quarters of a mile down the Potomac River before bellying into the drink. *These were the two best-known free flights of self-powered, unmanned aircraft in all of recorded history:* one by a two-ounce stick model and the other by a twelve-foot tandem-winged aerial steamboat. About the only thing the two models had in common was that they were both monoplanes. But this only added to the modeler's confusion, for most of the successful full-scale craft of the time were Pratt-trussed biplanes—a style foisted on the world, via the Wrights, by bridge builder Octave Chanute.

There was a tremendous amount of misinformation available, in 1910, to anyone persistent enough to ferret it out. The highly respected Samuel Langley, Secretary of the Smithsonian, had recently breathed his last, still believing with his whole heart that turbulence on windy days was what allowed birds to soar without flapping. (When you asked him how birds soared on calm days, he changed the subject.) The two bicycle mechanics from Dayton had convinced one another that rectangular struts with round corners created far less drag than any other shape. And white-bearded old Alexander Graham Bell, rich and respected and considered by many to be the chief aeronautical guru of the era, was still certain that "honeycomb" wings made up from hundreds of miniature tetrahedral kites was the only practical way for man to fly.

So where did a model builder of 1910 begin?

Birdcages

Usually with a scale model, or "flyer." From crude three-views, or sometimes just a fuzzy newspaper photo, he would put together, stick by stick, a three-foot pine-framed replica of a Wright or Curtiss pusher biplane. Because flying was still magic, the model would be complete down to the very last wing strut, the very last wire brace—who could know what was important and what wasn't?

He would cover this monster with silk or cambric or mom's old feed-sack dress, then whittle himself a pair of air-clubs for propellers—crude, twisted pieces of wood that would one day be considered "propeller blanks" rather than finished props. Next he'd add a couple of very un-scale motor sticks, to get a longer stretch for his rubber bands. After that, he'd wind the whole mess up, cross his fingers, and heave her off the roof.

Such a hefty contraption, all drag and no power, had about as much chance of sustained flight as a bamboo birdcage. The inevitable result was a long dive and a gloriously scale-like crash into the yard below. Where, with luck, the dog would finish it off, and the modeler would decide to take up fishing or golf. Or dog beating.

Drag was the number one problem with these "flyer" models. Drag goes up enormously as size goes down, making it far more debilitating to a model than to a full-size plane. All those wires

28

and interplane struts represented tremendous drag. When model builders began to figure this out, the monoplane racer, or "twin pusher," came into its own. Lacking most of the biplane's jungle-gym, the twin pusher represented a giant leap forward in performance.

Flying Machines

Cutting drag, however, did little for the number two problem of the era: weight. Modelers in 1910 were no dumber than you and I. They admonished one another constantly to build light, just as we do today. The trouble was, they simply had no concept of what "light" meant. Aeroplanes (in the U. S. the word was streamlined to *airplane* during World War I) were still referred to, and thought of, as "flying machines."

Flying machines. Think about that phrase. Today it has a kind of ironic, tongue-in-cheek sound—we can hardly use it except in quotation marks. But in 1910 it was a serious term. Aeroplanes, both full scale and model, were flying machines.

To a generation of people still living in the shadow of the nineteenth century, the word *machine* was a magic word, a tomorrow word—a word of awesome mass and power and possibility. To city folk it conjured up the slow, grinding intensity of the gigantic walking-beam steam engines that shook windows for blocks around and ran the factories of the day. To farmers it suggested some great, iron-wheeled steam tractor, or one of Cyrus McCormick's lumbering, tinny, horse-drawn reapers.

The pocket watch was about the lightest and most delicate instrument in common use in those days, but pocket watches weren't thought of as machines; they didn't have enough iron in them. Issac Singer's treadle-driven sewing machines were about the smallest machines around: seventy-five pounds of steel and oak and cast iron fleur-de-lis. Machines were many things in the year 1910, but they were not delicate, and they were never—in any modern sense—light.

The Height of Tech

Small wonder, then, that the designers of the first miniature flying machines sometimes covered their wings with mica (that's right: rock!), and almost always used brads (read: *nails*) to hold frame joints together. "Lashing," a process of binding joints with heavy black thread and then coating them with a glue made from melted fish, was just about the height of tech until the early teens, when little cans of orange-tinted Ambroid glue (originally spelled *Amberoid;* guess why?) first became common.

One of the biggest discoveries of the prewar era was "goldbeaters skin," a thin membrane that lined the stomach of an ox. Goldbeaters skin was originally used to separate layers of thin gold foil, to keep them from sticking. It had the look and feel and impermeability of a piece of doped Japanese tissue. It was light and strong and made a dandy wing covering, if only you could get it. Monokote may not be cheap, but it beats knocking an ox in the head every time you cover a wing.

The pioneer era in aeromodeling was a rude age, remembered fondly only by those who were very young at the time. (Proving once more that there's no bad time to be young.) Full scale aeronautical progress during this period was snail-slow. Modeling progress was, if possible, even slower. The big boys made some giant strides during the '14-'18 War, at least, while aeromodeling (as happens in every war) practically died.

The Prewar Clubs

A list of the nation's most active aeromodeling groups appeared in *Aerial Age* in 1915. Notice how they taper off as you move west from the big apple:

Aero Science Club of America (successor to the N.Y. Aero Club)
DeWitt Clinton Model Aero Club (NYC)
Harlem Model Aero Club
Bay Ridge Model Club (Brooklyn)
Long Island Model Aero Club
Model Aero Club of White Plains
Summit (NJ) Model Aero Club
Detroit Aero Research and Model Club
Illinois Model Aero Club (Chicago)

North Shore Model Aero Club (Chicago)
Milwaukee Model Aero Club
Minneapolis Junior Aero Club
Aero Club of St. Louis
Texas Junior Aeronautical Society (Ft. Worth)
Texas Model Aero Club (San Antonio)
Pacific Northwest Model Aero Club (Seattle)

Most of these groups faded away during the war and were never reorganized afterwards. The "junior problem," a favorite editorial subject ever since World War II, first surfaced right after World War I: kids of the early twenties simply weren't much interested in aviation, either full-scale or models. Radio was the hot fad of the day. Every boy worth his salt was busy winding a coil on a piece of broomstick, bending a hatpin over a lump of crystal, and stringing enough antenna wire across the roof to power the earphones of his home-made "crystal set." Radio, in 1920, seemed to be the wave of the future; it wouldn't be replaced by aviation until 1927.

Mail-Order Nationals

But the prewar clubs made a few lasting contributions to the sport. In 1915 the Aero Science Club sponsored America's first "nationals," a series of annual contests conducted by mail between recognized clubs for the possession of a perpetual trophy. The first two contests, in 1915 and 1916, were won hands-down by members of the Chicago-based Illinois Model Aero Club, a group that was by then beginning to steal the fire from the eastern groups.

After the war a third mail-order nats was held, in 1919, and when those rascals from Illinois once again swept the field, the trophy was retired—the rules said 'three wins and it's yours.' And so this first cycle of national contests came to an abrupt end. Nobody, at the time, had enough interest to initiate a new cycle.

The curious thing about these first three 'nats' is that the models that won them were framed entirely in what modelers think of today as hardwoods: pine and spruce and bamboo. Curious, because the heartwood of aeromodeling had already been discovered and put to use in flying models by members of the old New York Aero Club as early as 1911.

Lighter Than Cork

The wood, of course, was balsa, and the stories that surround its discovery are many and wonderful. Crude planks of the stuff were apparently being used as packing material for shipments of goods up from South America, around 1910, when some sharp-eyed Aero Club member first spotted it on the New York docks. Ralph Barnaby, who helped found the Soaring Society of America in the late twenties, modestly claimed to be that sharp-eyed modeler. Others attribute the discovery to a fellow Aero Clubber named John Carisi.

Still others embellish the legend with tales of a certain sea captain named Lundin, whose beautiful daughter sometimes accompanied him on voyages to South America. This daughter, it seems, ventured ashore one day in Ecuador, and simply knocked the socks off the barefoot natives. They decided to give a feast in her honor, and during the party somebody came strolling by with a thirty-foot log on his shoulder. A casual feat to an Ecuadoran, but it certainly got the attention of old Captain Lundin.

When the captain discovered that the secret of the trick lay not in the shoulder but in the log, he brought a load of this weird, weightless wood back to New York as a curiosity. And this, so the story goes, was the wood the Aero Club members found on the docks. (Whether the daughter came home with the load of wood or not, legend doesn't say. But it wouldn't have made much difference to the story. A modeler will rush right past a pretty girl to get first pick of a new balsa shipment.)

Raft

The word balsa is Spanish for "raft." It probably got this name in the sixteenth century, when the conquistadors discovered that it would carry more than four times its weight in pillage. That's because balsa is only 8% real, the other 92% being nothing but dead air space. So whatever you have to pay for a piece of balsa today, remember that it's really *twelve times* that expensive, because 92% of what you're paying for, and carrying home, and hacking and gouging and sanding upon, is dead air space: nothing at all.

Balsa trees grow like Jack's beanstalk. In four or five years they can reach three feet in diameter—too big to squeeze through your front door—and as much as *eighty feet* in height. Wow! But then they have to harvested quickly. Otherwise, they put down a taproot and suck up a couple of tons of water, completely filling all that dead air space. This makes them just as heavy as any other tree, but no stronger than they were; so that an old balsa tree, instead of growing wise, often collapses of its own stupidity.

I've had relatives like that.

World's Slowest Revolution

Model historians like to say that the discovery of balsa revolutionized the aeromodeling hobby. If that's true, then the balsa revolution was just about the slowest revolution in history.

Why it took so long is a mystery, but it almost surely has to do with the great millstone of nostalgia that hangs about the neck of almost every modeler. To a lifer, a true member of the aeromodeling fraternity, no models can ever quite match the models of his youth. Listen to Colonel C.E. Bowden, one of England's greatest modeling innovators, bemoaning the coming of balsa wood:

After the formation of the Society of Model Aircraft Engineers [in 1922] and up to the invasion of American methods and balsa wood, there was a very interesting period of model aircraft development along enclosed fuselage, hardwood constructional lines, [employing] gearing and silk covering. Many of the models produced make fine general purpose machines even now. In fact they were more durable and in many ways are more suitable for flying in our rigorous climate than . . . the all balsa and tissue type which requires such a lot of careful handling, and is so easily damaged by children who pick it up at the end of a flight, also by dogs, broken rubber motors, trees and so on.

Every time I read this, I picture the Colonel tugging at one end of a model, an English bulldog at the other. But what makes this anti-balsa sentiment so remarkable, and yet so completely understandable, is that it was published *after World War II,* in A.D. 1946. The "invasion" Col. Bowden refers to happened in 1930, when Joe Ehrhardt of St. Louis went to England and captured the Wakefield Cup for rubber models with a 2.5-ounce machine. (The previous year's winner weighed 10 ounces.) Sixteen years later, the Colonel—a man at the very forefront of gas modeling and low-wing design and rise-off-water flying and a dozen other major advances in the sport—was still not quite ready to accept the balsa revolution!

Later in the same text he grumbles that balsa requires "less skill and trouble" than hardwood; that it "sticks together with blobs of balsa cement instead of more skilled joints having to be made." The good Colonel, who came of age in the era of spruce and pine, had the same mixed feelings about balsa that a lot of older modelers today exhibit towards fiberglass and Kevlar and other forms of composite construction: *these newfangled materials may be OK in their place, but by doggies, they'll never replace the good old materials of childhood.*

A generation of American modelers, no doubt, agreed with the Colonel. So it should come as no surprise that balsawood, introduced into the Land of the Free in 1911, didn't come into really widespread use until after Lindbergh. For nearly twenty years it remained a specialty-house item, available only in large cities like New York and Philadelphia and Chicago.

Until toy and department stores began stocking limited amounts of modeling supplies in the early thirties, most people still ordered their balsa by mail. Or, more often, they merely read about it in the magazines, while continuing to cut their longerons and spars from spruce or pine or basswood. Model historian Jim Noonan of Milwaukee has accurately labeled the entire period 1907-1927 as "the pre-balsa era."

The Magazines

Still, there was some progress between Cecil Peoli and Lindbergh—it wasn't entirely the dark ages of aeromodeling. But like the European Dark Ages, the pockets of learning during these

34

years were scattered widely, with little communication between them. New knowledge was passed by mail among the elite. Some of it eventually found its way into the back pages of the half-dozen full-scale magazines and journals that catered, in an offhand way, to the art and craft of aeromodeling.

Among these magazines were *Aero Digest, Aeronautics, Aerial Age, Popular Aviation,* and one that must have confused the entomologists, *Fly.* Of these, *Aerial Age,* founded by former modeler William Stout, was probably the most receptive to model news. *Aerial Age* published not just new products and new designs, but the kind of gossip and scuttlebutt that both informs and inspires. A typical issue from 1919, for example, reports an out-of-sight flight (one of the first) from Golden Gate Park in San Francisco, made by a very light twin pusher covered with goldbeaters skin. How many modelers must have read that story—some by electric bulb, but many others by gaslight—and then sat staring at their own crude model, imagining it floating magically upward into those soft California clouds . . . .

Manufacturers

It was during that same year—1919—that lifer Charlie Grant, just out of Uncle Sam's Army, set about to design a series of flying models for the Ritchie Wertz Manufacturing Company of Dayton, Ohio. These Grant-Wertz models were unusual in two respects. First, they represented one of the earliest attempts in this country to mass-produce model planes on a Ford-like assembly line. (Grant designed all the production machinery himself—including an automated prop-carver that could turn out 1000 props a day.)

Second, these models weren't your customary twin pushers. They were single-stick tractors, with lightweight wings milled from solid sheet stock—early versions of the all-balsa R.O.G.s that Charlie Grant later became famous for. The entire series was marketed ready to fly, with an average pricetag around $3.50. This at a time when Henry Ford was 'overpaying' his autoworkers to the tune of five bucks a day.

Would you give 70% of a day's wages for a windup stick model? Surprisingly, people did. Some 100,000 of these little R.O.G.s were sold between 1919 and 1921, when production finally ceased.

Meanwhile, out west, an Oregon high-school kid had developed a similar line of stick models, and, after much refinement, began peddling them to his schoolmates and neighbors. The word spread to southern California, and soon the boy got a tentative order from an aspiring Hollywood actor named Reginald Denny. Tentative, because this fellow Denny was nobody's fool: he wanted to see the boy's models perform before he committed to an order.

The boy wrote back immediately, promising to send down "an agent," and then packed a boxful of models and booked himself onto a southbound train. It was the beginning of a forty-year career, for the boy, whose name was Jim Walker, went on to found the largest model aircraft firm in history, American Junior Aircraft of Portland, and to devote his entire life to the promoting of model aviation.

Stagnant Records

But the Charlie Grants and Jim Walkers of the hobby were few and far between during the early twenties. Perhaps the best comment on the era is contained in the list of national records published in the January 1928 edition of *Popular Aviation*. Not surprisingly, these records all belong to the Illinois Model Aero Club—that same bunch of nation-beaters from back in the 'teens. What is surprising is their dates:

Duration

Twin Pusher, handlaunch	10 min 14.2 sec	Robert Jaros	1924
Tractor, handlaunch	9 min 42.2 sec	Paul S. Smith	1924
Twin Pusher, R.O.G.	3 min 29.4 sec	Robert Jaros	1921
Tractor, R.O.G.	3 min 47.4 sec	P. Breckenridge	1919
Twin Pusher, R.O.W.	2 min 52.0 sec	B. Pond	1921
Tractor, R.O.W.	1 min 58.0 sec	B. Likosiak	1922
Scale, R.O.G. Indoor	21 seconds	Robert Jaros	1921

Distance

Twin Pusher, handlaunch	7,920 ft.	Robert Jaros	1924
Tractor, handlaunch	6,024 ft.	Paul S. Smith	1924
Twin Pusher, R.O.G.	4,029 ft.	Wm. Schweitzer	1919
Tractor, R.O.G.	2,685 ft.	P. Breckenridge	1919

Speed (300' course)

Twin Pusher, handlaunch	45 M.P.H.	W. Wakin	1920

So little progress was made during the years before Lindbergh that most national records were five or more years old by 1928. And this despite the fact that the oldest trophy in modeling—the trophy that is still awarded today to the contestant who racks up the highest time in any rubber event at the Nationals—had been in contention since 1923.

The Mulvihill

Bernard H. Mulvihill was vice president of the newly formed National Aeronautic Association at the time of the fourth annual "National Air Races," scheduled for St. Louis in September of 1923. That year Mulvihill proposed to add a little spice to the full-scale contest by including a duration event for model planes. Since he was providing the trophy, he got to call the tune, and the rules he proposed were wonderfully simple: every plane must be hand launched, rubber powered, and have no dimension over 40". His flight rules were even simpler: *the longest flight wins.*

"Tremendous Stimulant"

Here's what the program notes for the '23 Air Races had to say about this new event:

"The Mulvihill Trophy should be a tremendous stimulant to the youth of the country in building model airplanes. The annual competition for its possession should bring out new features in model airplane design which may conceivably have an effect on full scale production. At any rate, it may be assumed that the boys whose interest is thus aroused will contribute much to the progress of aeronautics a few years hence, as designers, mechanics, pilots or users of aircraft, and the drawing of their interest into the aeronautical field early in life presages a

longer career of usefulness in this field than would otherwise be possible."

It would be difficult to find a more succinct statement of the value that America placed—between Lindbergh and Sputnik—on the model airplane hobby. In one brief paragraph, hastily scribbled in the spring of 1923, Bernard Mulvihill managed to touch on almost every key point of modeling's public image, nearly five years before that image went public. The message that people like Bill Stout and Charlie Grant had been promoting for a decade—that modeling was the stepping-stone to aviation advancement—was at last being echoed in high places. The boy modelers of 1923, Mulvihill suggested, might well grow up to be future Edisons of the air.

It was a message that found a ready ear among the American public, for the myth of every-child-a-genius was alive and well in the U.S. in the early twenties.

The Sons of Thomas Alva

The myths that people live by seldom find their way into history books. And yet it is these popular belief systems that *create* history. 1492 couldn't have happened if Columbus and his circle hadn't believed in a round earth. 1776 would be meaningless without the Jeffersonian belief in the value of the individual. (While the Civil War, on the other hand, was rooted in an exactly opposite belief—the myth of federalism.) And so it goes. Every age has its myths, and its mythic heroes. Certainly the twentieth century—our century—is no exception.

The myth of the child genius has been one of the shapers of our times. Every American boy born into the first half of this century grew up in the long shadow of such a genius—a man who was the most prolific inventor in human history, a man whose formal education consisted of exactly three months of public schooling in Port Huron, Michigan, who nevertheless held more than a thousand patents by the time of his death at age 84, in 1931. That man was Thomas Alva Edison, the wizard of Menlo Park.

The incandescent bulb, the phonograph, the dictaphone, the electric railway, the carbon-button transmitter that made telephones possible and Alexander Graham Bell rich—Edison's inventions were everywhere. Even the waxed paper that five million modelers tacked over their plans was an Edison patent. Like his camping buddy Henry Ford, Tom Edison was both a role model and a burden to three generations of America's youth. The rags-to-riches myth that grew around Edison's life lay heavy on the shoulders of every child. No matter how stupid, no matter how academically inept you might be, you still had the possibility of growing into a famous inventor, a moneymaking manipulator of the great god Technology. Science, after the first world war, had begun to replace hard work and frugality as the way to wealth. All a child had to do was to pick a field and immerse himself in it until he made some new and unique contribution. Soon he would be as wealthy as Gail Borden or Harvey Firestone . . . or Thomas Edison.

It was a myth that dovetailed perfectly with the aviation madness kicked off by Lindbergh. Here was a brand-new technology: aeronautics. A field that was just beginning to blossom. What better arena to encourage children into, in order to test their creative capacity? Even if model building didn't lead them, in Mulvihill's words, to *contribute much to the progress of aeronautics a few years hence,* then at the very least they might become *pilots or users of aircraft,* and thus take their place in the great aerial future that was just beginning to unfold.

Every child an aerial Edison! It was a grand myth, and a useful one, and it carried an entire generation of kids across the dark chasm of the Great Depression, that long, bleak decade of poverty and pain. It was a myth that could be shared by parent and child alike, a myth that permeated the home atmosphere of millions of young modelers and gave them the solid support—financial as well as emotional— that led directly to the aeromodeling boom of the 1930s.

The Parental Nod

Ask anyone who has ever taught in the public schools about the relationship between a child's academic performance and the beliefs

39

his parents hold concerning education. It's a truism among grade school teachers, for example, that certain ethnic groups—Asian-Americans, for one—tend to believe strongly in the importance of schooling, and therefore encourage their kids to excel at book learning. And their kids seldom let them down.

In just this way, millions of American households during the thirties came to 'believe in' aviation. Millions of American parents of every race and creed, when their children expressed an interest in things that fly, gave them full support and encouragement. And it was sincere encouragement, too—an outgrowth of the parents' own enthusiasm for the air. After Lindbergh, nearly every citizen became to some degree "air-minded."

After Lindbergh, people invariably looked up when an airplane flew over. After Lindbergh, whole families would spend their Sunday afternoons parked outside the airport fence, watching the comings and goings of the most amazing variety of aircraft in history. Parasol-winged *Corbens* and bright-red Curtiss *Robins* and little Velie-powered *Monocoupes* hopped in and out like sparrows between huge, lumbering Ford and Fokker trimotors with their exposed cylinders and broad corrugated flanks. Army and Navy pursuits—colorful big Curtiss *Hawks* and midget *P-26s*—came and went like flocks of pigeons. By mid-decade there were the familiar yellow *Cubs*, and immense, thundering *DC-2s* and *DC-3s*—sleek, dolphin-nosed giants that became the prototype of all airliners for the next twenty years.

Lindbergh's flight had signalled the end for the rickety old 'flying machines,' those frail spruce skeletons from the days of the Great War that flitted about, dragonfly-like, with half their innards exposed and sometimes half their pilots as well. That marvelous summer of 1927 heralded the beginning of the "streamlined" age, a nationwide aerial ballet that lasted right up to Pearl Harbor—a long decade of speed and power and grace that was beyond question the most prolific and diverse in all of aviation history. The thirties were a sky's-the-limit era of open-ended creativity that permeated aeronautics from top to bottom—from the well-lighted loft of the aero engineer to the lowliest basement building board.

Aeromodeling during the thirties was fed by the spinoff energy of fullscale aviation, and so it ran just a little behind the full-scale curve in its achievements. But, as we'll see in the next few chapters, it followed the trajectory of that curve faithfully—depression or no depression—up and up and up.

A squadron of Comet RED RACERS from 1930 flies by.
The RED RACER kit sold for $1.00—but you could order
a Racer, a Comet Dipper (50¢), a Curtiss Robin (75¢) and
a 75¢ Army Pursuit biplane for just $1.75 factory direct!

Chapter Three

INTO THE AIR, JUNIOR BIRDMEN!

The Public Image of Aeromodeling in America

*When I was a kid in the early thirties there were more damn
model clubs to join than you could count on both feet!*
—Eddie Faria, Turlock, CA.

*I remember when I first became editor of MAN in 1931 how nearly
impossible it was to have our full scale aviation men and our
government men to consider models as anything but a toy.*
—Charlie Grant

WINS TOY PLANE TROPHY
Purchase (N.Y.) Youth Victor
Over 110 Boys in Model Contest
—*New York Times*, December 31, 1932

Child's Play

Modeling's public image was formed—cast in concrete—in the
years immediately following Lindbergh's flight to Paris. Like most
public images in this century, it was formed largely by the media of
the day (newspapers, magazines, radio) and by the advertising
dollars that control the media's every breath. It was a direct

outgrowth of the 'toy airplane' fad that crystallized in the wake of the *Spirit of St. Louis*.

But even the serious modelers, those hardcore designer-builder-fliers who had begun long before Lindbergh, and struggled along quietly, bending bamboo over candle flames and winning contests and advancing the art and science of aeromodeling despite the toy fad—even those people managed, inadvertently, to contribute to the image of model building as child's play.

It was probably unavoidable. For most of the aeromodelers of the twenties and thirties—serious or otherwise—were children.

Toy Airplane Mania

The model plane market just before Lindbergh was almost invisibly small. It consisted of a dozen or so legitimate kit manufacturers—Ideal, Wading River and Cleveland were among the biggest—and another dozen toy companies that put out almost-ready-to-flys (ARFs) of widely varying quality. Immediately after Lindbergh, though, this market simply exploded; within a year there were over two thousand firms in the field.

The largest of these newcomers, and in many ways the most typical, was the Metalcraft Corporation of St. Louis.

Few people today remember Metalcraft. But they were number one in the model airplane field during the late twenties. They were backed by the same three farsighted gentlemen (Messrs. Knight, Bixby and Dysart) who had put their money on Colonel Lindbergh before he was so much as a buck private. Metalcraft rode the tidal wave of the Lindy craze from its very inception, becoming, in less than a year, the IBM of the airplane hobby. In one month alone—October of 1928—they did $140,000 wholesale. (Multiply that figure by twenty to approximate its current value: just under three million dollars. *Wholesale.*)

Metalcraft's models were mostly scale: a *Spirit of St. Louis,* a Waco bipe, a Junkers *Bremen*, a copy of Admiral Byrd's Fokker *Trimotor*. The catch was that any one of these famous planes, plus nearly 500 other designs (so said their brochure) could be built *from the same kit*. What Metalcraft was peddling, through every department store, dime store and toy store in America, was an expensive box of aluminum sticks for clever children to snap together into a toy airplane—a kind of highly specialized, aerial Erector set.

Silver Ace

A short step up from Metalcraft's generic toys was the *Silver Ace*. The Ace was introduced by the Aero Model Company of Chicago in the summer of 1927—and copied shamelessly, within months, by at least a dozen other firms. A 30" semi-scale (*very* semi-scale) model of Lindbergh's Ryan, the Ace was an assembly-line ARF, with balsa fuselage sides and silk covering on top and bottom. It sold, all painted up and ready to fly, for a ten dollar bill—two day's pay for a working stiff. Within a year the price had crept up to $12.50, and you could purchase, in addition, a set of pontoons for $4.00, or an extra wing to make it into a bipe (everybody needs a Spirit of St. Louis bipe) for just $3.50 more.

The Silver Ace's wing spar, as well as its leading and trailing edges, were hardwood dowel, so the model's vaunted flying abilities were, at best, relative. Historian Jim Noonan has a soft spot for the Ace—and they *were* a razor cut above most ARFs of the day—but the truth is, nobody ever set any records with a Silver Ace. A well-adjusted Japanese wire-and-silk dimestore plane would outfly them.

Another typical model of the Lindy era was the little 12" Spirit of St. Louis kit put out by Mann and Benton of Chillicothe, Ohio and advertised for years in *Popular Aviation*. For fifty cents postpaid, Mann and Benton promised a "scientifically designed and very realistic" construction set for a model that "rises from the ground by own power and flies 30 feet, or more."

An eight-year-old Manteca, California boy named Duke Fox ordered one of these four-bit wonders, and when it arrived it was nothing more than cheap construction paper, worth maybe a dime at the most. Heartbroken, he built it anyway, but the flimsy fuselage collapsed the first time he tried to wind it up. Duke Fox grew into a lifetime modeler despite this early disappointment. For nearly fifty years he manufactured Fox U-Control and R/C engines—a tall, oblique man whose slow, careful speech masked a bright mind with marvelous recall. Duke told me his Spirit of St. Louis story in October of 1990, just a few months before his death. He was still angry at Mann and Benton.

And then there was the widely advertised *Dowae Stunt Plane*, $1.00 postpaid—yet another trap for the unwary. "Flies! Glides! Loops!" the ads promised. As well it might: with zero dihedral and the world's shortest tail moment, the miserably designed little Dowae was likely, after takeoff, to do just about anything at all.

Toy Airplane Era

This was the great toy-airplane era of the late twenties, when millions of air-minded American children (and their parents) were fleeced by hundreds of purveyors of scrap aluminum and dyed cardboard. By the mid thirties the fad had faded, and the model plane market reverted once more to the 'serious' hobbyists, who by now numbered in the hundreds of thousands. But not before countless parents had been taken for a memorable chunk of change, and countless potential modelers has turned away from model airplanes in disillusionment.

During this time, a well-intentioned magazine-sponsored club, The Airplane Model League of America, was able to reach thousands of kids with its 65¢ *Baby R.O.G.* kits and its syndicated essays on the 'science' of model aerodynamics. The AMLA's membership climbed to nearly half a million before the organization collapsed. But even an effort this size could do only so much to stem the tide of chicanery and opportunism.

Which, in the long view, may have been just as well. For it was the size of the toy fad—and the dollar figures from companies like Metalcraft—that first brought the model airplane to national attention. Numbers are impressive, but *dollar figures* have the real power. It was the dollar figures of the late twenties that got the attention of certain national corporations, and gave rise, ultimately, to the huge commercial clubs of the thirties, the clubs that rounded up kids by the hundreds of thousands, organized them into local units, showered them with buttons and badges and self-importance, and created the pool from which most of America's long-term aeromodelers ultimately sprang.

The Kiddie Market

Big business, in the Lindbergh era, was just beginning to recognize the influence children have on family spending. Corporations and their admen were on the verge, about 1930, of a major breakthrough in mass manipulation: they were just discovering that *one of the shortest routes to a family's pocketbook is through its children.*

Suppose, for example, you have a breakfast cereal to sell. It might be a breakfast cereal no different from a dozen other breakfast cereals, but naturally you want to sell more of it. You want, in the jungle metaphor of the business world, "a bigger bite of the market."

Radio, at the time, was a hot medium—a natural way to reach kids. And kids eat a lot of breakfast cereal. So you might start by creating and sponsoring some daily cowboy adventure show that kids would be attracted to—something, for example, like "The Tom Mix Ralston Straight Shooters."

Yeah!

You create this Tom Mix thing, and you sponsor it for a while, and pretty soon you find, by subtle questioning, that every time the redoubtable Mr. Mix and his thunderous wonder-horse Tony go galloping through a kid's head, the words "Ralston Purina" go galloping right along behind him. Just like a banner. Just like a horse's tail in the breeze.

So far so good.

But you can do better than that. You can print up millions of Tom Mix Trading Cards, and put one inside each cereal box, so that every kid who's *really* a Tom Mix fan will suddenly develop an insatiable appetite for Ralston Purina products.

And you can do even better. You can start, apropos of nothing, a "Tom Mix Straight Shooters Club," and print membership forms on every Ralston Purina box. Buy the cereal, clip the form, join the club. Children just love to belong.

Well and good—for Ralston Purina. But suppose you have an *adult* product to sell: something like Skelly gasoline, say.

No problem. Cowboy shows ("oaters," in the trade language) aren't appropriate for an oil company, though. So here's what you do: You cook up a kids' adventure program based on, say, *aviation.* Aviation is hot. And aviation has a natural tie to gasoline, because what burns more gasoline than an airplane, right? You can call your new program "The Air Adventures of So-and-So."

Pick a nice, clean-cut, blond-haired, middle-American name.

Pick . . . "Jimmie Allen."

Jimmie Allen

Make Jimmie Allen this handsome, corn-fed Kansas City kid, barely old enough to solo—a sort of budding Lindbergh, modest, a teenage (the word hadn't been invented yet) hero who gets into all the usual hair-raising tune-in-tomorrow scrapes, but does it in a cockpit instead of a saddle.

"The Air Adventures of Jimmie Allen." A gasoline oater. That should get the kiddies' attention, no?

Yes. But how does it sell Skelly gasoline?

Simple. As soon as the program is off the ground you set up, apropos of nothing, a "Jimmie Allen Flying Club." You tell the kiddies to have their dad or mom drop by their local Skelly station to pick up (no obligation!) a free membership blank. Be sure to do it this week, though, because next week the *free flying lessons* begin, and when that happens they'll want to stop by the station once more, for a copy of Lesson Number One.

Complete all five lessons and fill in the final exam (that's seven weekly trips to the local Skelly station) and you'll receive, pass or fail, a ready-to-fly sheet balsa R.O.G. with a big blue Skelgas emblem on the rudder! Wowie!

One more trip gets you a set of plans for the Jimmie Allen *Bluebird*, a high-wing rubber-powered 'pursuit' that looks something like the tried-and-true, three-year-old Comet *Dipper.* Build yourself a Bluebird, and then stay tuned for details of the "Jimmie Allen Air Races," coming soon to a city near you.

Wowie and hot damn!

Spectators

The year is 1933, and sixty thousand Jimmie Allen/Skelley Oil ROGs (kitted by Pop Schreiber at the Country Club Aero Supply, 59th & Holmes, Kansas City, MO) are flitting like mosquitoes all over the American midwest. The first 'Air Races' for Jimmie Allen *Bluebirds* take place down in Tulsa, before a crowd of ten thousand spectators.

Ten thousand spectators—ten percent of the Tulsa population!

Who would believe so many people would turn out to watch a bunch of children battle the Oklahoma wind with stick-and-tissue airplanes? But the following week—who knows why—*twenty* thousand gawkers show up at the Jimmie Allen contest in Kansas City. Then twenty-five thousand at Denver a week later, followed by thirty thousand at St. Louis . . . .

Heigh ho! Is this kiddie aviation thing *hot*, or what?

In no time at all, Richfield Oil of California has become the nation's second "Jimmie Allen" sponsor, followed by Pocahontas Oil and then Weather Bird Shoes and Mission Bottling and Town Talk Bread . . . and coast to coast the list grows on. At the peak of the Jimmie Allen fad, in late 1936, six hundred thousand club newspapers are being printed weekly, and the club's monthly magazine, *Air Battles,* hits a high of a million and a quarter copies!

Move Over, Jimbo

Just about this time, the late Mr. William Randolph Hearst of San Francisco and San Simeon, a man who was once (no, *twice*) the most powerful newspaper magnate in America, happened to be suffering one of those periodic reversals of fortune that, in the opinion of many of his contemporaries, couldn't happen to a nicer guy. The Depression had hurt him bad. He was finding it necessary to sell off some of his excess furniture—a couple of hundred rooms full—through a few select department stores nationwide. His bread and butter, the Hearst publishing empire, was perilously close to bankruptcy, and was locked into a nationwide circulation battle with its largest rival, the venerable Scripps-Howard chain.

Although not previously known for benevolence toward children, the seventy-year-old Mr. Hearst took a sudden interest, during the summer of 1933, in the Jimmie Allen phenomenon. What a marvelous thing for all those youngsters! Could something like it be organized through his papers?

Shaw Enough

It could indeed. Back east, on the staff of the Brooklyn *Eagle*, was a former modeler and youth enthusiast and high-minded idealist of the prewar variety by the name of Mr. Lawrence Shaw.

This Mr. Shaw, it seemed, was already neck-deep in the model airplane game. Four years earlier, in 1929, he had organized the *Eagle's* Junior Air Legion, and he had been running, every year since, the already legendary New York City Model Plane Derby, a huge *gummiband* contest traditionally held at Sheep Meadow Field, up in Central Park.

This Shaw fellow was known to be tough but fair, always pushing his boys to new challenges, always making the top dogs step down so that the also-rans had a crack at the prizes—which, in a Lawrence Shaw contest, were sure to be both many and lavish. Strong and opinionated and short and dictatorial, Lawrence Shaw struck Randolph Hearst as having the makings of exactly the kind of fascist that every good democracy needs at its helm.

The Junior Birdmen

And so in May of 1934, just a year after the first Jimmie Allen radio show blasted out over the Kansas prairie, the Hearst Corporation chartered a brand-new model airplane club. It was called "The Junior Birdmen of America, Inc.," and its National Director was Mr. Lawrence Shaw.

Seventeen Hearst newspapers in seventeen "wing cities" scattered liberally across the land began to run, every Sunday, a full page of Junior Birdman news and views and how-to's. Most of this material was generated by Lawrence Shaw himself, who also turned out, during that first, prolific year, four separate Junior Birdman handbooks for beginners.

Each of these handbooks guided the reader through the pitfalls of building and flying a simple, scratch-built balsawood model plane. The books were thick and meaty and deadly earnest, and sold at very close to cost: 10¢ each, postpaid. There was so much information to disseminate, so much ignorance to dispel! But Lawrence Shaw was up to the task. ("Model builder's cement," he advises the reader early in Handbook Number One, "is used for holding the parts of the model together. Nails are never used.")

A young New Yorker named Frank Zaic designed the four models presented in the handbooks; a cartoonist and future *Air Trails* editor named C.B. Colby did all the illustrations; and Lawrence Shaw himself wrote the building instructions. It was a near-perfect combination of talents, and the *Junior Birdman Handbooks* created new modelers by the score.

Half a Million

Seventeen major city newspapers reach a goodly number of Americans, and within two years Junior Birdmen membership, open to "all boys and girls living in the U.S. and its territorial possessions whose ages are 10 to 21 inclusive," was well over half a million—making it easily the largest and best-organized aeromodeling club in U.S. history. Shaw claimed to keep a dossier, in his New York office, on every single Birdman. And Lawrence Shaw was not known to lie.

It was a full eight months before Scripps-Howard, the Hearst chain's rivals, got together a similar group. They dubbed their boys the "Junior Aviators," and started doing their level best to copy, and then outdo, Mr. Shaw's Birdmen.

But the Junior Aviators never quite made up for their late start: 300,000 was their top enrollment figure, reached in late 1936. Headquartered at the Cleveland *Press*, the Aviators' most memorable achievement was their annual "Junior Air Races," a model contest held each year just before the full-scale National Air Races—sometimes in Cleveland, sometimes thirty miles south in Akron. Local sponsors sent their winners to the Junior Air Races from every corner of the country. It was a good meet, a well-run meet, and the best thing about it was that it always fell right at the end of summer, making it the last big blowout before school began in the fall. To win, you had to be good; but to enter, all you needed was a Scripps-Howard Junior Aviators card in your pocket.

Card Carriers

And so it was that the thirties became, for modelers, the Era of the Nationwide Clubs. Despite the fact that stick-and-tissue modeling is second only to writing for loneliness, an air-minded kid of 1935 could hardly avoid being a joiner, a card-carrier.

In addition to his Jimmie Allen Flying Club card, his Hearst Junior Birdman card and his Junior Aviator card from Scripps-Howard, he might well carry the cards of a dozen or more manufacturers—beginning, in 1928, with the old Lyonsport Aero Club, a promotion of the infamous Metalcraft toy firm. These manufacturers' cards, besides signifying loyalty to the firm and its products, sometimes entitled the bearer to a token discount (around 10%) on direct orders.

Then, too, your post-Lindbergh modeler would have to carry the card or cards of his local flying group(s), some of which grew to be almost as large and impersonal as the national clubs.

In Boston the Junior Aviation League, co-sponsored by the Jordan Marsh department store and the Boston *Traveler,* had more than four thousand members, and put out its own weekly newspaper. The Philadelphia Model Aero Association had nearly 200 chapters in Pennsylvania, New Jersey and Delaware, each with ten to twenty members. The Stix, Baer & Fuller club, out in St. Louis, boasted 1200 members, while Kresge in Newark (Ben Shereshaw, Director) claimed 1500.

City-sponsored clubs flourished, as well. From its start in 1926, the Detroit Department of Recreation was by the mid-thirties sponsoring twenty-two city clubs: 1500 boys who bought their supplies at cost and built an average of 500 planes a week. And that local-club-to-end-all-local-clubs, the Chicago *Times* Air Cadets, had more than 40,000 names on its rolls by decade's end.

Every magazine had to have a club, too. Forgotten publications like *National Glider,* with its Aviation Boosters of America, as well as the better-known American Sky Cadets of *Model Airplane News* and the *Air Trails* Air Adventurers Club (led by the bold and bombastic and utterly fictitious Commander Albert J. Carlson.)

Perhaps the most memorable magazine club, because its name was revived in the 1980s by a nation-wide group of rubber scale modelers, was the Flying Aces Club. The original Flying Aces Club was no more or less respectable than any of the others. To join, you just clipped three monthly coupons for your free Cadet wings, five more for your Pilot wings. (No need to learn anything, boys and girls. No need to build or fly anything, either. Just keep buying and clipping those *Flying Aces!*)

Cynical Ploys?

Looked at from one point of view, almost every one of the commercially sponsored clubs of the thirties were cynical ploys to exploit children—attempts to capitalize on their interest in the air and their need to belong. But whatever the economic motivation, most of these clubs still managed to live up to many of their professed ideals. They all promoted air-mindedness. They all disseminated aviation knowledge, both model and full-scale. They all encouraged interested youngsters to ban together locally. And they all created lifetime modelers.

Hearst and Scripps-Howard, in their race to outspend one another, sponsored contest after contest all across the country. So that if Randolph Hearst could be said to have taken advantage of Lawrence Shaw's enthusiasm for kids and aviation, then Shaw certainly returned the compliment in spades, spending Mr. Hearst's money liberally on America's budding model builders. And the Jimmie Allen program, after hooking a kid on flight with an all-balsa ROG, pushed him immediately into stick-and-tissue, the heart and soul of thirties model building.

Indeed, most of the commercial clubs ultimately fell into the pattern of giving as much as they took. Even the dubious-sounding "Cracker Jacks Air Corps," a candy-company gimmick, managed to come through with a trophy or two at some of the early Nationals.

Barefoot Boy with Windup Toy

What the card-carrying members of every one of these 1930s clubs had in common—had in abundance—was youth. The average model plane enthusiast of the prewar era (whether a serious modeler or simply a toy airplane owner) was a male child between ten and fifteen years of age. The public saw this image in the newspapers. They saw it at the local modelplane contests. They saw it in the vacant lot next door.

It is this sixty-year-old image of the barefoot boy tossing his rubber model into the blue that still haunts the aeromodeling hobby in America today.

The flood of toys that followed Lindbergh's flight promoted this kiddie image. The nationwide clubs, from the Birdmen to the Cracker Jacks Air Corps, did the same. And finally, even the Academy of Model Aeronautics, founded by serious, contest-minded adults in 1936, wound up promoting the child-modeler image as well. And, to an extent, it still does.

The A.M.A. was the brainchild of a small group of dedicated model enthusiasts, adults every one, who were dissatisfied with the NAA's on-again, off-again approach to "junior" aviation. What they envisioned was a nationwide scientific body that would act in an advisory capacity to the NAA's rulesmaking—an elite corps of experts who would collect data and promote research in the field of aeromodeling. It was to be a self-sufficient organization, supported partly by the dues of interested modelers and partly by the contributions of big business, both in and out of the hobby field.

But what these starry-eyed idealists discovered, in very short order, was that *nobody who wasn't a model builder particularly gave a damn about the art and science of model airplanes.* If the AMA hoped to get any sort of widespread publicity, any sort of outside-sponsor support for modeling, there was only one route available to them—what journalists call 'the youth angle.'

Kids and dogs sell newspapers.

Major contests, especially as the thirties wore on and the gas engine began to displace rubber, came increasingly to be dominated by older modelers. Thirteen was the average contestant's age at the beginning of the decade, nineteen by decade's end. At this point—about 1939-40—the postwar handwriting was already on the wall: it was becoming obvious that the "air-age youth" of America belonged predominantly to a single, Lindbergh-inspired generation. It was a broad generation, to be sure, and some of it was yet to be born. But by 1940 the bulk of the country's dedicated, long-term model airplane enthusiasts had already arrived on the planet. And their ranks, as they matured, were not being filled from below.

This situation would become increasingly hard to hide by the late 1950s, when the percentage of junior participation in national contests, despite the biggest baby boom in U.S. history, plummeted toward the single digits.

The AMA's response to these facts—and they had little other choice if they intended to survive—was to distort them. To play up, at every opportunity, the youth angle.

If they hadn't done so, who would have supported the National Model Airplane Championships after World War II? Not the Exchange Clubs, whose interest is youth. Not the U.S. Navy, whose interest is recruits. Not any one of the dozens of local corporations and civic groups who have traditionally helped foot the bill, over the years, for this annual moveable feast we call the Nationals. Almost every one of these sponsors has been recruited through 'the youth angle.' Who cares about grownups? Who wants to sponsor an adult sport that concerns, at best, less than one half of one percent of the population? Who wants to help a group of middle-aged men deepen their tans?

Kids and dogs sell newspapers.

Adult Hobby

The aeromodeling hobby today is predominantly an adult hobby. It has been since the end of World War II. Cost and complexity have closed it to all but the most determined—and talented—of kids. Not that there's no room in modeling for the interested youngster. There's plenty of room, even at the top. Unlike, say, baseball—where the most spectacular little leaguer ever born would play hell getting into a pro game—all of modeldom exults when a bright twelve-year-old goes to a Nationals and cleans everybody's plow. Or wins the local fun-fly. Or simply comes out to the field with his own model and makes it go.

But this happens less often than the AMA and the model mags would have you believe. The few kids among us are still given more than their share of press coverage—a legacy of the half-century-old debate over the 'junior problem.'

Where Are the Juniors?

Back in 1964, during one of the hobby's periodic paroxysms of guilt over whether it does enough to encourage young modelers, someone made the suggestion that all contest trophies and prizes be given to the junior (under 16) fliers. Let seniors and adults compete for glory alone, they said—give the kids all the loot, if you want to lure them away from TV and other distractions.

It was a noble idea, and it might have engendered a long debate, had it not been laid to rest with a single stroke of the pen by one Mike Bloore of Lansing, Michigan. Skipping the question of whether anyone can be 'lured' into the mastery of a hobby as demanding as aeromodeling, Bloore went right to the heart of the dilemma: "If we do not want our hobby considered childish," he wrote, "then it simply cannot be centered on the child."

Mike Bloore may not have spoken the final word on the 'junior problem' and the 'image problem' in American aeromodeling. But it has always sounded like it to me.

Roll Call: KITMAKERS

Next to the magazines themselves, it's the kitters who have kept the hobby alive for so long. Like the hobby shops, most of them have been small. Cottage industries, garage operations, mom-and-pops—call them what you will, they've supplied us with the raw materials of aeromodeling for over eighty years. More than two thousand have come and gone. Here's just a sampling, some total strangers, others heartbreakingly familiar. Almost all are defunct.

TWENTIES: Ace Aeroplane & Model Supply, Jersey City • American Model Aircraft, New Haven • August Schaefer's Model Airplane Supply, New Rochelle NY • Broadfield Model Planes, Hempstead, L.I.• Cleveland Model & Supply (1919)•Clinton Toy, New Haven•Comet Model Airplane & Supply, Chicago • Country Club Aero Supply, Kansas City • Eagle Model Airplane, North Haven CT • Hawk Model Aeroplanes, Chicago • Hawthorne (NJ) Model Aero • Ideal Aeroplane & Supply, NYC (1911) • Michigan Model Airplane Supply, Detroit • Midland Model Works, Chillicothe • Miniature Aircraft, New Brighton NY • Mount Carmel (CT) Mfg • Pioneer, Champaign IL • Scientific Model Airplane, Newark • A.F. Selley Mfg, Brooklyn • Simplex Air Model, Auburn MA • South Haven (MI) Model Airplane Supply • Southern Model Airplane Supply, Atlanta • Universal Aircraft, Detroit • U.S. Model Aircraft, Brooklyn • Zodiac Model Aircraft, Chicago.

THIRTIES: Airo Model Supply, Baltimore • Airway Model Plane, Bklyn • Allentown (PA) Model Airplane & Supply • Bay Ridge Model Airplane & Supply, Bklyn • Berkeley Models, Bklyn • Bunch Model Airplane, LA • Burd Model Airplane, Baltimore • Burkard-Stevens, Larchmont NY • Champion Model Aircraft, Columbus OH • Crescent Model Aircraft, Bklyn • Cyclone Aircraft, Bklyn • Dallaire Model Aircraft, Detroit • Dobe-Ott Model Aircraft, Chicago (became Joe Ott) • Douglas Model Aircraft, Seattle • Falcon Aircraft, Southbridge MA • Fli-Rite Models, Huntington Park CA • Golden Arrow Models, Pontiac MI • Heathe Model Airplane, Bklyn • H & F Model Airplane, Bklyn • Hub Model Airplane & Supply, Bronx • International Models, NYC • Korff Co, Indianapolis • Long Beach (CA) Balsa Syndicate • Madison Model Airplanes, Bklyn • Majestic Model Airplanes, Bklyn • M&L Model Supply, Oakland CA • Megow's Model Airplane Shop, Philly • Model Airplane Utility Co, Bklyn • Modelcraft, LA • Model Developments, Glen Ridge NJ • Modern Model Aircraft & Supply, Central Falls RI • Moskito Flier, NYC • National Model Aircraft, New Rochelle NJ • Pacific Model Aircraft, LA • Paul K. Guillow, Wakefield MA • Peerless Model Airplane, Lakewood OH • Red Bird, Omaha • Reliable Model Aero, Bklyn • Reginald Denny Industries, Hollywood • Reliance Model Aircraft, Philly • Skymasters Corp, Cincinnati • Star Model Aero Shop, Newark • Tilbury Model Racing Planes, Bloomington IL • Toledo Model Airplane Supply • Travis Model Airplane, Colo Springs • Tropical Model Airplane, Miami • Troy (OH) Model Aircraft • Truflight, Bridgeport CT • Victor Specialties, New Rochelle • Victor Stanzel, Schulenburg TX • Viking Aircraft, Hamilton OH • V.K. Model Airplanes, Williamsville NY • Washington (DC) Institute of Technology • Washington Model Aircraft, Seattle • Woburn (MA) Model Airplane Shop • Yalecraft Models, Hollywood.

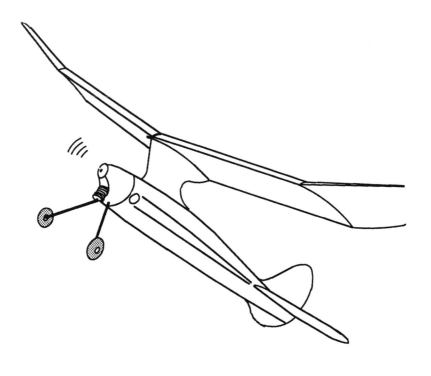

"You can tell it's a Zipper by the way it squats in the glide."

— Model Airplane News, *November 1957*

Chapter Four

FREE FLIGHT FOREVER

The Rise of the Gassie

Builds Tiny Motor
Monkeying Around
—Headline, Bill Brown story,
Philadelphia *Evening Bulletin*,
Saturday, May 30, 1931

*But the gas motor itself is the best selling point. It appeals
to the instinct that made you tinker with your bicycle or led
you to tinkering with the engine of the family car.*
—Gordon Light, *Air Trails*, August 1937

*Crashes provide much of the excitement and fireworks
at a gas-model meet.*
—*Popular Science Monthly*, December 1935

Alphonse Penaud's little *Planophore* of the early 1870s was the first man-made device, large or small, to balance on the wind and make repeated powered flights on its own, without guide string or tether: the world's first recorded freeflight. For power, the Frenchman (his assistant, actually, for Penaud himself was nearly paralyzed) twisted a long loop of rubber 'thread' and used its torque to spin a wooden airscrew. Fifty years went by—some would say closer to seventy—before anyone created a better power source for miniature flying machines.

Power to Weight

The problem, in those bad old days, was power-to-weight. In this respect, Penaud's twisted rubber band was hard to beat: it could store a terrific amount of energy in just a few grams of rubber.

Steam power (despite that one spectacular 4000' flight, in 1896, of Sam Langley's thirty-pound *Aerodrome #5)* was patently ridiculous. Compressed air engines seemed at first a solution. They were light, and multi-cylinder models were capable of driving propellers at impressive speeds. But they required huge, carefully-soldered sheet brass air tanks to store their energy. When you included the bulk and weight of an air tank—and you weren't going anywhere without it—compressed air's power-to-weight was right down there with a squirrel on a treadmill.

And then there was rocket power. Until they were finally outlawed, rocket planes would show up at every 'optional power' contest held during the late twenties, for amateur rocketry was yet another fad of the fad-ridden flapper era. The most successful of these rocket motors consisted of a drinking straw loosely packed with gunpowder: lots of push for very little weight. And quick, too, if speed was your thing. But gunpowder rockets had a couple of drawbacks. They set fire to things. And even when they didn't set fires, they were occasionally inclined to *extremely rapid oxidation,* the technical term for a loud bang.

That left gasoline—the internal combustion engine. A series of loud bangs, contained within a cylinder built to take it.

Internal combustion had been good enough for the brothers Wright. Internal combustion worked every day under the hoods of twenty-five million American cars: *pokita, pokita, pop-pop-pop.* Why, then, couldn't it be applied to model airplanes?

By 1930, thousands of aeromodelers were waiting impatiently for an answer to that question.

The problem was still the same: power-to-weight. Gasoline engines of the day were heavy and complex. Single-cylinder types were by far the simplest, but they weren't yet reliable; automobiles and airplanes had both abandoned the single cylinder long before World War I. With only one firing chamber, too much time elapsed between each bang—too much time for things to go wrong, too much time in which no work was being done.

How much was too much time? One-twenty-fifth of a second, at a modest 3000 RPM. Not very much time at all, by human standards. But this was the twentieth century, remember—the mechanical age—and human standards were all but passe´.

One-lungers

During the late twenties, when money and optimism were abundant, a number of experimenters began to revive the dream of a simple, lightweight, single-cylinder engine—most notably the folk who tinkered with motorcycles and outboards, plus a handful of sweaty souls who were tired of pushing their lawnmower. Occasionally one of the more 'successful' of these one-lung powerplants would be advertised for sale to modelers. Here's a typical engine ad from *Popular Aviation,* March of 1929:

But the time was not yet ripe, and engines like the Dynamic—it weighed closer to five pounds with batteries and ignition, according to former Indiana modeler Bill Swanson, and was, in his words "a marvel of unreliability"—never managed to make their way into the hearts of America's aeromodelers.

Bill Brown's Stovepipe

The first engine to do so was the one popularized by 1933 Nationals winner Maxwell Bassett of Philadelphia, and built by his flying buddy Bill Brown. It was an engine designed by a model airplane builder specifically for model airplanes: the Brown Junior. Tall and gawky and lincolnesque, the Junior quickly became known as "Bill Brown's stovepipe." It was the first mass-marketed U.S. engine, and the standard by which all others were measured; fifty thousand Browns were sold between 1934 and 1939. Its homely outline appeared on more sets of plans than any other engine in modeling history.

Bill Brown sometimes gets credit for 'inventing' the model plane engine, in the same way that Henry Ford is often accused of inventing the car. Neither party is guilty as charged. Old Sam Langley of the Smithsonian flew one of the earliest gas-powered models, way back before the turn of the century. Ray Arden's prewar skirt-chaser in Van Cortlandt Park was mentioned in Chapter Two. And in any event, the British had been keeping official records on gas-powered model flight since 1914—the year Bill Brown turned three.

So Brown was hardly the inventor of model engines. What he did do was to combine reliability, simplicity and lightness in a single-cylinder, two-cycle aircooled motor—and then reproduce it over and over in his dad's home workshop. And market it, finally, at a reasonable price.

Provided that you consider $21.50—one to two week's pay in 1934—a reasonable price for a ready-to-run .60 cubic inch motor.

Caution and Thoroughness

A charter member of the Philadelphia Model Aero Association, William Lykens Brown was a young man with an old man's caution and thoroughness. His first successful engine, a .28, was completed in 1929, while he was a sophomore in high school. But five years passed—five years of tinkering and refining—before Brown finally offered the .60 sized Junior for sale to the general public. By then, dozens of pre-production Browns were in the air, all up and down the east coast. By then Bassett had swept the '33 Nationals with his fleet of Brown-powered models; his win of all three outdoor rubber classes forced the NAA to separate forever the gas from the *gummiband* events. By then half a dozen other modeler-machinists on both coasts were experimenting with—and preparing to manufacture—their own engine designs.

Even after Bassett's grand slam in '33, the gas idea was slow to spread. At the Eastern States Champs in early 1934, only eight people arrived with engine-powered craft, of which two managed to put in official flights. Twenty-six showed for the Akron Nats that year, but only seven got airborne. Not even the experts, it seemed, could make these mechanical marvels run at will.

Two out of eight, seven out of 26. With the official, contest-proven odds of a successful flight hovering at around 25%, it's no wonder the gas fad struggled so long in getting off the ground. It didn't really begin gaining momentum until late in 1935, by which time the Brown had been on the market for well over a year, and already had at least two serious rivals—the big, expensive Forster .99, and Major Moseley's far better known .36 cubic inch Baby Cyclone.

Built out in Los Angeles by Moseley's full-scale aircraft firm, the 'Baby Cyke' was no imitation Brown. At $15.75 postpaid, it introduced the modeling world to the rear rotary valve, a decided improvement over the tricky little vacuum-operated mushroom valve on the earliest Browns. Unfortunately, it also introduced the world to the first crankcases made of magnesium alloy—a kind of silvery piecrust that two generations of modelers learned to call *pot metal*.

Between the Brown and the Forster and the Cyke—between New Jersey and Illinois and California—it would seem that the gasoline age had finally arrived.

Nobody's Dream

And yet surprisingly few modelers welcomed any of these engines at first sight. Even many of the people who had looked forward to a power source that would replace rubber were put off by the weight and noise and grease and complexity of this first primitive trio of gas-burners.

The modelers of 1935 were, after all, *rubber* modelers. What they had in mind, what they might have described as ideal, was an ounce or two of metallic magic, worth a couple of hours' pay at most—a motor that would start with a flip, run like a demon, and haul a 36" rubber job straight up into the clouds. In short, what they had in mind was the *half-A glow engine*, something that was still fifteen years in the future.

Instead, what their week's pay got them, in 1935, was a huge lump of machined steel screwed into the middle of a fourteen inch maple propeller—total weight just under a pound. If that combination wasn't offensive enough, then add a spark coil the size of a baby's fist, a fat condenser, two pencell batteries in their aluminum tray, a switch and a plug and a great snarl of copper wire that was supposed to tie everything together and make it all work.

To the average modeler peering into a Brown or Forster or Baby Cyke box for the first time, the metallic melange that greeted him looked more like spare parts for a Model T than something meant to fly a model airplane. Alien objects, these—objects from another world, the harsh and noisy world of machinery. If this was what the gas engine was like, then it was utterly incompatible, in many modelers' eyes, with the light and delicate dream-world that American aeromodeling had so recently become.

The Modern Model of 1935

For the model airplane had changed radically in the six or seven years between Lindbergh and the Brown Junior. Two decades of

64

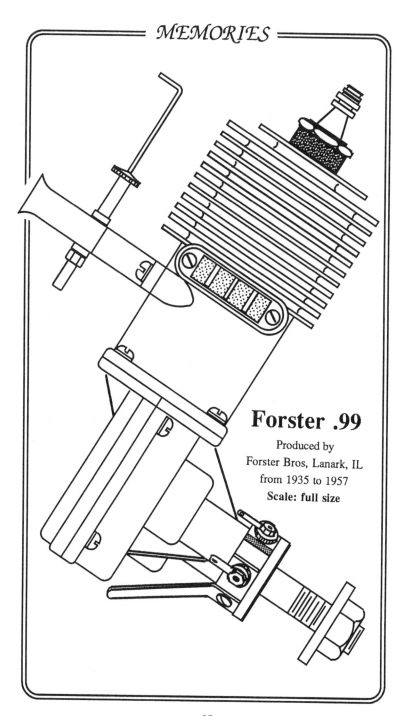

Forster .99

Produced by
Forster Bros, Lanark, IL
from 1935 to 1957
Scale: full size

near-stagnation had given way, during the early thirties, to a period of rapid evolution. Aeromodeling had grown overnight from a sport of hundreds to a sport of thousands, perhaps millions, and the best of these new minds had little or no nostalgia for modeling's past—even its recent past.

This new wave of post-Lindbergh modelers saw no inherent virtue in spruce and pine and beautifully wrapped thread-and-glue joints. They took one look at the venerable old twin pusher, a planform that had been serving the hobby faithfully since 1894, and consigned it instantly to the aerodynamic scrap heap. These new modelers peered into the future, and saw that it was streamlined. They put their best energies into skinny, balsa-framed tractor designs—long, lean versions of the *Spirit of St. Louis*—and in a brief few flying seasons they created the modern model airplane. The lifting stabilizer, key to lightweight freeflight performance (and something Charlie Grant had been advocating since 1919) suddenly became the norm. Polyhedral began to replace vee-dihedral—Carl Goldberg introduced it on indoor models as early as 1930.

Between 1927 and the mid-thirties the "scientific" model airplane—meaning the all-out performance machine, as opposed to the scale model—evolved from a hardwood-and-muslin A-frame pusher into a lovely streamlined creation with teardrop fuselage and dragonfly wings, a sleek marvel of structural engineering that was built with a gram scale and balanced on a pencil point and powered with a machine-perfect paulownia-wood prop. The best models of 1935 weighed under two ounces ready to fly, had huge, efficient freewheeling propellers (folders were just appearing), and were capable of three to four minute still-air times.

A World Divided

To trade such refinement and delicacy for a pound of shrill and cantankerous steel struck many modelers as something less than progress. And no wonder: the ignition engine of 1935 was a gross and dirty and shockingly noisy device—an ear-rattling roar in the previously silent world of rubber and glider and compressed air. Some people loved this roar, but many didn't. Like the streamlined automobile, which came into being at almost exactly the same time, the "gassie" divided its world into two antagonistic camps. And sometimes that dividing line went right down the middle of an individual.

Charlie Grant was one of those divided people. Grant was, first and foremost, a rubber modeler. When Bassett made his famous prediction at the '32 Nats (the year he entered only one event, and finished fourth) that gas would eventually replace rubber, the normally opinionated Grant simply reported the remark in *MAN* without comment. And yet, before the decade was half over, Charles Hampson Grant had become probably the best friend the gasoline engine ever had—Bassett and Brown not excepted.

Grant moved into the editor's chair at *Model Airplane News* in the winter of 1931-2. He was 37 years old, a trained aerodynamicist and amateur boxer who was, by all reports, already something of a middle-aged curmudgeon. Fortunately for the hobby, he would live to be an old one.

In 1932, the great changeover from twin pusher to tractor was just getting under way. Grant was pleased by this change, and he took no pains to hide it. For once history was on his side. He had never believed in twin pushers anyway—he'd always been a tractor man. A scrappy, sawed-off little out-of-work aero engineer, seldom without a strong cigar and an even stronger opinion, Grant took the *MAN* editor's job intending to stay for a year or so, until the engineering field picked up again. He wound up staying eleven years.

Now I Are One

Like so many engineers of his day, Charlie Grant was only semi-literate. He thought "Aeronca" was spelled the way most people pronounced it: Aronica. He never did learn that Sal Taibi's name wasn't Sol, and he insisted on ending Joe Raspante's surname with an *i*. But for all his faults, Charlie Grant was just possibly the most ardent believer in the American Air Age—and modeling's indispensible role in it—that ever came down the pike.

Like every aeromodeler of his generation, Grant had grown up building rubber models. But unlike most of the others, Grant approached his hobby with High Seriousness. He was hell-bent to make it into a science—make it respectable in the eyes of the world. By 1932, nearly twenty years of his life had gone into collecting data on the performance of model aircraft—*rubber-powered* model aircraft. He didn't care much for gliders, and in 1932 there wasn't any third choice. Rubber was all he knew.

Furthermore, he could see at a glance that Bassett's newfangled "gas" models were economically out of reach of millions of youngsters, and likely to remain so. And youngsters were important to Charlie Grant. Youngsters represented not only the future of modeling—and hence the future of the magazine that fed and clothed him—but also, he sincerely believed, the future of all American aviation.

Missing Link

Yet at the same time, Grant was fascinated by Bill Brown's stovepipe. By the time the Brown Junior hit the market in '34, he had dropped all pretense of editorial neutrality. He praised it to the skies. Borrowing a highly-charged phrase from the religious debates of the day, Grant declared the Junior to be nothing less than the "missing link" between model and full scale engineering.

And so, in a way, it was.

Rubber, despite its light weight, had never been an entirely satisfactory form of power for any model that even approached scale dimensions. Full-scale aircraft, designed around powerplants that represented half or more of their empty weight, were invariably short-nosed. But rubber models needed *long* noses for balance. Build a true-scale rubber job and you almost always wound up adding weight to the front—dead weight. The gasoline motor, huge and ungainly though it was, solved the twin problems of balance and power simultaneously.

So Grant, as a model designer, couldn't help being attracted to this new field, despite his years of rubber expertise.

When a man is divided between two loyalties, economics can easily tip the balance. Perhaps Grant the editor saw the handwriting on the wall—saw that one Brown Junior, at $21.50, was the economic (read: *advertising dollar*) equivalent of a hundred rubber-model kits. Perhaps he decided that the younger modelers, who could never in a million years afford a twenty-two dollar engine, would still buy *Model Airplane News* to read about Brown Juniors and dream. Or perhaps Grant the engineer was simply captivated by this new and totally unexplored design field.

Perhaps all three.

The K-G Gassie

In any event, Charlie Grant threw the entire weight of *Model Airplane News* behind the gas movement. He began by publishing his own design, the Kovel-Grant *Gassie*, as *MAN*'s first gas job, in the spring of 1935. The K-G was a rubber modeler's gassie—an eight foot airplane constructed with unbelievable amounts of 1/32" sheet balsa. But the K-G's layout was sound: parasol wing, long tail, large stab, small fin. *(The small fin was the touch of genius. Rubber models need large fins, gas models small ones. How did Grant know that in 1934? By watching Maxwell Bassett's spiral dives?)*

The K-G was an immediate success. Orders for plans poured in from all over the English-speaking world. Its high wing and high thrustline quickly became the touchstone for all stable, conservative free flight layouts of the 1930s.

And then, for reasons known only to himself, Grant followed up the K-G with one of the homeliest model airplanes ever conceived. Published as the Loutrel *Sportster,* the plane was originally—and far more appropriately—dubbed the *Mudhen.* Fans of the legendary Ben Shereshaw don't like to remember that the Sportster was at least partly Shereshaw's design, a flying test bed for his buddy Pete Loutrel's converted boat engines. But then, fans of Pete Loutrel don't like to remember that the Loutrel engine (a good runner, by most accounts) was later mass-produced in a grease-laden hell-hole up in the Bronx slums under the trade name "GHQ."

Oh, That GHQ!

No history of American modeling can avoid the initials GHQ. The G.H.Q. Model Airplane Company was, in 1935, a respectable subsidiary of the oldest and largest mail order hobby house in the country, Arthur and Bernie Winston's *America's Hobby Center,*

69

Inc. GHQ, like Ideal and Cleveland and Comet before them, manufactured inexpensive flying scale rubber kits. Their line was fairly extensive. By mid-1935 they were advertising eighteen different 24" models at two bits each, plus a couple of 36" fifty-centers, as well as three 60" jobs (still rubber) at a buck apiece. Not bad kits, in most people's memory. But the GHQ engine— which hit the market in early '36 and lasted, unfortunately, through 1944—was the undoing of the company's good name.

Over a hundred thousand GHQs were sold, and almost every engine collector today who really wants one can find one—often in mint condition. Few GHQs ever wore out, because so few were ever successfully started. Some said the engine was ported to run clockwise. Others claimed it had no porting at all—a fuel-saving measure that was years ahead of its time. Bernie Winston was naturally touchy on the subject of the GHQ. During the late thirties he ran Saturday workshops for frustrated owners, and claimed, sometimes a bit shrilly, that he never failed to start an engine that was brought to him.

Gresham's Law (the one that says bad money always drives out good) seems to apply equally to model plane engines, for the GHQ was virtually the only engine that was continuously available throughout World War II, when supplies of metal—even pot metal—were government regulated. In fact, the only time in the engine's nine-year history that the sturdy old GHQ was out of production was a brief period when the entire production shop—a local motorcycle gang—were caught spiriting engines out the side door in their lunchbuckets and fired, *en masse* and *non obstante*.

Advertised in the July 1936 issue of *MAN* in kit form at $8.50, or ready to run for $12.50, the GHQ certainly looked good on paper compared to the $21.50 Brown, or even the $15.75 Baby Cyclone. Thousands of readers bit. Two years later the kit price had fallen to a modest $5.00 as the word got around.

But the GHQ wouldn't die, and when the '42 war shortages halted production of virtually every U.S. engine except a handful of Herkimers from upstate, thousands of modelers forgot having been bitten. Orders began pouring into the little plant in the Bronx once more. Soon GHQ had the engine market pretty much to itself, and the price climbed up and up and up, reaching a high in 1944 of $20.00.

Price gouging? Look at it this way: what would *you* pay, in wartime, for brand-new engine that was almost certain to last forever?

The model mags wisely stood clear of the GHQ controversy. Truth-in-advertising has never been a crusade that editors of low-circulation periodicals could afford to join—even fiery, opinionated editors like Charlie Grant. Besides, there were plenty of other battles to fight. Just a few months before the GHQ's introduction, the largest model airplane organization in America had abruptly and quite unexpectedly *banned gas power from all of its contests, and begun a nationwide campaign to have the gasoline model airplane outlawed entirely!*

Publishing the Bans

During the summer of 1935, Mr. Lawrence Shaw, national *fuehrer* of Hearst's Junior Birdmen, chanced to witness the screaming death-dive of a berserk gassie during a JB meet in New York City. Not an unusual occurrence, actually. Death dives were fairly common in '35, when wheel launches of gas models still exceeded wheel landings by a comfortable margin. But these were the days when newspapers headlined model meets, and spectators turned out by the thousands—drawn, often as not, by reports of just such death-dives. The crash that Shaw witnessed narrowly missed clobbering some of those trustingly upturned spectator faces.

As the dust settled and the screams died out, Mr. Shaw had a sudden and terrifying vision. He could see the 660,000-member Junior Birdmen of America, Inc., his wonderful one-man empire, crumbling in the jaws of a King Kong sized lawsuit. He could see the bejowled countenance of his boss of bosses, Mr. William Randolph Hearst himself, pronouncing the dread words *can him . . .*

71

Shaw didn't particularly like gas models anyway—didn't know anything about them, and wasn't anxious to learn. He was a rubber man. Gas was false doctrine to him, a distasteful new schism in the sacred religion of aeromodeling, an impurity that ought to be wiped out before it spread. Lawrence Shaw decided that he was the man to do it.

Banning gas in Birdmen contests was merely the first step. Shaw immediately brought his own weight, as well as that of the entire Hearst newspaper chain, to bear on the United States Department of Commerce, the government branch in charge of aviation. His goal: nothing less than a federal ban on all gas modeling in America, sport or otherwise.

Hoo-ee!

By mixing a powerful imagination with a dash of redundancy, Shaw was able to come up with four distinct arguments against gassies, to wit:

1) *They are a menace to persons and property.*
2) *The storing of gasoline in the home is a hazard.*
3) *Gas modelers trespass and violate the personal and property rights of others.*
4) *Gas models are a hazard to [full-scale] aircraft.*

Specious though they may sound, Shaw repeated these points over and over until a number of people began to mistake them for fact. Fortunately, none of these people worked in the Department of Commerce. Shaw kept the pressure on month after month, but month after month Commerce—which had bigger fish to fry—continued to turn a deaf ear.

A couple of eastern states, impatient with this flagrant federal footdragging, passed anti-gas laws of their own. *"No model aircraft,"* the Connecticut Commissioner of Aeronautics decreed in July of 1937, *"shall be flown in or over the State of Connecticut if powered by means other than rubber bands."* Within weeks, Massachusetts announced a similar ban.

Hornet's Nest

Shaw may have thought he was making progress. But by bringing the rubber-versus-gas controversy out in the open, he had stirred up a hornet's nest. And not surprisingly, the chief hornet turned out to be that pugilist-turned-engineer-turned-editor, Mr. Charles H. Grant himself, by now three years into the editorship of *Model Airplane News*.

When Grant got wind of the Birdmen ban, the last vestiges of his editorial neutrality dropped away. He became a crusading gas man. Pictures of gassies had already been infiltrating—threatening to take over—*MAN*'s monthly "Air Ways" rotogravure. Now Grant started a second roto section, this one strictly for gas models. He called it "Gas Lines." It first appeared in February 1936, and quickly became the rallying point for America's small but growing number of 'gasoleers.' Grant used this new column to found yet another magazine club: the International Gas Model Airplane Association, or IGMAA.

No self-serving publicity gimmick, the IGMAA was founded as a political pressure group, pure and simple. Influential New York modeler Nathan Polk spearheaded its organization. Every dollar the club collected went to lobby for sane legislation— meaning no legislation—of gas modeling. Dozens of local chapters, called 'units,' were formed. Their job was to beat the bush for new recruits and to help influence public opinion on the grassroots level.

Within twenty months of its founding the IGMAA had 4500 dues-paying members—more than enough to make the National Aeronautics Association, whose funding came largely from dues, sit up and take notice. And just in time, too, for the two-state gas ban was in full force, and an overzealous aviation inspector at Springfield, MA had recently made headlines by 'busting' five fliers at a local gas contest. *Flying Aces* columnist Phillip Zecchitella reported the bust with a moan: model builders, he warned, were about to be lumped with commercial aircraft manufacturers, who were already buried under a snarl of federal red tape. "In short," Zecchitella predicted, "we are going to be licensed . . . . "

Bleak November

That was in bleak November of 1937. But even as Zecchitella's column hit the newsstands, the gears of self-interest were beginning to mesh behind the scenes. Charlie Grant had something the NAA

73

coveted: 4500 dues-paying IGMAA members. And the NAA had something Grant needed: the power to stop Lawrence Shaw.

A deal was cut, and the following spring the IGMAA—suddenly and quite unexpectedly, in the eyes of many of its members—was absorbed into the NAA, which august body began dutifully and noisily licensing both gas modelers *and their individual gas models!* Just exactly as Zecchitella had predicted!

This flurry of licensing, as it turned out, was all a grand charade, staged largely for the press and public. But to many of the modelers involved it seemed that their worst fears were already coming true: the great government octopus was reaching out to their very building boards. They screamed like stuck pigs.

Meanwhile, by way of holding up its part of the bargain, the NAA went to work on the Shaw problem. It was short work. In less than three months, Lawrence Shaw's nationwide anti-gas movement was stopped dead in its tracks.

Exit Shaw

Stopping Shaw, as it turned out, was no great trick—a mere matter of politics and posturing. Then as now, the NAA was the mother hen of all American aviation. Once it saw fit to support the gas flyers, it simply exerted its hen status. It stood up and cleared its throat and ruffled its bureaucratic feathers importantly. It assured all concerned parties that it was thoroughly in charge, and that the organizations under its wing would be self-policing. Finally, it promised with a loud squawk *never to issue a flying license for one of those terrifying gas models to any citizen under the ripe age of sixteen.*

It was as simple as that.

The nation's legislators were satisfied: somebody else had taken the responsibility. Immediately they turned their attention to other menaces, and forgot model airplanes completely. (Two years later, with the public spotlight elsewhere, the gas licence age was quietly dropped to fourteen; by war's end the age clause had disappeared completely. And as for the licensing of individual models . . . will the people who registered every gassie they built during this period please stand up?)

74

The NAA's actions left the states of Connecticut and Massachusetts—not to mention the National Director of the Junior Birdmen—out on the proverbial limb.

The legislatures of these sovereign states couldn't simply back down. That would be to lose face to the feds. So they waffled awhile. Finally Connecticut agreed to issue a certain number of gas-flying permits, strictly for 'scientific' purposes. Massachusetts decided magnanimously to permit any gas model, scientific or otherwise, to fly, provided both model and modeler were licensed through its own department of aeronautics.

Unpopular laws, history shows, are simply ignored. Few people troubled either state for a flying permit, and yet gas experimentation in both states went on pretty much as it did elsewhere. Within a couple of years, the Connecticut and Massachusetts laws faded quietly into oblivion.

Lawrence Shaw too refused to back down: no gassie ever again flew at a Junior Birdmen meet. In regions where gas interest ran high, whole squadrons quietly defected, keeping their JB structure but renaming themselves as independent clubs. John (Old Time Plans Service) Pond's Junior Birdmen Squadron #153, for example, left the fold to become "The San Francisco Vultures."

By his opposition to the gas engine, Shaw had placed himself and his organization out of the mainstream of American modeling. Birdmen membership peaked in 1937 at nearly two-thirds of a million; after that it began to taper off steadily. The final JB 'nationals' took place in 1939. By the end of the decade, Shaw's empire had returned into sand—destroyed, exactly as he had feared, by the gasoline engine.

Local Bans

And so the ban-the-bombs period of opposition to gas faded into history. About the only bans that stuck were local bans, and these were for the most part reasonable, based upon real threats to public safety.

Van Cortlandt Park, in upper Manhattan, had been the scene of dozens of near-catastrophes with gassies ever since Ray Arden's prewar model attacked his future bride. Van Cortlandt was simply too small and too crowded for gas flying—less than a thousand feet, east-to-west. It was easily New York City's most miserable flying site . . . except for all the others. Almost everybody who grew up in the Big Apple before the war flew there at least once.

But toward the end of the decade gas flying was outlawed in Van Cortlandt—and the ban was actually enforced. By the beginning of World War II you didn't even have to fire up an engine to get a ticket from the Van Cortlandt cops; you could be fined for merely *having a gas model in your hand.* (The charge was never clear; "possession with intent to test glide," maybe?)

A few other cities outlawed gassies from specific parks and public areas—regulations that, like Van Cortlandt's, usually made sense. But for the most part, prewar free flighters were few and far enough apart to escape the eyes of the law. It wasn't until the late forties and early fifties, when every park and vacant lot in America began to vibrate to the unmuffled roar of the sport controlliner, that cities really cracked down on model plane flying. Most of the anti-model ordinances still on the books today date to this wild and woolly postwar period of mindless and unmuffled U-Controlling.

The Great Divide

The great rubber-versus-gas battle went on right up to the war. History was on the side of the gasoline engine, but that fact was far from obvious at the time. Birdman Shaw may have lost the battle, but he certainly wasn't alone in his aversion the strange new shape—and sound—that aeromodeling was taking. Dick Korda and Jim Cahill were two of the biggest names in rubber during the late thirties. Both were international Wakefield winners. Of the two, Korda chose to make the transition to power before the war. Cahill held out until the late fifties.

Cahill, James B.

No one typified the diehard rubber fan of the thirties any better than Indianapolis modeler Jim Cahill, whose *Clodhopper II* won the

1938 Wakefield Cup in France with a single flight of just over 32 minutes. (For the record, the little ship was down below twenty feet at the three minute mark, when it picked up a lucky bubble and bobbed back up for another 29 minutes OOS—causing a hell of a row over whether the timer had or had not used binoculars. This, according to Ron Moulton of *Aeromodeller*, was the flight that set the International Wakefield Committee to thinking about the advisability of unlimited flight times.)

As early as 1937, Cahill already had a bellyful of the overbearing attitude exhibited by some of the born-again gas jockeys of the era. "These experts build up the delusion that just because a model is larger, you can have more fun with it," Cahill grumbled in *Air Trails*. "And, too, that a larger model will lift you above the general run of modelers . . . ."

His attitude never changed. When that same magazine asked him, in the early fifties, to name his favorite model, he unhesitatingly harked back to his old 1937 Clodhopper, the model that copped both the Moffett and the Wakefield trophies in one year. Not surprisingly, nothing ever took its place in his heart.

On the Run

In fact, rubber experts like Cahill had been on the defensive ever since Bassett's shocking gasoline sweep of all three rubber events at the 1933 Nats. Who today remembers the names of August Ruggeri or Vernon Boehle? Ruggeri and Boehle were the real winners—and also the real losers—of that long-ago Roosevelt Field Nationals where rubber first began its long decline. It was Ruggeri and Boehle who flew the *gummiband* models that Bassett's fleet of gassies elbowed into second place.

Vernon Boehle was doubly cheated, for he came second behind Bassett in both the stick and the cabin events—which meant that the Mulvihill and Stout trophies, two of America's oldest and most prestigious outdoor cups, slipped right through Boehle's deserving fingers and fell into the arms of that young upstart greasemonkey, that smiling and likeable little disturber of the peace from Philadelphia, Maxwell Bassett.

In the cabin event, Boehle's score was what even the staid *New York Times* called "remarkable:" eight minutes and forty-three seconds for his single best flight. In 1933, this was a world record for rubber, but how could it stand up to a gasoline engine with no fuel restriction—an engine that might drone on, when everything went well, for twelve to fifteen minutes?

Boehle's response to his '33 defeat was classic: he went back to Indianapolis and ordered a set of castings to hack out his own Brown Junior. For years Vernon Boehle continued to fly—and win—rubber events. But by 1935 his name had begun to appear in the gas listings, as well. (Today he's best known as the designer of the *Boehle Giant*, a Baby Cyke powered fifteen-footer that was meant to win the Texaco fuel-allotment event simply by *staying in sight* longer than smaller planes!)

Boehle made the transition—bridged the chasm between rubber and gas—and remained in the hobby. The cheerful little red-headed August Ruggeri, on the other hand, stuck doggedly to his *gummibands*, and, despite his heroic name and his near-genius ability to make a twin pusher perform, slipped quietly from sight within just a couple of years after that fateful Nationals of 1933. (According to old time flier George Oswald, Ruggeri 'retired' to a shop on East 73rd Street, NYC, where he cut beautiful balsa.)

The Road Less Traveled

August Ruggeri, like Jim Cahill and his under-appreciated brother Bob, had chosen the road less traveled—the road that ultimately narrowed down to about what it is today: a few hundred dedicated rubber modelers who build Wakefield (and Unlimited, and Coupe d'Hiver) for competition among themselves and with a few hundred of their counterparts across the Atlantic. "Real Modelers Crank 'Em Backwards," their teeshirts proclaim. More than most of today's modelers, these rubber men are aware of their history, their long, unbroken tradition. They know that, as *gummibanders*, they carry the banner first raised in 1909 by a young lad named Percy Pierce, whose twin pusher, launched from the starting line, regularly began thumping the far wall of the armory

78

some two hundred feet away, forcing the New York Aero Club at last to move its indoor contests outdoors.

Nothing Good Ever Dies

And yet, despite widespread defections to gas, rubber flying went on—before, during, after the war. It was after the advent of gas that a youngster named Earl Stahl began to design, chiefly for *Flying Aces*, his endless series of simple, efficient little rubber scale jobs, so popular today among Flying Aces Club members.

It was after the advent of gas that two young men from Chicago, Wally Simmers and Ed Lidgard, joined Cahill and Korda and all-round modeler Hank Struck to create the handful of pre- and post-war contest rubber models we still consider to be the classics of the genre: the *Jabberwock* and *Gollywock,* the Comet *Sparky,* the *Clodhopper* and *Korda Wake* and *Flying Cloud.*

Rubber flying went on, because aeromodeling is a hobby of accretion, and few aspects of it ever die completely. But after Bassett, the great mass of American modelers, the thundering herd of the late thirties, turned slowly but inexorably toward the new challenge of gas.

On the Trail of the Herd

Chicago hobby shop owner Carl Goldberg was typical. Best known for his expertise in the light and filmy world of indoor rubber, the 22-year-old Goldberg became, during the summer of 1935, one of the founders of a brand-new club called The Central Gas Model Plane Society. Central was an earnest young group, open (according to its bylaws) "to any modeler, male or female, sixteen years or older, of good moral character and able to present to the club's Executive Committee within six months of their date of acceptance tangible evidence of their sincerity."

Tangible evidence presumably meant a gas model.

How Carl himself satisfied that requirement is unclear. He was an exceedingly slow and cautious experimenter. Nearly two years passed before he appeared in public with his 'first' gassie, the monstrous *Valkyrie*—an underpowered tribute to both indoor construction (every wing rib was built up) and the conservative force arrangement of Charlie Grant's by-now-ancient *K-G Gassie.*

Carl Goldberg. Here was the quiet radical of aeromodeling, the tireless innovator, the man who had introduced polyhedral to the world in 1930, falling back now on first principles—for the Valkyrie, like the *K-G* before it, sported a simple vee-dihedral wing. (Bassett, in his *Miss Philadelphia* series, had alternated between poly and vee and tip dihedral—sometimes at the same contest. Max Bassett was an inveterate wing-switcher.)

The Valkyrie had a lifting stab, but in other ways it was a painfully conventional design, little more than a streamlined *K-G.* Only its wing mount was radical—so radical that for years it didn't have a name. (Even Comet, before the war, never called a pylon a pylon: their Zipper ads referred only to the model's "automatic pilot wing mount.")

And yet the Goldberg Valkyrie was the first small step of a design revolution that ultimately rocked the freeflight world—split it as profoundly as gas had split rubber—into two antagonistic camps. By the time war came to America in December of '41, you were either a cabin buff, and your hero was Charlie Grant, or else you loved the pylon look of the *Zipper* and *Interceptor* and *Playboy*, and your heroes lived 'out west,' in Cleveland and Chicago.

Transition

It was an exciting time, designwise, this long transition period from rubber to gas. In the six or seven years between the long-nosed, big finned, Curtiss-Robin-like *Miss Philadelphia II* and the squat, high-pyloned Goldberg *Zipper,* there occurred a wide-open era of raw experimentation, when more progress was made in the field of model aeronautics than in any comparable period before or since. (For a design-by-design account of these times, just thumb through Frank Zaic's marvelous *Yearbooks* of the thirties.)

80

Like the Renaissance in Europe, this was a time when the old rules had been found wanting and the new rules hadn't yet been formulated. So anything seemed possible. And almost everything was tried.

Particularly toward the close of the decade there occurred a great blossoming of original designs. From down in Little Rock came H.A. Thomas and John 'Kingfish' Sadler with their sleek low-wingers, starting a trend that culminated in the Peerless *Panther*, with its curious amalgam of underslung polyhedral and open cockpit. Chuck Hollinger, who later designed the 72" J-3 *Cub* for Berkeley (the grandaddy of today's *Sig Cub* kits), had already begun the development of his *Nomad*, a pod-and-boom shoulder-winger that you can see at a glance owes nothing to anyone. About this same time Joe Weathers out in San Diego and Winnie Davis back in Kansas City—both prolific designers—each went through a gull wing phase.

Out east, Leon Shulman and Frank Ehling took to building "flying wedge" fuselages that carried Grant's CLA rules almost to the point of parody. And hot on their heels was Henry Struck's *Record Hound*, with its anhedral stab and single landing wheel built into a gentler, rounder version of the wedge. Carl Hermes of Connecticut produced his *Hayseed*, a sleek missing link between cabin and pylon models, while Roy Marquardt of Iowa flew nothing but twin-boom models, both pusher and tractor—some of them sporting newfangled tricycle landing gears.

Along more conventional lines, 'Berkeley' Bill Effinger's *Buccaneer* series, begun in 1935, remained the classic cabin jobs of the era, while Shereshaw's teardrop-shaped *Cavaliers,* also kitted by Berkeley, set the all-time standard for streamlined grace.

On the west coast, high-wing scale models suddenly became popular, while elsewhere Goodyear-like racers appeared: New Cyclone's shoulder-winged *Lancer,* and the Scientific *Varsity* and the Megow *Soaring Eagle* and its chubby cousin the Comet *Golden Eagle.*

All these unique aircraft—and a hundred more—helped to make the late thirties the Golden Age of model design. And all of them were ultimately laid to rest by the rules changes that led to Goldberg's late-1938 *Zipper*.

Scale

The sheer weight of the engines, during this long transition period, opened up a brave new world of giant-scale freeflight. The age-old prejudice against low-wing scale jobs, enhanced by some of Charlie Grant's stability theories, at first confined scale gassies to high wingers: *Corbens* and *Robins* and Taylor *Cubs* and Stinson *Reliants*. But soon a rash of low-wingers began to appear— sometimes in imitation of fullscale racing or military planes, sometimes in imitation of mere dreams. More than a few were takeoffs on Frank Tinsley's illustrations from the Bill Barnes fiction yarns in *Air Trails*.

Modelers got bolder and bolder. By 1938, pictures began to appear in the various mags of gorgeous, ten-to-twelve-foot, twin engined DC-3s—pictures taken, one can't help but suspect, before the model's maiden flight. (Imagine turning a true scale twelve-foot DC-3 loose upon the winds: six month's work and three weeks' pay, gambled on three degrees of dihedral, a miniature stab, and *double* the normal torque!)

Vee dihedral, polyhedral, gull wings and swept wings; twin tails, vee-tails, tee-tails, no tails—during the late thirties every variation on the basic flying machine had its day. Grant, in the *MAN* "Gas Lines" section, snorted and harrumphed at everything that didn't conform to his Center of Lateral Area theory. But the pictures continued to pour in, and he published them anyhow, if only as an excuse for more snorting and harrumphing.

Gadgets

This latest fad, the gasoline engine, opened up more than just a new field of aerodynamics. It introduced into modeling a brand new world of gadgetry, as well. And do we Americans love gadgets? Hey, now! Who do you think invented the word?

One of the cleverest of this avalanche of gadgets was the 'automatic' starter. Firing up a spark ignition engine had been, right from the beginning, a daunting task. By the summer of 1938, however, a bright young man named Carl Turner had the answer. He began marketing a flashlight-sized metal tube with a fat torsion spring inside. You simply wound up the spring and pressed it against your propeller hub and released the catch, spinning the prop over smartly half a dozen times. Assuming your engine was just about ready to start anyway, this often made it happen. Since then, more efficient ways of grinding down the front of crankcases have been devised—but Turner's "Cadet" starter of 1938 was one of the earliest commercial devices for that purpose.

The biggest problem with the gas model, though, had already proven to be not *starting* the engine but *stopping* it. Following the pattern set by the Brown Junior, most thirties engines came with an integral gas tank: a little bubble of metal or celluloid that hung down below the intake pipe, which traditionally protruded from the rear of the cylinder. This little tank didn't hold much—a couple ounces on average. But two full ounces of white-gas-and-#70-oil could run a .60-sized mill for a small eternity, especially if the model happened to be dangerously out of trim. (As every free flighter knows, there's nothing like a few wild loops followed by a death spiral for throwing the very last drop of gas into the pickup tube of a fuel tank.)

Engine Killers

Clearly, the first thing needed was a consistent five to ten second engine run, for testing purposes. One of the earliest solutions to the problem (January '36 *MAN*) was elegantly simple, at least on paper: just tie a string to a knife switch in your ignition circuit and run alongside the model as it ROGs, prepared to jerk the string and kill the spark if things go wrong.

Ever try to keep up with a .60-powered gas model on takeoff?

Even if you managed to stay alongside, and the ship didn't turn on you accidentally, jerking a string tied to its nose was almost certain to give it the idea. One attempt with this system (two, for slow learners) led people to conclude that some sort of *mechanical timer* might be more practical. At this point, something like half the gas fliers in America had the same idea simultaneously: the 50¢ watch.

A cheap pocket watch with a sturdy second hand could be modified very simply so it would short out the ignition or cut the battery juice after a predetermined number of seconds. All it took was a set of Rube Goldberg contacts, cobbled up out of hairpins and soldered in place above the second hand. To avoid the problems of grease and engine vibration, guys in Southern California took to mounting these touchy little devices in their wings. Properly cared for, they functioned reasonably well—between crashes.

So well, in fact, that the cheap pocket watch—one of the few good things to come out of the Great Depression—soon became the mainstay of every gas jockey in America. A few hardy souls groped about for more sophisticated solutions: air-driven timers that used miniature fan blades like the generators on full scale planes; fuses; rubber-powered escapements that unwound at a (supposedly) fixed rate. But most of the early gas fliers settled for the pocket watch. It reigned supreme until the spring of 1938, when a spate of specially-designed clockwork timers (by Scientific, by Polk's, by Berkeley and Bay Ridge and one Nathan R. Smith of Los Angeles) hit the market almost simultaneously.

Goodbye to Fuel Allotment

And not a minute too soon, either—for the 1938 NAA rulebook practically mandated some sort of engine timer. In addition to raising the wing loadings, the '38 rules summarily dropped the old allotted-fuel system in favor of a simple thirty-second maximum engine run.

Before 1938, almost every gas event had been flown by 'fuel allotment': a certain amount of gas for each pound of airplane weight. The Texaco oil company had originated this practice, by sponsoring at the '33 Nationals the first Texaco Trophy for the longest flight made on 1/4 ounce of fuel per pound. (Bill Northrop of *Model Builder* loves to point out that those early Texaco trophies were probably the biggest bargain in the entire history of American advertising. The company dropped its sponsorship after only three or four years, yet half a century later it still gets free plugs everywhere oldtimer events are flown!)

When the NAA sat down, in early 1934, to write up the country's first gas rules, it incorporated Texaco's "quarter-ounce per pound" allotment. But every year gas models and gas modelers kept improving, until by the summer of 1936 any ship that didn't crash outright was almost certain to fly out of sight on that much gas. (Seven pounds was the maximum allowable weight for a model at the time, and a lot of guys would actually ballast their models up to seven just to get the full one-and-three-quarter ounce allotment.) So in '37 the NAA cut that allotment in half, to 1/8 ounce per pound. But still models disappeared over the hill. The answer, everyone hoped, was 1938's heavier wing loading requirements, coupled to a flat thirty second engine run.

This had to be an improvement. No more time-consuming weigh-ins before each flight, with the allotted amount of fuel doled out by a contest official. No more cranking your engine up, tuning it, then wasting even more of that precious allotment while you strapped cowlings back in place and switched from starting battery to airborne pack before releasing the plane for its takeoff run.

Now everybody was entitled to exactly the same engine-on time: thirty seconds from release of model. Gone forever were Max Bassett's slow, circling fifteen-minute engine runs. Gone were the giant east-coast models with their teeny, gas-miser engines—models that took all morning to climb to two hundred feet. Freeflight design from the two coasts, which had gone off in separate directions from the very start, might finally be able to re-converge around these new rules. Or so it was hoped.

Because among the growing schisms in the aeromodeling fraternity, none was sharper than the division between East and West.

Never the Twain

Ever since the first hardy, stinking old oxcart pioneer struck California, and hawked and spat, and defiantly refused to shave off his travelling beard, America has been divided into East and West. So why should modelers be any different?

Western gas designers had, right from the beginning, favored smaller models than those built out east. As early as 1936 the Southern Californians had already gotten their fill of long, floating, out-of-sight flights; they were starting to build smaller, heavier models, and look for ways to limit their engine runs.

From L.A. came the first 'precision' contests, in which models took off from the center of a set of concentric rings, attempted to do a predetermined number of circles in both climb and glide, then land back within the target. Precision flying quickly became popular all up and down the west coast. Even though the largest of the circles was traditionally only around 700 feet in diameter, some contests would see an astounding 60% or more of the entries landing within the target! (To get the calm weather needed for such an event, a few hardy contest directors even held their meets at night.)

The east, in general, is windier than the west. In the wind, big planes stay in sight longer than small ones. And ride light lift better, too. So easterners tended toward giant floaters. When they, too, got bored, they began to put these giants to good use in 'payload' contests, lifting everything from lead shot to booster batteries (a foreshadowing of the postwar weight-lifting events sponsored by Pan American Airways.)

Meanwhile, up in Portland, Oregon, kit manufacturer Jim Walker and his cronies were busily experimenting with 'programmed' freeflights: models that performed certain simple maneuvers dictated by a clockwork timer hooked to the control surfaces.

The sky was the limit during this period, not merely in design and gadgetry, but in flight performance itself.

Modeling Reborn

In many ways, the mid to late thirties were like 1909 all over again. The world of gas, it turned out, was almost as different from the world of rubber as rubber had been from full scale. Just as the first modelers had had to discover that their path to performance did not run parallel to that of full scale, so the gas fliers of the thirties found they had to forget much of their rubber-design knowledge. This new field that Bassett and Brown had pioneered in 1932 was—quite simply—modeling reborn.

From the perspective of sixty years, it's not easy to appreciate Maxwell Bassett's achievement. It's not easy to reconstruct, even in imagination, the broad chasm Bassett had to bridge. There's no way for those of us who came later, those of us who grew up in the long shadow of the air age, to recapture the ignorance and uncertainty of 1932. It's so deceptively easy today to poke fun at those first stumbling, stalling flights of the boxy and pig-ugly old *Miss Philadelphia II* (originally called *Fleetwings*—see page 90.)

But to make a gassie fly at all, in 1932, was akin to balancing it on a cue stick in front of an oscillating fan. At the time, the only person on earth who seemed to have the edge on Max Bassett was the English modeling genius C.E. Bowden. While Bassett's *Miss Philadelphia* was looping and spinning its way to fame in the U.S., Bowden's *Kanga* biplane—its outlandish big rudder offset by two deeply dihedraled wings—was turning in flight after consistent flight over in the U.K.

The constantly changing torque of an erratic engine, the broad speed range and the incredible mass and inertial forces of eight to ten-foot airframes—these and a dozen other factors (shall we talk about precession?) were shoving the gas model back in the direction of full-scale aerodynamics, a direction from which rubber had been for twenty years steadily retreating. Bassett's propeller alone, at the 1932 and '33 Nationals, outweighed most of his competitors' entire models.

Compared to the rubber models of the day, the *Miss Philadelphia* was an unguided missile. To make such a monster balance on the wind, and remain airborne without any other help than a few built-in warps and twists, would seem utterly impossible.

Except that, by now, we've all seen it done a thousand times.

You Can't Do It Again

Which brings us to a simple but seldom-acknowledged principle of history: *the unrepeatability of first experiences.* Once a feat—any feat—is known to have been accomplished, there's no possible way to recreate the uncertainty of the pioneers who first attempted it. As soon as Roger Bannister broke the four-minute mile, dozens of other sprinters suddenly found it possible. After the Wrights were known for certain to have flown, experimenters on three continents magically found their wings. Where Bassett finally succeeded, hundreds followed.

It seems that once a thing has been accomplished, some mental barrier is broken that can never be re-erected. Let's take a more current example: Everyone knows that perpetual motion is 'impossible.' And yet, if someone were to discover its secret tomorrow morning, within the year four or five additional (and totally different) methods of achieving perpetual motion would be found, and patented, and written up incomprehensibly for *Scientific American.* That's simply the way the universe works. Certainty is the mind's most formidable barrier.

For this reason alone, I have little patience with folk (beginning with Glenn Curtiss in 1914) who spend their energies trying to recreate Langley *Aerodromes* and Whitehead *#21s* in order to "prove" whether these machines might have flown before the Wrights. The most such experiments can ever prove is that these machines *can be made to fly now.*

But now is not then. It's simply impossible to recreate the aerodynamic ignorance that surrounded those original experiments. It's impossible to reenter that mental atmosphere, that fog of derision and doubt and disinformation that Langley and Whitehead (not to mention Wilbur and Orville) stumbled through. Innocence lost is gone forever. Such attempts to reenact the past seem as ludicrous as the Gypsy's chant in *Camino Real:*

> *"Tonight*
>> *the moon will restore the virginity*
>>> *of my daughter Esmerelda."*

The game of Who Was First has always been a fascinating one, particularly in the field of aeronautics. But it isn't a game you can play with replicas.

"Engine-Launched Gliders": A Footnote

By the end of the 1930s, the world of model airplanes had changed beyond all recognition. The era had begun with simple rubber models, and only two types, at that—stick and commercial. It was a division that went back to the 'flyers' and 'racers' of 1910: stick models were for pure performance, while commercial models looked something like man-carriers.

The era began with rubber models, and now it was going out with the *Zipper*, a skyrocket with wings, a flying machine that resembled a full-scale, man-carrying aircraft only as the mist resembles the rain. The *competition model airplane* had become, as Roy Clough noted in a 1947 *Air Trails* article, "very suddenly an engine-launched glider."

Not everyone at the time liked the idea of engine-launched gliders. Not everyone does today. But fifty years have passed, and the engine-launched glider has yet to run its course.

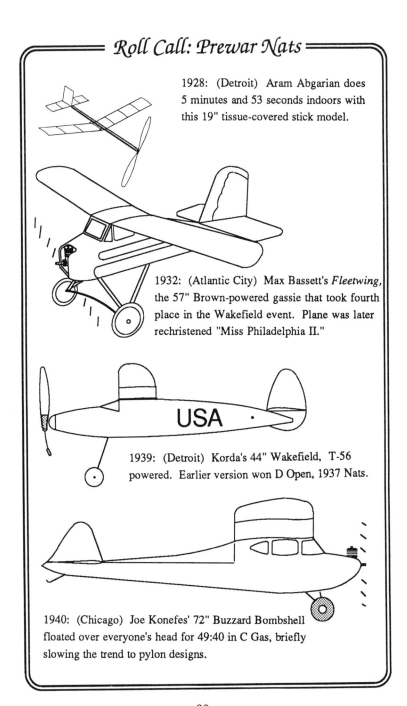

1928: (Detroit) Aram Abgarian does 5 minutes and 53 seconds indoors with this 19" tissue-covered stick model.

1932: (Atlantic City) Max Bassett's *Fleetwing,* the 57" Brown-powered gassie that took fourth place in the Wakefield event. Plane was later rechristened "Miss Philadelphia II."

1939: (Detroit) Korda's 44" Wakefield, T-56 powered. Earlier version won D Open, 1937 Nats.

1940: (Chicago) Joe Konefes' 72" Buzzard Bombshell floated over everyone's head for 49:40 in C Gas, briefly slowing the trend to pylon designs.

Chapter Five

THE PREWAR NATIONALS
Gathering of the Clan, Part One

The hum of the tiny motor, like that of a full-scale plane in the distance, and the soaring spirals of the red monoplane as it rose ever higher, finally to play hide and seek in the gray clouds and islands of blue sky some 3,000 feet above the field, held spellbound more than 175 boys from many parts of the United States and Canada, assembled for the first day of the National Championship Model Airplane Meet.

—*New York Times*, June 28, 1933

The most fair and satisfactory method of timing outdoor contests is for the judges to follow the models in flight in an automobile accompanied by the contestant.

—*Popular Aviation*, May 1929

The National Model Airplane Championships is, with the possible exception of Mr. William S. Winter himself, the most ancient and venerable institution in American aeromodeling. In many ways, the history of the Nats IS the history of aeromodeling. The Nats predates our oldest magazine, *Model Airplane News*. The Nats predates even its own sponsor, the Academy of Model Aeronautics, which grew out of a pow-wow held during the ninth Nationals, back in Detroit in '36.

Lies and Technology

The Nationals has always been both more and less than a contest. It is, to borrow a phrase from free flighter Bob Stalick,

91

who borrowed it from Frank Zaic, the annual Gathering of the Clan.

A good Nats is something akin to the yearly conventions the old mountain men used to hold, a century and a half ago, up in the Rockies above Taos Pueblo: a time for greeting old friends by arm-wrestling with them, a time for swapping lies and technology, a time for getting a glimpse of the clan heroes—past, present and future. Without the Nationals there would be far less unity among us, far less sense of identity, far less of that invisible bond that Lindbergh had in mind when he said, "If we fly, we all speak the same language."

Today, when one of the clan says he's going to "the Nats," everybody knows what he means. He means the AMA Nationals. But this wasn't always so. Back in the stick-and-tissue days of the early thirties, just before the advent of gas, you had your choice of three or four national model airplane championships, each with a different sponsor, and each calling itself "the Nats."

The Junior Birdmen of America—company club of the Hearst newspaper chain—had its Nationals. So did the Scripps-Howard Junior Aviators. So did the American Legion and the Y.M.C.A. So did the Playground and Recreation Association. And so did a long-forgotten magazine called *The American Boy*.

The First "Nats"

The very first Nationals to crystallize out of the wake of Lindbergh's epic flight took place in Memphis, Tennessee, on Saturday, October 8, 1927, less than five months after the Lone Eagle landed at LeBourget. Officially titled "The National Playground Miniature Aircraft Tournament," it was sponsored by a nationwide organization of city park-and-recreation departments. Park & rec folk were among the first to notice the sudden mania for model planes that was sweeping America. And since they already had an organization in place to deal with such manias, it's not surprising that they were first to put a national competition together.

The 'Playground Nats' of 1927 was an eliminations contest. To qualify, you had to pull a first place in one of the regional meets held in a dozen or so cities and towns across America. These Regionals consisted of ten events, five indoor and five out. The top score from each event was whipped off by mail to a panel of national judges—a panel that included, supposedly, such heavy hitters as Orville Wright, Teddy Roosevelt and Colonel Lindbergh himself. Five finalists in each of the ten events were then selected and brought to Memphis, expenses-paid, for the big October showdown.

Five entrants, ten events. So the Playground Nats wasn't a monster of a contest, the way later Nats got to be; it was limited to fifty fliers. But they were, in theory at least, the top fifty fliers in the country—the cream of the cream of America's stick-and-tissue model builders.

Fifty entries meant that each flier at Memphis got a lot of personal attention. It also meant that the contest could be completely planned in advance, so it would run smoothly and efficiently. Which was a good thing, since only a single day was allotted for the whole shebang. Outdoor was held in the a.m., indoor in the p.m., followed by the customary way-past-midnight awards banquet—and then goodbye.

As it turned out, only about half of the qualified fliers were able to make the Memphis trip. And not one of them complained (as people in later years did) about the length of the awards banquet. Longwinded speakers not withstanding, nobody was in any hurry for the evening to be over. It had taken everybody much too long to get there.

Six Days on the Road

Travel, in October of 1927, was by train, bus or rickety car. (Model T's were everywhere, but the first Model A was still two months in the future.) So your average contestant at the Playground Nats spent about six days on the road in order to get in his half-day of flying. One modeler came all the way from Hawaii, sponsored by the Honolulu *Star-Bulletin*. He was nearly two weeks getting to Memphis, by boat and train, and another two weeks getting home. These guys were young and supple and loved their hobby.

All the trophies and most of the publicity for this first Nats were provided by the magazine *Popular Aviation*. *PA* was a general aviation mag, but like many general aviation mags of the time, it carried a small modeling section. Before Lindbergh, this section had been conducted by one Paul Edward Garber of the Smithsonian Institution, one of modeling's earliest Friends in High Places. After Lindbergh, the section was expanded and taken over by an enthusiastic young hobby dealer and compressed-air fanatic from the midwest by the name of Bertram Pond.

Bert Pond was proprietor of the Peru Model Airplane Shop, at 69 East Main Street, Peru, Indiana—a crossroads farming village up in the tall corn above Indianapolis. Before the Depression, Ringling Brothers and a few lesser circuses had their winter quarters in Peru—giant barns out along the banks of the Wabash, full of tigers and elephants and bright red peanut wagons. An unlikely place, Peru, Indiana, to go looking for a lion in winter. But an even more unlikely place, in the mid-twenties, to go looking for a hobby shop. Most of Bert Pond's business was done by mail.

IMAC

Peru (Bert pronounces it PEE-roo) and its Model Airplane Shop were 140 unpaved miles southeast of the magnificent and sin-laden city of Chicago. Neverhteless, Pond's allegiance resided with a Chicago-based group of fliers called the Illinois Model Aero Club—the very club that had dominated those first three mail-order nationals back in the 'teens. If many of Pond's *Popular Aviation* columns read like publicity releases for this club, that's only because, before 1930, Chicago's IMAC, founded in 1912 by a young lad named Bill Stout, was by far the most enthusiastic and creative bunch of aeromodelers in America—miles ahead of the boys on either coast.

At one point in 1928, for example, IMAC members held every national (they liked to say "world") record for rubber and compressed-air powered model aircraft, both indoor and out, both tractor and pusher. (Pond himself won the Mulvihill rubber trophy the third time it was contested—in 1925.) Duration, distance, speed, rise off water, rise off ground, handlaunch—IMAC

94

members held them all. And Bert Pond took the reins at *Popular Aviation* just in time to begin broadcasting the club's secrets to kids all over America who were preparing for that first big Nats in Memphis.

'Playground and Rec,' the New York based sponsor of the Memphis Nats, was an old hand at organizing youth movements, and raising money from local businesses, and just generally doing things up right. And so, when it came off, the Memphis Nationals had a lot going for it. It had events for handlaunch and rise-off-ground and rise-off-water, both indoor and out. It had cargo events. It had glider events. It had optional-power events, to encourage experimentation with just about anything besides the miserable, cantankerous black "para" rubber that everybody used in those days. Furthermore, this Nationals totally ignored Solid Scale, those inert little blobs of dust-gathering wood, carved and painted to look deceptively like airplanes but hopelessly incapable of flight.

Orville, Teddy, Lindy, and no flightless blobs—how could the Playground Nationals go wrong?

Wrong and Wrong Again

Two ways, as it happened. First, it was just for kids. It made no provision whatever for fliers over the magic age of 21. And in October of 1927, just as today, some of aeromodeling's wealthiest and most influential and most fanatical fanatics were well over 21.

Second, the Playground people failed to kowtow to a group of Washington-based bureaucrats collectively known as the National Aeronautic Association. The NAA was charged with governing all aviation in America, big or little, and it had been doing so with rigor since its founding in 1922. (When the Mulvihill trophy was first offered, in '23, the rules stated that every contestant "must be a member of the Junior Flying League of the NAA.") But for some reason, the Playground Association omitted to get their Nationals sanctioned—a secular term meaning *blessed*—by the gods of the NAA.

In America, you can sometimes fly in the face of wealth and get away with it. And occasionally you can even defy the bureaucracy and survive. But to attempt both at once is suicide. The Playground Nationals came off as advertised in Memphis in '27. And again in Atlantic City in 1928, and in Louisville in 1929. And then it was heard of no more.

The Nats That Became THE Nats

Some eight months after that first Playground Nats, another group held its first Nationals, up in Detroit. This was the Airplane Model League of America, a "house" club created out of thin air by a now-defunct youth magazine called *The American Boy*.

The AMLA was the first of literally dozens of commercially-sponsored model clubs that sprang up in that fourteen-year period between Lindbergh and Pearl Harbor, the period that has come to be remembered as aviation's golden age. Some of these clubs were mentioned in Chapter Four. Their sponsors included newspapers, magazines, department stores, toy and candy manufacturers, airlines, oil companies, radio stations, butchers, bakers, candlestick makers and any number of other enterprises that would seem to have little or no connection with aeronautics.

The vast majority of these so-called 'clubs' weren't really clubs at all, in any meaningful sense of the word. Most were little more than public relations gimmicks designed to capitalize on young people's romantic notions about aviation and their desire to belong. (Send in the sailor boy labels from two Cracker Jack boxes to receive your very own Cracker Jack Air Corps wings . . . plus a catalog full of opportunities to buy more Cracker Jacks and win more 'free' gifts.)

But the AMLA, thanks to two men—a Detroit shop teacher named Merrill Hamberg, and *American Boy* editor Griffith Ogden Ellis—became much more than a gimmick. It grew, almost overnight, into the country's first truly national association for the promotion of aeromodeling.

Gusher

Hamberg, a little round middle-aged fellow with wire-rimmed glasses and a Charlie Chaplin moustache, started it all. In January of 1927 he inserted a brief contest announcement in *American Boy*. The contest he proposed was for a simple little 12" rise-off-ground rubber model of his own design. In his innocence, Hamberg even offered to send a free set of plans to anyone who wrote and asked for them.

A week after publication the hapless shop teacher was buried up to his moustache in mail. Letters poured in from every state in the union. And with each plans request came a litany of questions—questions that ranged all the way from how to carve a propeller to how to form a model airplane club.

Hamberg had tapped a gusher. This was still early spring, remember—weeks before the epic flights of Lindbergh and Chamberlain and Byrd. If America was just on the verge of going air-crazy . . . and it was . . . nobody in the country was aware of it at this point. But Mr. Merrill C. Hamberg of Detroit was beginning to suspect.

Hamberg went reeling to the *American Boy* offices for help with his bulging mailbags. He and editor Ellis were still busy licking stamps and shaking their heads over the matter when May came and the *Spirit of St. Louis* hit the headlines. Overnight, Hamberg's stream of mail turned into a torrent.

Griffith Ogden Ellis was the first to recover from the shock, the first to recognize the potential of this new fad. Here, he declared, was "a new boy's avocation that promises to be even bigger than radio!" And he seemed to know instinctively how to handle it. While Hamberg ground out copy by the ream, Ellis began disseminating it—not only through the pages of *American Boy,* but through a hastily formed syndicate of local newspapers all over the country. From New York City to Sweetwater, Texas, America was soon flooded with Merrill Hamberg's articles on building techniques, Merrill Hamberg's plans for prizewinning model aircraft, Merrill Hamberg's tips from the experts for better performance.

For 2¢ Plain

And still the torrent of letters continued to pour in. In an effort to set up some kind of system of stock answers for stock questions, the Airplane Model League was formed in September of that year. All it took to join was an unused 2¢ stamp. What you got in return was a membership card, a lapel button, the right to fly in AMLA contests, and the privilege of pestering *The American Boy* with any aviation question Dad couldn't answer. And Dad, in 1927, didn't know jack-doody about aviation. Two hundred thousand kids sent in their stamps immediately.

The League defined for itself four main objectives: to answer questions, to furnish hard-to-find materials, to help organize clubs, and to link America's air-minded youth with America's aviation leaders, many of whom were former model builders themselves.

The first such leader to agree to this link was IMAC's founder, William Stout. Stout was all grown up by now, and famous as well: he was the designer of the Ford Tri-Motor, the owner of Stout Metal Aircraft, and president of Detroit-based Stout Air Lines, one of the country's earliest commercial passenger carriers. He agreed to serve as president of the AMLA.

He also agreed, when talk turned to holding a national meet, to sponsor two perpetual trophies, one for indoor fuselage and one for outdoor fuselage events ('fuselage' in 1927 meant *enclosed fuselage*—as opposed to simply a stick. Such models were also called 'commercials.') His only stipulation was a good one: the Stout outdoor rules, he declared, must always be identical to the English Wakefield rules, in order to give Americans practice in flying this newly-formed international event.

The AMLA was off to a flying start.

The First Mail Order Discounter

Outside of the major cities, modeling supplies were still scarce in 1927. So the AMLA quickly put itself in the kit business, selling mail-order 'construction sets,' at cost, for almost every plan it published. (One of their primary goals, remember, had been to disseminate hard-to-find supplies.)

The League's first kit, a little long-nosed Hamberg rubber job with a stick fuselage and a diamond-shaped stabilizer, was called the "Baby R.O.G." (R.O.G. means rise-off-ground—as opposed to rise-off-water, say, or hand-launch.) Simple and sound and ugly as sin, the Baby R.O.G. was such a good performer in a day of predominantly bad performers that it quickly winged its way into the hearts of thousands of modelers. It sold for 65¢ postpaid.

What your 65¢ got you was a set of plans wrapped around a packet containing wire, sticks, wheels, rubber and tissue—plus a little corked test tube full of banana oil and another full of glue. Not one but *two* propeller blanks were included in the package, because prop-carving was by far the trickiest aspect of modeling in those days, and everybody, shop-teacher Hamberg felt, was entitled to one mistake.

Like every subsequent AMLA offering, the Baby R.O.G. was a true *construction kit* in the most basic sense—a direct contrast to the ready-to-fly models that had already begun to flood the toy market. The AMLA frowned on ready-to-flys, and not just because they cost ten to twenty times what a kit cost. Right from the start, the League policy was to create model *builders*—"junior engineers," in the phrase of the day—and not merely model fliers.

It was an excellent policy. Quite inadvertently, the AMLA and *The American Boy* began preparing an entire generation of air-minded children for the hard times to come—for that long Depression decade in which a box of sticks and a tube of glue, bought at the local drugstore for less than a quarter, could keep a young child dreaming and building and happy for a week or more.

And despite the popularity of ready-to-flys, the market was there, even in affluent 1927, for construction kits. The League mailed out over 75,000 Baby R.O.G.s in less than eight months. As the orders poured in for this little model, it must have occurred more than once to Mr. Griffith Ogden Ellis—as it has to every modeling editor since—that the kit business might well be a more lucrative enterprise than the publishing business.

Heroes

But the magazines, then as now, were far more important than any line of kits. They were—and are—the life blood of the hobby. *American Boy* not only published its monthly plans and building information and flying tips, but sponsored local and national

99

contests, and—perhaps most important of all—*reported on the winners*, thus providing the new sport of aeromodeling with its first national heroes.

All across the country, modelers read of the exploits of Jack Loughner, Ernest Marcoullier, Aram Abgarian, Donald Burnham, Louis Proctor, Joe Ehrhardt, Gordon Light. No sport is complete, no sport is compelling, without heroes—and the AMLA created them through its contests and publicized them every month through its syndicated columns.

And then ran out of money.

The Great Depression, which began with the stock market crash in the fall of 1929, finally caught up with Ellis and *The American Boy* in the spring of '31. During the runaway prosperity of the late twenties, the magazine had not only been footing the bill for the totally non-profit AMLA, but had been sponsoring its Nationals in Detroit each year, and then spending thousands to send the three top winners, plus their models and chaperones, on gaudy, six-week European tours. (Young Joe Ehrhardt of St. Louis was able to win the 1930 Wakefield Cup for the U.S. only because he 'happened' to be in England at contest time—as a guest of *The American Boy*.)

But when the great bubble of 1920s prosperity burst, everybody in America got soap in their eyes. All across the country, philanderers and philanthropists alike found themselves suddenly having to tighten their belts.

The American Boy maintained its commitment to modeling through the 1930 season, but in the April '31 issue it reluctantly bowed out. *Due to financial difficulties,* Ellis announced sadly, *there will be no 1931 Nationals in Detroit.* Many of the local sponsors of the contest had reneged, and the magazine, although still solvent, simply couldn't afford to foot the entire bill alone.

The Depression had arrived in modeldom. Rubber modeler Earl Stahl, looking back at this era sixty years later, summed up the times perfectly: "Money and hope," Stahl said, "were scarce."

It looked as if the AMLA Nationals was just about to go the way of the Playground Nationals, victims both of hard times.

100

Wanner to the Rescue

Enter, stage right, the George D. Wanner Company of Dayton, Ohio. Although long forgotten today, George Wanner was a big-name kit manufacturer in 1931—bigger than Comet, which was then only two years old; bigger even than Ideal, which had been in business since 1912. In addition to a fairly extensive line of flying scale models, Wanner kitted, almost as a sideline, every one of those thousands of official AMLA models sold at cost to League members.

When Wanner learned of the AMLA's difficulties, he decided that this just wouldn't do. Depression or no, there *had* to be a Wakefield contest in '31, because America held the cup. And there had to be a Mulvihill contest, too, because it was purely American, and three times older than the Wakefield. And of course there had to be a Stout contest, because bushy-browed William Bushnell Stout was a good guy, and president of the AMLA, and yet another of modeling's Friends in High Places.

So Wanner agreed to sponsor a 1931 Nationals for these three rubber events. Not in Detroit—that was *The American Boy*'s home town—but in Dayton, Ohio, Wanner's home town. Sorry about indoor, Wanner said; no auditorium in Dayton big enough. But he did agree to include some prizes for those funny little flightless blobs again, because . . . well, because, technically, solid models *were* model airplanes, after all. And since they didn't fly, they didn't take up a lot of contest time or space.

And so, thanks to George D. Wanner, the 1931 Nats came off as promised, despite the hard times. Only about 157 fliers made it to Dayton for the affair. (Earlier AMLA Nats had been drawing over 250 contestants.) During the meet, Joe Ehrhardt recaptured the Wakefield Cup, partly because the English entries had to be flown by proxy, but mostly because Ehrhardt's model, compared to the English ones, was incredibly light. The U.S. was still miles ahead of the rest of the world in the 'balsa revolution.'

Twenty-nine Minutes Plus

But the hero of the Dayton Nats wasn't Wakefield winner Joe Ehrhardt. It was a young Detroit flier named Emanuel Feinberg,

101

who took the Stout outdoor trophy with a time of twenty-nine minutes, thirty seconds—an incredibly lucky flight that must have raised suspicious eyebrows east of the Atlantic, where thermals had yet to be invented. Feinberg's winning model, a stick and tissue 'tractor', was published soon after in *American Boy*.

The Feinberg model was nothing magical, just a typical design of the era: a kind of elongated teardrop for a fuselage, vee-dihedral, simple rounded wingtips and a gawky two-wheel landing gear that was encumbered, *a la mode*, with a full-length axle between the wheels. (Wind tunnels from Gottingen to Wright Field had long since demonstrated that *a round wire in an open airstream has about the same drag as a streamlined strut ten times thicker*. But this basic aerodynamic rule was slow to register on model builders.)

The Wanner Company, bless their long-forgotten souls, delivered on every one of their promises. And Mr. Edsel Ford, old Henry's handsome kid, not only sponsored the Dayton victory banquet, just as he'd done for each previous AMLA Nats, but also agreed to fly the top four winners and their models to Washington D.C. in a company Trimotor, where they put on a miniature aerial circus for President Hoover and a dozen press cameras, right out on the White House lawn.

A four-hour flight to Washington might not be quite so lush a prize as a six-week European junket, but, considering the times, it was just dandy. *American Boy* gave the Wanner meet as much pre-publicity as time permitted, and then did its customary follow-up on the winners, making sure that the Dayton contest was still referred to officially as "The AMLA Nationals."

25 Million Questions

But unofficially, the Airplane Model League of America was on the skids. By now it had over 400,000 members, each of whom had contributed exactly 2¢ by way of dues (they hadn't been asked for more.) The League had distributed roughly four million plans sets, at cost. It had answered between twenty and twenty-five million mail-in questions—one for every six U.S. citizens in 1931. It had interviewed winners and collected data and awarded merit certificates and encouraged the formation of over three hundred local clubs. It had done its share, and more, to establish the sport of aeromodeling in America. And now it was broke.

The summer of 1932 came and went with no mention, in *American Boy* or elsewhere, of another Nationals. And then, once again, deliverance arrived at the last minute. From the L. Bamberger Department Store of Newark, New Jersey came a late-July offer to sponsor a national meet in Atlantic City in September. Bamberger proposed to fly every one of the official NAA events—Wakefield, Mulvihill, Stout indoor and outdoor—and seemed willing and able to foot the bill. All the AMLA was asked to contribute was its good name. Which was about all the AMLA had left to contribute.

So who were these guys from Joisey, these *easterners,* and what was their game, anyhow?

Nat and Irv and the B.A.C.

The Bamberger Aero Club was by that time one of America's oldest and most successful department-store clubs. It was the brainchild of two brothers, Nathan and Irwin Polk, a couple of "demon modelers" (in the phrase of the day) who would later found the country's second-oldest mailorder hobby store, Polk's Modelcraft Hobbies of New York City.

The Polk brothers' long careers weave in and out of aeromodeling history like the lifeline thread in a Navajo blanket. Thanks mostly to the Polks, the Bamberger club already had a solid history of meet sponsorship behind them. If anyone could pull off an east coast Nationals, surely it was Nat and Irv and the B.A.C.

Center of Power

And wasn't it about time for a nationals in the East? So far, every AMLA contest that had billed itself as a "nats" had taken place out on the prairies. The Mulvihill Trophy, America's equivalent of the Wakefield, had been contested for chiefly in the midwest. Despite the East's overwhelming population edge, the center of power in American aeromodeling during the late twenties and early thirties had remained solidly in the prairie states. It seemed to hover about a long, deeply-cambered curve that connected Detroit and St. Louis by way of Chicago.

The Detroit-based AMLA was partly responsible for this, as was the IMAC group from Chicago, as well as a hyperactive department store club down in St. Louis, C.E. Carmichael's 'Stix, Baer and Fuller' boys. But there was also the matter of publicity. Because midwestern fliers had ready access to midwestern publications—*American Boy, Popular Aviation, Popular Science, Popular Mechanix*—they often seemed, during the late twenties and early thirties, to get the lion's share of national publicity.

This situation was just about to change, however, with the change in editorship of a small, struggling east coast pulp monthly called *Model Airplane News*.

The Atlantic City Nationals

So Bamberger made its last-minute bid for an eastern Nats, and got it—if only by default. With Irwin Polk as CD, and a lot of support from the Atlantic City Exchange Clubs, the meet came off on September 9 and 10. Billed as "The Fifth National AMLA and NAA Championships," it drew only about 150 entrants, the smallest Nats in Nats history.

Charlie Grant, *MAN*'s new editor, later recalled the 1932 Atlantic City meet as "the last stand of the twin pusher"—the first major contest in America that was totally dominated by single-prop 'tractor' models. Gordon Light remembers the Atlantic City Nats for the Wakefield cup he won there, and then had taken away from him by the governing committee in England, on the grounds that the contest had been held without sufficient notice to European entrants.

Indoor fliers remember Atlantic City as the first 'microfilm' Nats, when frail balsa airframes covered with a one-molecule-thick mixture of nitrate dope and banana oil simply mangled the old endurance records. If the American domination of Wakefield competition left any doubt about the importance of lightness in model plane performance, those 1932 indoor times dispelled it. By the final day of the Atlantic City Nats, it was obvious to all that paper-covered models simply couldn't compete with the 'mikes.' Paper models would either have to be put in a separate category, or else relegated to the dustbin of history.

Sound and Fury

But most modelers today tend to remember the '32 Nats not for its microfilm or its outdoor tractors, but for the performance of a tall, shy, baby-faced kid from Philadelphia, a kid whose model finished a modest fourth in the Wakefield event. The Wakefield winner, Gordon Light, turned almost eight minutes, while this fourth-placer staggered and stalled and looped around the sky for a mere two minutes and fifty-five seconds.

It wasn't the duration—or even the aerobatics—that made this fourth-place model so memorable. It was the ungodly racket the thing made, for the flier, a seventeen-year-old named Maxwell Bassett, had found a loophole in Lord Wakefield's rules. Although Bassett's model, a vaguely Curtiss Robin-like affair sometimes called *Fleetwings* and sometimes *Miss Philadelphia II*, had the same oversized rudder that all the other rubber-powered models had, it wasn't rubber-powered. Mounted on Miss Philadelphia's stubby nose was a single-cylinder gasoline engine—a tall, finned stovepipe that would later be marketed worldwide as the Brown Junior, the first successful production gas motor for model aircraft.

Bassett was fresh from having won what may well have been the very first gas-model contest in history, held in Philadelphia on May 10, 1932. But his hopes, when he signed up for the Atlantic City Wakefield event, weren't flying too high. In the Philly contest he'd beaten out the other three contestants with an official flight of exactly nine seconds—one whole second ahead of the number two finisher, engine designer Bill Brown. In fact, the sum of all the official flights registered that day was *under twenty seconds*. Gasoline powered model airplanes were in their infancy.

And so, when the dust settled at Atlantic City, Bassett was pleased with his fourth place in Wakefield. As well he might be. Two minutes, fifty-five seconds was actually a terrific performance, considering how very little was known, in September of 1932, about how to make a gas model fly.

What's to Become of the Nationals?

Few people who witnessed the flight took Miss Philadelphia's performance seriously. After all, loophole-seekers had been showing up at competitions with 'alternative' power sources for years. Compressed air, clock springs, even rocket motors had been tried. (Frank Ehling, a notorious rule stretcher, once won a contest in New York City with a glider tied to a pigeon's foot, because the rules hadn't specified an *internal* power source.)

So a person might get lucky with one of these mechanical freaks—might even make it into the top five at some important meet, as Bassett had just done. A person might do that once. But your big winners, your consistent fliers, had always been powered by a twisted rubber band. The thermal gods, in the year 1932, seemed to prefer it that way.

To most eyes, the big issue of '32 wasn't the gasoline engine at all. The big issue was, *What's to become of the Nationals?* And the question hung fire all winter. By the time the summer of 1933 arrived, the good old AMLA was down for the count. *American Boy* magazine had backed away completely from sponsoring any more contests. Absolutely nothing remained by way of a national organization capable of administering model aircraft competition in America. The public interest was there; the need was certainly there; but the money simply wasn't.

And money was the whole problem. Despite the widespread enthusiasm for aviation, the model airplane hobby before the advent of gas was, at best, a nickel-and-dime affair. While devotees of the sport might run the age gamut from twelve to eighty—might even include a few movers and shakers, a few captains of industry—the great mass of the country's aeromodelers in the early thirties were still school children, long on enthusiasm but short on clout. And doubly short on cash.

There was, after all, a Depression on.

Private enterprise had sponsored the first five Nationals. But now it was 1933, the very bottom of the country's economic slump. Twelve million Americans were out of work, and there seemed to be precious little enterprise, private or otherwise, left. Wheat was a major American export, and the price of wheat on the world market was at its lowest point in three centuries. Money and hope—in Earl Stahl's words—were still scarce. Under such conditions, who could be found to sponsor anything so frivolous as a National Model Airplane Championships?

The Age of Bureaucracy

Certainly not the model airplane business—it was down for the count. And not the government, either. At least not directly. This time—1933—modeling's White Knight turned out to be none other than those Washington-based quasi-governmental rulemakers known as the National Aeronautical Association.

Infused with some of the new energy and hope that the Roosevelt administration brought to town in January of '33, the NAA had suddenly been reborn. In early spring of that year it appointed a brand new Committee on Model Airplanes. It began to take a renewed interest in its 'junior' contest rules and national records. It began issuing, to anyone interested, model flying licenses in the form of inexpensive junior NAA memberships.

I say the NAA did all this, but of course bureaucracies do nothing. It's one or two determined individuals within them that occasionally, against great odds, get something worthwhile accomplished. And the individual behind this sudden new life at the NAA was the chairman of that revitalized Model Airplane Committee—a hard-driving, self-effacing, retired naval aviation lieutenant named H.W. Alden.

A skilled public relations man and yet another of modeling's Friends in High Places, Lieutenant Alden was destined, in just a few years, to become one of the founding fathers and critical parents of the American Academy for Model Aeronautics—today's AMA. Meanwhile, from NAA's headquarters on Dupont Circle, Alden set out to hold the modeling movement together with one hand, while

107

casting about with the other for a new patron saint for the Nationals.

The new saint, as it happened, was close at hand. *Model Airplane News,* like the federal bureaucracy, had recently gotten its own infusion of springtime energy—in the form of editor Charlie Grant. Grant went to work on his boss, a young publisher named Jay P. Cleveland, and within weeks Cleveland had agreed to co-sponsor, hand in hand with the NAA, the 1933 Nationals.

And so, in another last-minute save, the Gathering of the Clan, the great mother of all U.S. model contests, was on once again.

The Roosevelt Field Nats

The date was June 27-28, 1933. Fliers from eighteen states and Canada showed up (including one determined young fellow named Art Snyder, who bucked the Dust Bowl tide of western migration by hitchhiking all the way from Burbank, California!)

It was a fabulous meet—"the first modern Nats," in Bill Winter's words. Outdoor models took off from the very runway that Lindbergh had used on his flight to Paris. Indoor models flew at a high-roofed armory downtown, where the best time was recorded—on an unofficial flight, as luck would have it—by a quiet young New Yorker named Carl Goldberg, who wound up second in the final standings. (Goldberg had to enter seven Nationals—and this was only his sixth—before winning his first event.)

1933 was the year that Max Bassett, that shy, baby-faced engine expert from Philadelphia, really got his act together. He aced the Mulvihill, Stout and Moffett—all three of the traditional outdoor rubber events—as well as a brand new duration event sponsored by Texaco for gas models. ("And now," crowed *The American Boy* from the sidelines, "the gasoline-powered model airplane rules the skies!")

After Bassett's clean sweep of the outdoor events at the '33 Nats, the NAA rewrote the rules to separate gas and rubber models. Not by simply banning gas models from the traditional

108

rubber events. Oh no—that would have been far too simple. Instead, they separated all models into classes according to wing area, using the following formula:

Class A	0-30 square inches
Class B	31-100 square inches
Class C	101-150 square inches
Class D	151-300 square inches
Class E	over 300 square inches

Class E planes—and every gas model of 1933-34 fell into this category—were of course ineligible for the other events. But no one was prohibited from building a giant rubber model to compete (lots of luck!) with the gassies of E class.

Confusion

These rather arbitrary wing area classes, which became law in March of 1934, hung on practically forever—despite the fact that, within just a few years, gas engines had appropriated that same "A-B-C-D" terminology for a totally different purpose. To gas fliers of the late thirties, "Class A" meant any engine under .20 cubic inch displacement. "Class B" referred to engines between .21 and .30, "Class C" was .31—.60, and "Class D" was . . . the Forster .99.

As a kid in the late forties, I remember making the confusing discovery that the "B" in my *Thermic B*, a 20" handlaunch glider, meant that it was a "Class B" glider. What did that have to do with the Thor and Ram and Judco ignition engines, which were then being advertised (dirt cheap!) as "Class B" motors? Did it mean they'd fly my little Thermic? Even to a seven year old, this didn't seem likely.

Open Class

But the '34 NAA rules had one bright spot in them. For the first time since the pre-Lindbergh years, provision was made for competition between 'open' class fliers—people over 21 years of age. (At least two veteran clan members must have breathed a sigh of relief: Carl Goldberg was born in 1913 and Frank Zaic a year earlier. Thanks to this rules change, both of them were able to fly—and place—at the '34 Nats in the newly-created Open Class.)

And so once again adults were welcome at the picnic. The aeromodeling hobby was finally beginning to see itself as something more than child's play, something more than just another antidote for juvenile delinquency. The Clan was beginning to come of age.

1934: Wherinhell is Akron?

Primary responsibility for the next Nats, in 1934, fell once more upon the NAA—which is to say, upon Lieutenant Alden. With help once again from *Model Airplane News*. *American Boy* had by now slipped completely out of the picture. *Popular Aviation,* a supporter of the defunct Playground Nats, was easing away from the modeling field, and the two other magazines that might have put their shoulders to the wheel, *Air Trails* and *Flying Aces,* were still, in 1934, oriented toward fiction and full-scale.

This left Charlie Grant's *MAN*—the only magazine published exclusively for modelers—firmly in the saddle. *MAN* was by then running a regular "NAA Junior Membership News" column, full of rules changes and contest info and instructions for forming local modeling "chapters," which was the NAA's term for clubs.

The '34 Nats were held in the Goodyear blimp town of Akron, Ohio, under the local sponsorship of the Akron Chamber of Commerce and two of the city's senior NAA Chapters. Nearly two hundred fliers attended, seventeen of them in the newly-formed Open class. The Nats' first-ever towline glider event, sponsored by the Akron *Beacon-Journal*, was won that year with a flight of 23 minutes and thirteen seconds—a record never broken in that class. Carl Goldberg, a bridesmaid for six years running, finally came out on top in indoor stick, with a time of twenty-two minutes and fifty-nine seconds—a new world record.

Bill Atwood and Irwin Ohlsson, a couple of budding young engine manufacturers from California, camped their way from Los Angeles to Akron in a Ford Model A, accompanied by Ohlsson's hardy mom. At the time, U.S. 66, Steinbeck's 'mother road' from Chicago to the Pacific, was still gravel and mud. The trip took them nine days, and they were feeling pretty cocky about the feat until they ran across a pair of rubber fliers from up in Buffalo, NY, who had pedaled down on a 1901 model tandem bicycle, pulling a trailer full of models and camping gear. One of the two was so badly sunburned on arrival that he needed medical treatment.

All this for a two day contest—outdoor on Thursday, indoor on Friday. Plus free admission to the local wrestling matches (hot *damn!*) on Thursday evening.

Who Can Ever Surpass Such Records?

Of the twenty-six gassies present at Akron, only seven put in official flights. Bassett won again, with a time of nearly 22 minutes, while Brooklyn's Joe Kovel came second with 14:02, flying the parasol-winged *K-G Gassie* designed for him by Charlie Grant. The only west coaster to get off the ground was Irv Ohlsson, who managed a 36 second flight that netted him next-to-last place. In 1934, the great east-west rivalry in free flight was not yet a nose-to-nose affair.

Akron was a good meet, but not a great meet. Charlie Grant felt otherwise. "Twenty-three minutes indoors, models flying out of sight outdoors!" he trumpeted in the September *MAN*. "Who can ever surpass such records?" Part of his wild, cigar-chomping enthusiasm might have been simply pyrotechnics for his new boss, publisher Jay P. Cleveland, who had only recently purchased the magazine. If so, it was probably unnecessary. Jay Cleveland, though not himself a competitor, was already a hardcore supporter of aeromodeling—and remained so until his death in 1975.

1935: St. Louis

In '35 the big meet, which had by now become a moveable feast, landed at Lambert Field, St. Louis, where it drew more than 300 competitors, varying in age from twelve to 43. This time registration was held on Thursday, with flying on Friday and Saturday. The Nats was growing, and trying hard to become a weekend affair, but Sundays were still holy days in middle America.

Indoor times at the marvelous St. Louis arena, with its unobstructed 135' ceiling, set the high-water mark for all prewar Nationals. Twenty years later, in 1955, when indoor was at a low ebb and facing the prospect of being dropped from the Nats schedule, critics loved to harken back to the St. Louis Nats, pointing out that times had improved but little, and models had changed but little, in the intervening two decades. (This was just before Messrs. Bilgri, Foster, Andrade, et al, combined their talents to make U.S. indoor events respectable—and competitive—once again.)

Outdoors, the Lambert Field weather was calm and bubbly and nearly perfect both days, and a fifteen-year-old New York City kid named Leo Weiss finally knocked the redoubtable Max Bassett out of the winner's circle by posting an hour and four minute flight in Texaco. Weiss' time was just 28 seconds short of Joe Kovel's then-current world record of 64:40, set a couple of months earlier at the Eastern States Champs.

1936: Wayne County Forever

The next year it was back to Detroit, home of the old AMLA meets. Wayne County Airport, twenty miles southwest of town, was the outdoor site, and there the Nationals remained for four straight years, from 1936 to 1939. By the end of that four-year siege the Clan had so thoroughly worn out its welcome in Motown—seven of the first twelve Nats were held there—that half a century has gone by and we still haven't been invited back!

1936 was the Nats where they gave an R/C event and nobody came. The meet as a whole drew about 250 fliers, 78 of them in Open. Bob Cahill (brother to Jim 'Clodhopper' Cahill, who was to win the Wakefield in France in '38) showed up with one of the earliest folding props. It had no stop, and lousy hinges—but at least it showed that the rubber boys still had tricks up their sleeve.

Outdoor rubber entries, in fact, outnumbered gas by more than two to one in '36. But the big gassies, some of which weighed as much as fifteen pounds, seemed to get all the attention—in the magazines, in the newsreels, and especially in the live radio coverage.

Because Gordon Light—by now an *Air Trails* staffer—had gone to England and captured the Wakefield Cup the year before, the '36 Nats included among its events the Wakefield World Champs. The British had by this time become wary of the proxy business. They sent a six-man team to Detroit to win back their cup—and they did. But just to prove that *proxy* wasn't a four-letter word, Bert (Peru, Indiana) Pond put up a remarkable three-flight total of 44:14 to capture America's Moffett Trophy . . . for New Zealand!

Headquarters for the '36 Nats was the classy Hotel Book-Cadillac in downtown Detroit. A plush layout, as its name suggests—but perhaps not the best choice for a Nationals headquarters. Within three short days, the combined adolescence of two hundred rambunctious and highly-charged modelers had overwhelmed the management, alienated most of the regular clientele, and absolutely guaranteed a change of venue for the following year. (Frank Zaic still remembers the consternation of the *maitre d'* when hordes of young men and their models poured out of a mere handful of rented rooms. By separating mattresses and springs, and by judicious use of the bathtub, up to nine guys were bedding down in rooms rented to two people.)

AAMA, Eh?

Before the Clan was booted out forever, though, a small group of them went into a huddle in one of the Book-Cadillac's conference rooms and laid the foundation for a new national modeling organization. They called it, rather pretentiously, the "American Academy for Model Aeronautics," or AAMA.

The AAMA was to be an elite, science-oriented group of modelers, not open to the masses at all, as so many other national clubs were. Entry was to be restricted to modelers who had done "at least two minutes indoors or one minute outdoors" (presumably with some form of rubber model—a type of flying that was already on the wane.) The official symbol of this new organization was a

113

torch of knowledge with wings on it, centered within an eye-shaped oval which may or may not have had Masonic overtones.

Open your AMA membership packet today and you'll find that very same symbol—on patches, on decals, on tie tacks and lapel pins and belt buckles and tee shirts. It's just about all that's left of the high ideals of those founding fathers of 1936. For the AAMA—it became simply "AMA" the following year—never had time to pursue its lofty scientific goals. Its hands were full from the very beginning in trying to solve the social and regulatory and public-relations problems of American aeromodeling. And they still are.

1937: The Fort Shelby Years Begin

In '37, contest headquarters shifted to Detroit's long-suffering Hotel Fort Shelby, later home of the Plymouth Internats, and featured in a memorable 1950 *Saturday Evening Post* picture-story entitled "Don't Build Airplanes in the Bathtub." Unlike the Book-Cadillac, the Fort Shelby's management seemed to understand a young man's need to toss the occasional firecracker into the occasional shower room—to smear glue on elevator buttons—to attach delicate streamers of Japanese tissue to houseflies and turn them loose by the dozen in the hotel lobby.

Right from the start, the Fort Shelby's house rules were soft on practical jokers and midnight engine tuners—a real modeler's hotel. Although, as the *Post* title suggests, they drew the line at microfilm-making in the hotel bathtubs. But people poured their film in the tubs anyway, because everybody knew the best 'mike' models were completed the night before the event—and what's more convenient than your very own bathtub? (The film, it seems, left an invisible slick on the porcelain that could break the bones of the next guest.)

People came to the '37 Nats, according to *Air Trails*, by "busses, trailers, boats, automobiles, motor cycles and airplanes." There were over 500 entries, only three of whom were female. (Women didn't begin entering the Nationals in appreciable numbers until the fifties, when their count rose once or twice to nearly a sixth of the total.)

This was the first year of rubber flying scale, and it drew only two entries. The *Literary Digest,* covering the meet with the impartial eye of an outsider, observed that model aircraft appeared to be divided into two general categories, Scale and Non-scale. "The scale models," said the *Digest,* "do not fly . . . . "

Farmer Brown

1937 is remembered by the outdoor fliers as the first 'Farmer Brown' Nats. The drift at Wayne County Airport in '37 was consistently back towards town—exactly as it had been the year before. But town was twenty plowed and cultivated miles away, and this year, the farmer whose land bordered the airport wasn't caught off guard. His '36 crops had been trampled by hundreds of panting and sweating trespassers—madmen apparently, eyeballs rolled upwards as if near death, tearing diagonally across his fields in single-minded pursuit of small specks in the sky.

Brown didn't understand all he knew about these madmen, but one thing was clear: they had cost him big bucks in crop damage in 1936, and he wasn't up for a repeat performance. As soon as the '37 flying began, he posted his property lines and sent his family out to do the retrieving, charging 10¢ for every plane returned.

The modelers, halted in their tracks by Brown's NO TRESPASSING signs, were incensed. They were young and idealistic and mostly city bred, and they hadn't yet absorbed the idea that every inch of America belongs to somebody. They screamed like stuck pigs.

The newspapers covering the meet took the fliers' side and had themselves a field day, painting the farmer as a reactionary ogre and the modelers, some of whom were well past middle age, as the heroic and dew-bespangled cream of American youth. But 'Farmer Brown'—it wasn't his real name—was unmoved. He studied the news reports carefully, discovered the value of some of these crazy-looking toys, and responded the following year by raising his prices: two bits for power models, ten to fifteen cents for rubber jobs and gliders.

1938: Deja Vu

Economically, these price hikes proved a good move on Brown's part, for the next Nats, in '38, was the first one in which power actually outnumbered rubber and glider: 400 of the 700 contestants signed up to fly gas. Engine runs had by then been limited to 30 seconds, but that didn't keep the gassies from drifting downwind in flocks and gaggles and coveys. Farmer Brown had his most profitable year by far.

Times were changing, however. Thirty-eight was the first Nats in which official timers were deprived of their binoculars. More important, it was *the first Nationals in history in which the timer wasn't permitted follow the model.* Before 1938, contests had begun to look more and more like a Keystone Cops movie, with dozens of honking, careening autos full of wild-eyed contestants and squinting officials zig-zagging down the field in pursuit of the models.

Loss of Wheels

At least two entrants, Bill Effinger of Berkeley Models and a chap from Des Moines named Clifford Hodge, made quite a stir this year by using small motor scooters to retrieve their ships—but in general the loss of wheels in freeflight was well received. Most modelers, in 1938, still couldn't afford a car, anyway, and this put the poorer ones at a competitive disadvantage. The prolific rubber designer Henry Struck, for example, didn't get his first car until 1941—and then wrecked it twice the day he bought it! ("Hey, bum, how did you get your license?" Gordon Light asked in *Air Trails*.)

Even without wheels, though, Struck still managed to win flying scale in '38, with a beautiful little *Caudron* monoplane. It was a feat he was to repeat with a new design almost every year, until Effinger's Berkeley line featured a complete stable of Struck's Nats-winning scale jobs.

"Acted As a Helicopter"

Carl Goldberg, after winning indoor stick again, came skipping onto the Wayne County field just ten minutes before the final bell in Open Gas. He had under his arm a curious little plane with a Dennymite up front. It looked to be dangerously overpowered. According to legend, the design came about as the result of a bet that he couldn't fly "60-60"—a .60 engine on a 60" airplane. The Dennymite was only a .56, but the model had just 46" of wing. If it flew, he'd win the bet with ten inches to spare.

For reasons that soon became obvious, Goldberg dubbed the final version of this strange-looking airplane the *Zipper*. A picture of the model appears in the October 1938 *Air Trails* coverage of the Nats. Described simply as Goldberg's "latest parasol gas job," the Zipper (John Pond labels this early version the *Gas Bird*) raised very few eyebrows. Only the Argus-eyed Grant seemed to pay any attention to it:

> *One of the most remarkable flights was made by a little six foot [sic] model which literally tore off the ground and spiralled itself vertically upward at an angle of about sixty to eighty degrees. Actually it acted as a helicopter, the propeller pulling it nearly vertically. It climbed to an elevation of about 600 feet before the motor cut.*

Goldberg and his "latest parasol" (the term actually refers to *strut-mounted* high wings, but pylons didn't yet have a name) got in only one flight, failed to place, and was quickly forgotten.

By now the Exchange Club of Detroit was solidly behind the Nats, providing manpower and business sponsorship and contacts in high places. Exchange clubs had for years underwritten local and regional model contests, but it was the Detroit club that first aligned the Exchange solidly behind the Nationals—a quiet and under-appreciated sponsorship that was to continue for decades. Even the huge 'Navy Nats' of the fifties almost all had the strong and silent backing of the National Exchange Clubs.

1939

Despite all the Exchange could do, however, the Clan's welcome in Detroit was wearing thin by '39. The soldiers from nearby Selfridge Field were getting tired being 'volunteered' as timers, spending days staring into the July sun with stopwatch in hand. The Hotel Fort Shelby was getting tired of the same noisy adolescent pranks, repeated year after year. And the local business firms—including all three major auto manufacturers—were getting tired of picking up the lion's share of the tab.

Plymouth Motors had underwritten the traditional, last-day "victory banquet" in 1938, hiring an entire lake steamer for the big event. But on opening day of the '39 contest, no one had yet been found to sponsor that year's banquet, and right up to the last minute it looked as if only the first-place winners were going to be fed.

Nationals victory banquets had always been for everybody—win, lose, or draw. But this was beginning to look like the end of the tradition. Then, just hours before the Saturday evening affair, Irv Polk ran into Roy Howard of the Scripps-Howard newspaper chain (they were still sponsoring their own 'Junior Aviator' Nationals) and by the time Polk stopped talking, Howard had agreed to foot the bill for the blowout. So close was the '39 Nationals to financial collapse.

Watershed

But all that happened behind the scenes. Out on the field, where the gassies now truly did rule the skies, 1939 was a memorable meet—a real watershed in modeling history. Timed engine runs (as opposed to fuel allotments) meant more flying and less processing. On Saturday, the final day, 1100 official flights were logged in seven and a half hours. The wind, for once, didn't blow toward Farmer Brown's fields. Goldberg's *Zipper* (and his slightly smaller *Mercury)* made hash of every power event, putting an end to the four-year reign of the cabin model and reviving once more the ancient battle between the people who feel that model airplanes should be required to resemble full-scale craft and those who hold that aeromodeling is its own science and ought to be unrestricted as to design.

Carl Goldberg was the hero of the hour. His designs (although not, as *Time* magazine erroneously reported, Goldberg himself) won five out of six possible first places in gas.

Goldberg was by now working full time for Comet, kitter of the Zipper and Mercury. And Comet was a major advertiser in *Model Airplane News*. This severely restricted what the pugnacious

Charlie Grant—whose sympathies lay solidly with the cabin-model crowd—could say about this turncoat easterner and his funny-looking pylon ships which flew (all too well!) in the face of Grant's much-publicized Center of Lateral Area theories. You can almost hear the teeth grinding in Grant's terse comment on the Zipper's success:

> *Many of the events were won by this type of ship. This manufacturer is indeed fortunate in the fact that the new rules, passed by the Academy of Model Aeronautics, encouraged this type of model . . . .*

Years later, after he was safely out of the editor's seat, Grant was free to bemoan the fact that Goldberg's pylon had changed forever the face of freeflight. In a 1948 *Air Trails* article he recalled the '39 Nats as "the greatest model aviation show in history . . . because of the variety of model designs." Probably he was blurring the '38 and '39 meets together in memory, for by '39 the field was beginning to be dominated by kit designs—other people's airplanes. 1939 was probably the first Nationals in history in which more people flew kits than originals.

Grant was far from alone in his nostalgia for the pre-pylon era. Many modelers saw the Zipper as a mixed blessing at best. Here's clan member Walt Leonhardt, writing in *Model Builder* almost fifty years later:

> *Little did I know that when I saw Carl flying the Zipper way back then that it was the beginning of the end of variety in free flight . . . All our club members went home and bought Zippers.*

But variety didn't disappear all at once. At the very next Nats the high-pyloned Zipper got its wings clipped, if only temporarily. And it happened right in Goldberg's new hometown.

1940: The First Chicago Nats

Chicago is barely two hundred miles west of Detroit, but in most people's minds it's much more centrally located than the

Motor City. To Californians, Chicago is the epitome of midwest, light-years closer to them than the 'eastern' city of Detroit. At the same time, New Yorkers don't see it as being all that much further away—while many southerners, especially back in the railroad days of 1940, still thought of Chicago as 'their' shopping town.

And so, when the '40 Nats were announced for the windy city, just about every hotshot modeler in America declared his intentions of going. And a surprising number of them did.

People came from 42 of the 48 states, plus Canada—almost 1200 registered contestants, all told, and nearly double the number that had been coming to Detroit. But Chicago was ready for them. Some six years earlier, a longtime modeler named Frank Nekimken had infiltrated the city's Park District bureaucracy. Nekimken spent those six years wisely, running local meets and promoting flying clubs and model building programs, and just generally doing what he could to orient the youth of Cook County to the air age.

Nekimken took on the CD job for the Chicago meet, and he tossed a four-day winging that even Charlie Grant had to admit was the smoothest and most professional in the entire history of the Nationals.

The outdoor site was a huge piece of parkland down on 79th Street near the present Chicago Midway, then called simply Chicago Airport. It was undeveloped land, and broad runways were cut through grass so deep and lush that gas models were seen to crash in it without breaking a prop.

Nothing was overlooked. For the first time in Nats history, spectators were actually controlled: kept rigidly behind ropes and away from the launching aircraft. Timers—trained Park District employees—were plentiful. Even the noontime box lunches arrived on time—every single day!

All of the pre-registration and publicity, as well as the tab for the huge victory banquet, was handled by the Chicago *Daily Times,* one of those marvelous newspapers of the thirties that was radically committed to aeromodeling. (Ten cents in stamps, forwarded to the *Times*, got you half a dozen Nats entry blanks plus an equal number of rules booklets.)

120

Bombshell

But the highlight of the Chicago meet was the appearance of a one-design freeflight club led by a local modeler named Joe Konefes. Like Carl Goldberg, Joe was an employee of Comet Models; but unlike Goldberg, he didn't fancy the functional ugliness of pylon models. Joe was a cabin man—with a following. Joe's group called themselves The Buzzards, and they fielded somewhere between twelve and twenty (these guys moved so fast nobody ever got an accurate count) boxy-looking cabin models called *Bombshells*. The club specialty was mass launches of these big ships, every one of which had identical orange and black paint schemes, and some of which would be sent off into the clouds on unofficial, just-for-the-hell-of-it flights towing long, snapping banners that said BUZZARDS.

Show biz had come to modeling, in the form of Konefes and the Buzzard Club. Their numbers alone were almost enough to upstage "Goldberg's Army"—the dozens of folk who had arrived with Zippers and near-Zippers and Zipper spinoffs. But what happened on C Gas day—the day the Bombshell fliers had been waiting for— simply put the icing on the cake.

C Gas was flown on July 4, and the morning dawned wet and overcast and windy—the absolute worst weather of the entire meet. Undaunted by such skies (it was their home town, after all) the Buzzard Club turned out *en masse*. All morning the lousy weather held—nobody was getting any decent times. Then Joe Konefes himself, the Bombshell's designer, spotted an approaching hole in the clouds, and turned loose an official flight just seconds before the twelve o'clock whistle.

Lunch Hour

Now lunch hour was sacred at a Frank Nekimken contest. Once that noon whistle blew, no one not already in the air could launch an official until after the 1:00 'all clear.' It was a good rule, even though the contestants—who traditionally don't care, during Nationals week, whether they eat *or* sleep—grumbled about it. It was a rule meant to give the 140 park district employees who were running the show a solid sixty minutes of midday sanity.

121

The Konefes Bombshell lifted off and climbed out dead ahead, fast and steep. Just about then the whistle blew, and the engine cut, and the model nosed over into what other fliers came to call "THAT glide." Immediately it hit lift, and leaned over into it. And then (here's what makes the story) *the wind died*—the infamous Chicago wind simply up and quit!

For more than forty-nine minutes that big halloween-colored airplane bounced and drifted in easy circles around the field, accompanied only by one of Wally Simmers' little rubber jobs, tossed up at about the same time for an unofficial test flight. Both planes just hung there, spinning slowly like a pair of Paul Klee mobiles. In July of 1940, no one had ever heard of a dethermalizer.

One thousand other competitors, many with their sleek, streamlined *Zippers* (and *Mercurys*, and *New Rulers,* and lovely big Cleveland *Playboys*) sat around in the grass, glumly eating their baloney sandwiches and watching Joe's Bombshell and cursing fate. At last the big creature dropped out of the lift and descended, bouncing to a stop right at the edge of the field. The timer clicked off his watch, and the weather closed in once more. Ten minutes later the all-clear whistle sounded and a thousand fliers went back to an afternoon of mediocre three to four minute flights.

Within months Joe Konefes' *Buzzard Bombshell*—all seventy-two squarish, old-fashioned inches of it—was on the market in kit form. It was a design that scaled down well, and Class A versions were soon being given away free with a year's subscription to *Air Trails.* For the next year or so everybody had to have a Bombshell, and the Goldberg Zipper was temporarily eclipsed.

The '41 Nats: "Unwieldy"

Despite defense mobilization and the beginning of wartime shortages, the 1941 Nats, held once again in Chicago, drew an even bigger crowd—over 1300 this time. Perhaps word had gotten out about the quality of Nekimken's contest organization. Or perhaps America's model builders—most of whom were draft age—had simply glanced into the crystal ball and decided it was time to eat, drink and be merry. The war in Europe was drawing closer every day. Even though Pearl Harbor was still six months off, and the mood of the country was still strongly isolationist, few Americans really believed that war was not in their future.

Beginning on Wednesday morning, July 2, Nekimken and his faithful park department crew clicked off twenty-seven separate events in four days. It was another flawless contest, the "greatest" Nats ever . . . and yet, to many of the old timers present, something seemed to be missing.

Was it simply that the thing had gotten too impersonal, too big? For the first time, said Charlie Grant, it seemed "unwieldy, more like a lot of smaller meets being run in the same location without the contestants contacting anyone outside of their own sphere of activity." Thirteen hundred fliers! This was the first Nationals in history where old friends searched for one another day after day without ever making contact.

Specialties

The Nationals, just like the hobby it symbolized, had begun inevitably to fragment into specialties, the top contestants into specialists. Performance levels in every one of those twenty-seven events had soared up out of reach of the neophyte—even the lucky neophyte. To win in 1941 meant to specialize, and everyone was beginning to recognize this fact. "It is now impossible," former Wakefield champion Dick Korda observed wistfully, "to build 'everything.'"

Rubber seemed a world apart from gas, and only tenuously related to glider. And indoor—what about indoor? In '41 it was moved from the 133rd Infantry Armory to the much larger International Amphitheater downtown. There Gordon Cain of Boston won 'cabin' (the latest term for fuselage) for the second straight year. Korda himself took outdoor rubber with a dethermalizer-equipped model, one of the first D/Ts to appear at a Nats. (A pneumatic timer in the fuselage released a rudder tab, spinning the model in. Fine for rubber, but not the answer for your four-pound gassie.)

123

Sal Taibi won C Gas with a Bombshell-like cabin model—his deep-bellied, Grant-pleasing *Pacer.* The design had already appeared in *MAN* and was currently being kitted by Bay Ridge Models of Brooklyn, a gung-ho freeflight firm that would switch entirely to controlline after the war, changing its name to Consolidated.

R/C in '41 drew an even dozen entries, and was won by a pipe-smoking thirty-seven-year old toy manufacturer from up in Portland, Oregon—a jittery, high-strung fellow named Walker, whose main passion in life seemed to be demonstrating an ugly little .29-powered solid model that he swung around his head on a wire. Or was it two wires?

The man was tireless. Morning and night he was out there flying that thing—around and around and around in those same dull, dizzying circles. His was one of the first engines fired up every morning, and it was the very last engine heard on the field as the 1941 National Model Airplane Championships—the final prewar Nats—drew to a close.

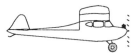

Control Issues

The '41 meet was an appropriate ending to a series of fourteen consecutive Nationals—contests that had themselves come full circle. Beginning in June of 1928, when the model airplane hobby had stood facing the barely explored world of 'free' flight, they had progressed year by year to July of 1941, when most of the secrets of balancing a model on the wind were known to all, and the next great challenge lay not in *free* but in *controlled* flying.

Whether that control was exercised directly, through wires, like the fellow from Portland was doing, or indirectly through invisible radio waves, the issue, in 1941, was still one of human will: *how can a model plane be made to do exactly what I wish?*

The question was appropriate. It came at a time when a whole generation of modelers was just coming of age. A whole generation was about to shed its youth, in France and North Africa and the

124

islands of the South Pacific—shed its youth and take up the powers and responsibilities of adulthood. *To take charge*, whether of your model or your life, is to learn to assert your will, to begin to find ways to influence the flow of events around you. Control is only a dream, an ideal, for a child. But it's a real possibility for an adult.

Grown Up

By 1941, the National Model Airplane Championships had grown up, and a whole generation of modelers had grown up with it. The baby-faced children who had, each July, ridden the chartered busses like schoolkids from hotel to flying field and back—who had chased models all day and then stayed up all night talking and goofing and playing practical jokes—these same kids were beginning now to arrive in cars of their own, some with wives and families in tow. The enthusiastic and wide-eyed fourteen-year-olds of 1932 had matured into the dedicated open-class competitors of 1941.

The era of aeromodeling's youthful freedom was drawing to a close, and with it the era of "free" flight as well. The stage was set, in 1941, for control: not just control over engine runs and length of flight, using timers and fuses, but control over entire flight paths, from takeoff to landing. The stage was set for U-Control and R/C.

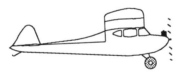

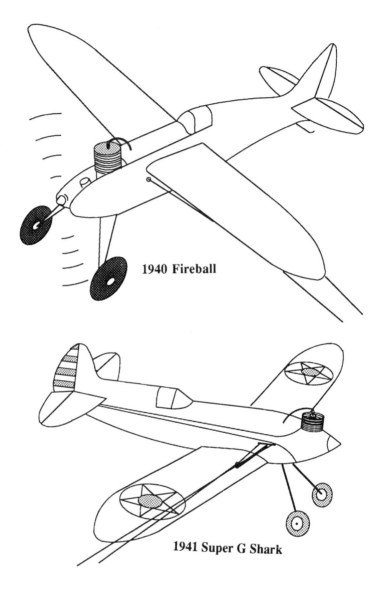

1940 Fireball

1941 Super G Shark

The first control line kit on the market was Jim Walker's Fireball,
patented in 1940 as a "controlled, captive-type toy airplane." Next
came the Victor Stanzel Super G Shark in 1941, a two-line
modification of their 1940 single-line whip-control models.

Chapter Six:

CONTROLLED CAPTIVE-TYPE TOY AIRPLANE

Before the war, free flight was dominant; now it is U-Control.
—*Model Airplane News,* December 1947

Petitioner shows . . . particularly on Sundays and holidays, large numbers of persons come upon said area and there hold regatta with miniature airplanes of various types and descriptions . . . The exhaust from the engines driving such planes, and the flying of propellers, and the swift movement of said machines through the air, in circular motion and cutting and buffeting air currents, make screaming and nerve-wracking noise . . . .
—from the suit of J.C. Baldwin vs. the
County Commission, custodians of
North Fulton Park, Atlanta, GA, 1948

No one likes to strike patents down, and, where possible, you like to give validity to a patent, even if a limited validity.
—Hon. James M. Carter, Judge,
U.S. District Court, Los Angeles, 1955

There's a way of looking at the history of technology that suggests a kind of inevitability to the march of progress, a sort of historical determinism at work behind the scenes. Certain ideas seem to appear not merely at random, but just exactly when the

127

world is most in need of them. Dr. Fleming's penicillin, for example. Or Jim Walker's U-Control.

Cynics, of course, have a ready explanation: *when somebody sees a chance to make a quick buck, they put on their thinking cap.*

But it's rarely that simple. If you look into the background of almost any "new" product or idea, you usually find that it's not really so new at all—that it's been around for decades, just waiting for its time. And you often find that, when its time finally comes, the idea doesn't present itself to just one individual, but pops up in two, three, maybe half a dozen minds at roughly the same time. It's almost as if the *zeitgeist*—the spirit of the times—whispers some new need into a thousand ears, and out of that thousand, a handful sit up and and take notice. Usually only one or two of that handful wind up getting the credit—not to mention the profit.

Case in point: the electric garage door opener. As an 'invention,' it made one of its first public appearances during the late 1920's, in a tantalizing little half-page story buried in the back pages of *Popular Science Monthly.* (A similar story described a guy hooking his Dictaphone to his telephone so it could take messages while he was out.) Thousands of American readers saw that garage door opener story—including, no doubt, a few who had already 'invented' something similar.

But did this national publicity make the garage-door opener an overnight sensation? Hardly. It had to lie dormant for another quarter-century, waiting to be reinvented when its time had finally come, a decade or so after World War II. (Ditto the phone-answering machine.) When garage-door openers finally did make it big, during the affluent and gadget-happy 1950's, their latest 'inventors' fought long and expensive patent battles to decide who stole what from whom—the kind of battles that make lawyers grin, as my father used to say, "like a goat eating razor blades."

If you're beginning to feel that I take a dim view of the verb *invent*, you could be right. For a book called *Galloping Bungalows* (Shoe String Press, 1991) I spent about eighteen months piecing together the technical and social history of the American house trailer. During that time I interviewed at least a dozen people whose grandfathers or uncles or next-door neighbors had "invented" the very first automobile trailer in America, and then had been cheated out of the glory by some promoter like Glenn "Aerocar" Curtiss or Wally "Airstream" Byam.

Again: Just last fall, while back at the AMA Library rooting up truffles for this book, I happened across a curious picture in a 1940 *Model Airplane News*. It showed a winch for towing freeflight gliders that was made from a child's tricycle turned upside down. You removed the front tire and used the wheel rim as a winding reel, cranking the pedals by hand. This is almost exactly the same idea that I innocently 'invented' some twenty-nine years later, and published in May of 1970 —in the very same magazine.

No New Thing

Still not convinced? Then call up from your modeling memory one of your own pet creations. Pick the weirdest, most unlikely *original design* you ever made fly. Now sit down with a full set of the Zaic *Yearbooks* from the 1930s, and start turning pages. Odds are, before you're halfway through the set you'll find a three-view of some model that's disgustingly close to yours. Does this make you a plagiarist? Not in my eyes. It simply confirms what that old curmudgeon wrote in Ecclesiastes: *There is no new thing under the sun.*

And so, when clan heros Dale Kirn and Charles Mackey assure us, in the November 1981 issue of *Model Builder*, that a genteel and soft-spoken old Oregon watchmaker named Oba St. Clair—and not Jim Walker—was once declared by a Los Angeles judge to be the true 'Father of Control Line Flying' . . . well, forgive me if I'm not knocked off my chair.

The Peerless Pilot from Portland

Nevilles E. "Jim" Walker was once a familiar name to everyone who spoke model airplane. Like Bert Pond, the compressed-air magnate of Chapter Five, Jim Walker was not merely hooked but already a dealer and manufacturer—already trying to scratch out a living from this crazy hobby/sport/obsession of ours—well before

Lindbergh's flight. His company, up in Portland Oregon, started life in the twenties as Junior American Aircraft.

Now, "Junior American" may sound just fine to you, but it grates upon my large and delicate ear. I grew up in the forties and fifties when it was *American Junior,* the famous "A-J" of the red, white and blue boxes found in every dime store, drug store, and hobby shop in the forty-eight states:

A-J Fighter
A-J Bomber
A-J Ceiling Walker
A-J Interceptor
A-J Hornet
A-J Pursuit
A-J Firebaby
A-J Firecat
A-J Fireball

These were the kits that—beyond question—started more kids down the primrose path of model aviation than any others in history. Some 232 million of them were produced under the American Junior label before the firm was sold to Pactra Chemical (the Aero Gloss dope people) in 1962.

But back in the late twenties, like it or not, the name was "Junior American." And Junior American's specialty was a line of ready-to-fly stick-fuselage rubber models with built-up, silk-covered wings. These wings—hand built, hand covered, hand doped—were invariably dark blue, because that was the color Jim could buy, cheap, in 55-gallon drums. Walker's very earliest products were *flying* models, not *building* models, and he never abandoned that philosophy.

Ready To Fly

When magazine editors in the 1950s began to wring their hands over what they called "the ARF question"—whether Almost-Ready-to-Fly airplane kits were or were not destroying our sacred hobby—Jim Walker just turned aside with a wry grin. His record spoke for itself. If a child had any love at all for things that ride the invisible air, that child could not help but be captivated by Jim's dime gliders, by his folding-wing *Interceptors*, by his all-balsa R.O.G. models. They went together in seconds. They had simple, clear instructions printed on sturdy boxes. They were invariably cut from the lightest, straightest balsa, and dyed in the most exciting colors. They were inexpensive. They were available everywhere. *And they flew.*

Walker understood the child's dream of flight: the spiralling climb of some made object out of your own hand and up into a clear blue sky. He knew that if you wanted to hook a kid forever on things that fly, you didn't put hurdles in his way. You didn't teach him that he had to earn his wings by bending over a dusty building board for hours. That would come later. What he needed first was to *see something in the air,* and that's where Walker's stuff came in. Here's Larry Conover, a lifetime modeler from out in windswept Iowa, recalling his earliest exposure to aeromodelling:

> *"The first one I saw was a ready-made all-balsa ROG*
> *with a red celluloid prop and fin. I watched a boy fly it*
> *on a corner lot, at least 20 feet high. It was wonderful*
> *and I was a model enthusiast from that time on."*

Independence

After a decade of struggle, Walker's ever-expanding line of simple rubber and glider models at last rewarded him with a degree of financial independence. By the late thirties his company was on its feet and running—running so smoothly, in fact, that the boss was able to live every modeler's dream: he could design and build and fly from morning till night, all in the sacred name of "research and development." And he did.

The man's interests and enthusiasm were boundless. He toyed with radio control (and won the Nationals four times.) He toyed with sonic control, in a doomed attempt to circumvent the almighty F.C.C. and bring some license-free form of 'remote control' to the masses. He toyed with small-field free flight, focusing on engine timers and pre-programmed auto-surfaces as ways to keep the models from flying away.

And he toyed with tethered flight.

By the 1930s, tethered model airplanes were hardly a new idea. The earliest on record appears to be a compressed-air model flown by one Victor Tatin, of France, back in 1879. The first gasoline powered 'round-the-pole' model, a scale Antoinette, performed before a large audience in a Paris velodrome in 1911. And by the late twenties, a Britisher named F.B. Thomas was successfully flying crude gas-powered models around a pylon, controlling both elevator and engine from outside the circle.

Speed and Noise and Excitement

When miniature gasoline motors became widely available in the U.S. during the mid-thirties—'miniature' at that time meaning two pounds or less—people who didn't immediately bolt these monsters to the nose of a free-flying model plane would often shoehorn them into the smallest, lightest, fastest car or boat model they could build. Boat racing mania swept the city of Los Angeles in 1936, and all across the nation there began the ululating roar of little open-throated race cars—a roar that didn't taper off until well into the 1950s. This new mass-produced miracle, the single-cylinder spark-ignition engine, opened up a whole world of speed and noise and excitement for car and boat addicts. And 99% of this racing, whether on land or water, was done in circles—at the end of a short, taut string called a tether.

So the stage was set for some kind of tethered airplane racing, as well. Free-flight speed events, popular back in the *gummiband* days of the twin pusher, had fallen out of favor even before gas came along. Free-flying speed jobs had become, in the blunt, official words of the NAA, "too hard to time." And indeed, clocking a 60-mph model through a two hundred foot course (60 mph being equivalent to 88 feet per second) provided far more scope for stopwatch error than for design improvement. And twin pushers were already pushing 60 by 1930.

But beyond timing difficulties, freeflight speed simply made no sense. Free-flying models are too vulnerable to stray gusts of wind, too hard to control, too dangerous to spectators, too easily destroyed. The rubber-speed idea still resurfaces periodically—as a kid I got suckered in by a nifty-looking little mid-fifties *Flying*

132

Models design called the "FM Racer." But people who try it usually find that it isn't all that great.

And yet, to many folk, speed has a fascination all its own. All those boat and car guys were obviously having too darn much fun, going around and around in their endless circles: *varoom, varoom, varoom* . . . .

The time was ripe for control line.

Things on Strings

And so the *zeitgeist* whispered this new need into thousands of ears—whispered it, perhaps, in Texas German, because the first to respond commercially were a couple of young model-building brothers, Victor and Joseph Stanzel, down in Schulenburg, Texas. Victor owned a small company that had for years been puttering about the sidelines of model aviation with a line of solid scale models, those little flightless blobs that the AMA, in 1938, finally banished forever from its Nationals.

But solids were boring even to manufacturers, and so in January of 1940 the Stanzel brothers unveiled their first flying model. It was the *Shark*, a racy-looking low-wing gassie. A gassie, *but not a free flight,* as virtually every other gas kit in the world was. The Stanzel Shark was a 'tether' model. A rock on a string. A sort of winged racecar.

With a twist.

Instead of being tethered to a pylon, the way cars and boats usually were, the Shark's single control line was attached to the end of—a fishing pole! And the fisherman . . . er, *pilot* . . . stood right out there in the middle of the circle spinning around with the plane, raising and lowering the tip of his pole to control—after a fashion—the model's altitude.

Varoom, varoom, varoom . . . .

At first it sounded downright silly, but—by jingo!—this Stanzel thing not only worked, *it was a whale of a lot of fun!* Suddenly touch-and-go landings were possible. Suddenly scale was possible. Oddball designs were possible. And best of all, *speed* was possible—and measurable, too! All it took was a fishpole and thirty feet of stout line.

Simple. Elegant. And exactly the sort of thing that kids had been doing for nearly three decades with those miserable, worthless, flightless little *solid models,* after they got tired of dusting them, or hand-flying them, or holding them out of car windows to make their little aluminum props go *whir-r-r.*

G-Line

Stanzel called this marvelous new invention "G-Line," and claimed to have applied for a patent on it—a patent on a fishpole! Experiments showed them that, because of the excess speed (and hence lift) of a gas model, the attach point for the G-line needed to be, not out at the wingtip as you might expect, but somewhere up towards the front of the fuselage. But the line still had to be attached somehow to the wingtip, to stabilize the model in the roll mode. So the Stanzel Shark sported a piece of rigid music wire jammed into the leading edge of its inside wing panel, something like a pitot tube. At the end of this wire was a small loop for the G-Line to pass through on its way to the fuselage.

From this arrangement it would seem like only a short step to the idea of using a *pivoting* pitot tube—pivoting and bent 90° and running down the full length of the leading edge, terminating in some sort of control horn with some sort of cable or pushrod back to the elevator. Then, when the pilot raised or lowered the tip of his fishpole it would pivot the line guide up or down, and tweak the elevator up or down, and thereby exert a little genuine aerodynamic influence on the model. Like so:

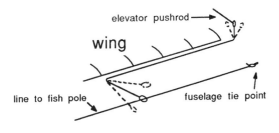

Surprisingly, nobody took this short and seemingly obvious step. (In fact, I just "invented" it while writing that last paragraph.) But no matter—even if they had, the idea would have been quickly outdated, because just seven months later, in September of 1940, the American Junior Aircraft Company of Portland Oregon introduced "U-Control."

Patent Number 2292416

If I were forced to pick the three most significant advances in aeromodeling that occurred before World War II, I would have to say: balsa, gas engines, U-Control. This is not due to any personal bias toward U-Control. It's true that I can see three ukies from the desk where I now sit—one flown to death, one awaiting its first flight, the third yet uncovered. (For the record, I can also see three rubber models and an equal number of handlaunch gliders, six gas freeflights, three R/C sailplanes and two R/C power models.) Still, I believe I can state without fear of perjury that *I am not now, nor have I ever been, Senator McCarthy, a member of the Controlline Party.*

I dizzy, I sicken, I fall on my prat too easily.

And yet, though it may never be my first love, my hat is off to U-Control. Not "control line." That phrase refers to the entire field of tethered flight. I mean *U-Control*—the system covered in Jim Walker's United States Patent number 2292416, labeled "Controlled Captive-Type Toy Airplane."

The essence of the Walker system is two wires and a bellcrank. Simplicity itself. Without Walker's two wires and a bellcrank, it is just possible that American aeromodeling would have dried up to a trickle sometime during the late fifties, before the mid-sixties influx of inexpensive, ready-to-install R/C units came along to resuscitate the magazines, and with them the hobby.

Our monthly model mags are the glue that hold us together— the creators of our heroes, the shapers of our collective self-image, the seed-catalogs of our dreams. And these magazines, bless them every one, run strictly on advertising dollars, something that would have been in disastrously short supply during those lean years after

Sputnik . . . if Jim Walker's 1940 *Fireball* hadn't opened up an entirely new world of model aviation.

Fireball in the Sky

And yet that first kitted Fireball of 1940, for all its historical and nostalgic value, was far from wonderful. Its wing airfoil was, for all practical purposes, flat bottomed. This meant that it would "loop the loop," as people were fond of saying in those days, but it wasn't partial to inverted flight. Also, because the Fireball was created by a free flight modeler for other free-flight modelers, it had dihedral. Not a bunch of dihedral, mind you—too little, actually, by free flight standards. But a whole lot more than necessary, as it turned out.

A one-piece wing with zero dihedral would have been simpler and stronger and cheaper to produce, and would have performed just as well—better, really—at the end of a set of control lines. But, to the generation of modelers who were Walker's potential customers in 1940, an airplane with no dihedral was no airplane at all. So the Fireball had dihedral.

The Unbanked Turn

Another of the Fireball's shortcomings was its pair of patented control-wire guides on the bottom of the wing. (Just about everything on that model was patented: 2292416 covered *nine separate aspects* of the Fireball and its control system.)

These two little guide loops, copied straight from the line guides on a fishing pole, were located too far inboard—much closer to the root than the tip of the wing. This allowed the Fireball, despite its dihedral, to fly around its endless circle *with its wings level*—a feat impossible for an untethered aircraft of any size, and a rich source of ridicule among diehard free flighters and self-appointed aero-aestheticians everywhere. *Who needed an airplane that didn't even bank in a turn?*

But of course if you set up your leadouts so that the model banked realistically, then wing lift would try to tighten that bank, causing your lines to go slack. And God help you, my U-Control friend, if your lines go slack! You could be chased all over a vacant lot by an aggressive Bunch Tiger. You could lose an ear, or some more critical appendage. Legend has it that only J.C. 'Madman' Yates, the famous forties stunt pilot from Southern California, could fly with slack lines—sometimes nearly a half-circle of slack. Lesser mortals needed tension, and lots of it.

Tight lines are almost the whole trick. Every one of the early control-line experimenters—Jim Walker included—vastly over-estimated the importance of aerodynamics in this new form of flying. The overriding principle in tethered flight is *centrifugal force*. Out on the highway it may be true that speed kills, but in the controlline circle, speed cures. For half a century the chief problem of the serious U-Control stunt flier has been to find, for each individual model, that elusive airspeed that's exactly slow enough to be elegant in the bloodshot eyes of the judges, and yet fast enough to keep those damned lines taut in vertical maneuvers.

"Enlarges the Entire Concept of Power-Model Flying"

Walker's first series of U-Control ads, in the fall and winter of 1940, didn't exactly set the world afire—particularly along the eastern seaboard, where all the modeling magazines were published. In 1940, free flight was king. Goldberg's pylon had just become the wave of the future; the skyrocket climb was everything; and who needed a solid model on a string, created (God knows why) by some obscure toymaker out at the far end of the Oregon Trail?

The deliberate vagueness of those first Fireball ads didn't help, either. They were illustrated with drawings rather than photographs. Centrifugal force was conspicuous by its absence: the model in the ads seemed to be soaring about like a free flight, somewhere high above the pilot's head. Although the C-shaped control handle in the flier's hand was clearly visible, the lines themselves wandered off into space, entering the plane at a thoroughly misleading angle.

Nothing was shown, or even hinted at, of the bellcrank-and-pushrod system that was the heart and soul of U-Control. Readers were left completely in the dark about the plane's innards. Was this new system electronic, with a relay and slave motors to move the elevator? (Freeflight champ Leo Weiss had developed such a system while a freshman at MIT in 1936.) Or did the lines simply slide through curved tubes, going back to a double horn on the elevator in the manner of full-scale linkages?

This vagueness in the ads was intentional, for the impetuous Walker didn't get around to submitting drawings to the patent office for his "Controlled Captive-Type Toy Airplane" until the day after Christmas, 1940. That he had been flying Fireballs in the Portland area for a year or better is well documented—*Model Builder* columnist Francis Reynolds recalls demonstrating one in 1939 as part of a Clipper Gasoline promotion.

Walker had even taken a model to the 1940 Nationals in Chicago without attracting much interest. But after the first couple of ads in the fall of '40, Polk's Model Hobbycraft in New York City jumped on the Fireball, not merely stocking the kit but actually featuring it in their own advertising—an endorsement from the all-important eastern establishment that couldn't be ignored.

Meanwhile, Walker loaded a station wagon with Fireballs and made a long, meandering demonstration tour down the west coast, ending up, like so many other wandering dreamers, in the city and county of Los Angeles, state of California. There the Fireball was an instant hit. Competition—eyeball to eyeball competition—has always been the first order of business in the great smogwashed L.A. basin. And here was a brand new form of flying that lent itself perfectly to competition!

A New Spin on "Precision" Flying

It was in L.A. that free flighters had popularized, back in the mid-thirties, the first "precision" flying: those contests mentioned in Chapter Four in which gas models took off and landed inside a giant, 700 foot diameter bullseye, executing while airborne an exactly predetermined number of climb and glide circles.

To fly Precision, you metered your fuel, filed your flight plan with the judges ("four power circles followed by three-and-a-half glide circles") and then set her on the ground and turned her loose with a prayer. Precision freeflight was just about as tough an event as modeling had seen, up to that point. It required you to do your homework—to build straight and true, know your plane and engine perfectly, know exactly what to expect from any given weather condition. And then be lucky, as well.

But this U-Control thing! Why, here was a whole new game, a game that required you not only to do your homework, but to *actually pilot your model through its entire flight.* Here was a chance to compete not just on the designing and building and trimming level, but on the piloting level as well. Eyeball to eyeball.

Control!

And it eliminated much of the luck factor, too. It gave you control over the entire flight. And a wonderful sense of oneness with the model: you could actually feel your plane lose energy in a climb, feel it speed up in a dive. You tugged at a U-Control ship and it tugged right back at you, just like a living thing.

Unlike free flight, ukies could be flown almost anywhere: in a vacant lot, on a ball diamond, right out in the street in front of your house. (The neighbors rarely complained. Strange as it seems today, model airplanes, before World War II, weren't noisy. They were *interesting.*)

And here was the best thing of all: with those lines attached to it, *your plane would never fly out of sight and be lost!*

By the fall of '40, Los Angeles modelers were already starting to feel the pinch of prewar gas and material shortages—already becoming aware that engines were getting too valuable to lose. They took to Walker's "captive-type toy airplane" like hogs to muck. Well before Pearl Harbor, speed and stunt events had become regular features of the Southern California contest circuit. Within a year of its introduction, this U-Control gimmick had become—in the Los Angeles area at least—a roaring success.

That Patent

The model magazines, ordinarily quick to jump on a new fad, sidled up to this one with caution. For one thing, there was the ticklish question of that patent. Nobody in the model business had ever made such a big thing over a patent before. Nobody in the model business seemed to know, in the year 1940, just exactly what "patented" meant.

Were the mags forbidden to publish drawings or photos of Walker's system? Were individual builders forbidden to duplicate the Fireball's controls in their own planes?

The first magazine to venture into this uncharted territory was Charlie Grant's *Model Airplane News*. In the April '41 issue Grant published plans for a model called *Controlled Lightning*. The *Lightning* looked something like a scaled-up Comet *Dipper*, minus the parasol wing mount. (Its designer, Cleveland modeler Bill Schwab, was a free flighter known for his winning ways with Joe Elgin's *Playboy*.) Control for the *Lightning* was provided by a crude—though unarguably original—two-line system.

In place of Walker's simple C-shaped handle, Schwab used a kind of erector-set "joystick" that was hinged comically to the flier's beltbuckle, something like a prosthetic penis. The control lines attached directly to this joystick, with the 'up' line on top and the 'down' line somewhere below bellybutton level.

Pull back on the joystick and the plane climbed. Push forward and it dived. Take a deep breath and it simply wobbled.

Neat.

Inside the *Lightning*, things were more primitive yet. The two control lines, with a couple of inches separating them, ran through eyelets and then did a prompt 45° turn toward a common fastening point on the elevator pushrod, like so:

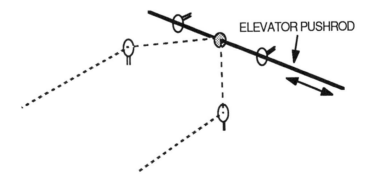

Now, this system looks pretty good on paper: pull on one dotted line while slackening the other, and the pushrod should slide in the direction of the tight line. *Should.*

In the real world, however, the friction in the *Lightning's* control system was deadly. This friction was directly proportional to the centrifugal force: the heavier and faster the plane, the worse the friction. And the worse the friction, of course, the more sluggish and prone to freeze were the controls. "Lightning" turned out to be the perfect name for Schwab's model: you could never tell where it was going to strike next.

Controlled Lightning was, when everything worked, a slight improvement over the Stanzel G-Line. But it was patently not the answer to the Walker patent.

License

Within a few months, the word about 2292416 got around. Anyone, it seems, was free to duplicate Walker's bellcrank system, *but not for profit.* If other manufacturers wanted to put out U-Control kits, they'd have to pay American Junior an annual licensing fee for the privilege. The fee wasn't much—"Berkeley" Bill Effinger, one of the earliest and most faithful licensees, still maintains that he got more than his money's worth every year, just by being able to use Jim Walker's name in the Berkeley Models ads.

But a lot of the other manufacturers balked. It wasn't just the money. It meant that a person had to be reasonably honest with himself—and with Jim Walker—about the number of kits he expected to sell each year. And this was something that manufacturers—then as now—tend not to be reasonably honest about. (It isn't, after all, anybody's business how little money there is in the model airplane business.)

Rumor

And then, there was another reason the manufacturers balked. All through the war, and all through the late forties, a vague but persistent rumor kept floating around the industry—"Don't quote me on this, but I heard it from a guy that's supposed to know about

141

these things"—a vague but persistent rumor that said, almost in a whisper:

The Walker patent isn't worth the paper it's written on. It'll never stand up in court!

For these and other reasons, a number of manufacturers simply defied American Junior. They began advertising and selling controlline kits that copied Jim Walker's "U-Control" system brazenly, piece for piece.

One by one, each of these manufacturers received a certified letter from a certain law firm in Portland, recommending that they cease and desist. And one by one, each of them ceased and desisted.

With at least one exception.

A gentleman named R.W. Pinckney, owner of Model Industries of Melrose Park, Illinois, was one flagrant violator who chose to ignore Walker's warning letter. Thus it was that, in January of 1948, Pinckney found himself in Federal District Court, Chicago, charged with patent infringement.

Despite the fact that Pinckney was the father of a darling little nine-year-old girl named Skippy—a girl who'd learned to fly U-Control in less than ten minutes, and won junior controlline events all over the country, and was America's current sweetheart of speed, and had been interviewed fetchingly on ABC radio as the youngest contestant at the '46 Wichita Nats—despite all this, the federal judge in Chicago was unmoved. He found for Jim Walker and American Junior Aircraft.

Model Industries picked up the tab for Jim's lawsuit, and the American hobby industry pricked up its ears. *The Walker patent had held up in court.* This fellow from Portland might have a disarming grin—and he certainly was a tireless showman and promoter of the hobby—but he obviously took 2292416 seriously.

Your Favorite Control System

The cheapest way around the Walker patent, of course, was to put out a bare kit, without any controls. After all, kits didn't normally include engines and fuel tanks and such, so why should they include bellcranks and pushrods and leadout wires? On the plan, you could simply draw a big arrow to the point where the bellcrank axle belonged, and mark it "install your favorite control system here."

Dozens of manufacturers did this, and dozens of manufacturers found that their kits didn't sell. This was a brand-new field, and ambiguity made buyers nervous. They wanted their ukie kits be complete. Kitmakers who refused to bow to this public demand had to settle for a miniscule share of the market. By the end of the decade, the eight largest manufacturers—Berkeley, Guillow, Testor's, Scientific, Top Flite, Modelcraft, McCoy, and Megow— were all licensed to produce and sell 'genuine' U-Control models.

Alternative Systems

A second way around the Walker patent was to come up with an alternative control system of your own, as the designer of the *Controlled Lightning* had done. Half a dozen such systems hit the market during the forties—systems just different enough from U-Control to avoid infringement. Some of the best known of these were the "Jem Automatic Pilot," "Cam-A-Matic," "Flight Controller," "Roller Control," I.M.P.'s "NU-Control," the 'Camtrol," and Stanzel's "Super G-Line." Many of these alternative systems were themselves protected by U.S. patents. And yet each of them, despite its patentable uniqueness, had one common characteristic: compared to U-Control, it was junk.

Who Needs Wires?

But then, to the average modeler who read those first Fireball ads in 1940 and '41, Walker's U-Control system was junk, too. Outside of a few madmen in the L.A. basin, who needed it?

All across America, the first-ever generation of gas modelers had finally begun to master the complex aerodynamics of free flight. They had finally begun to learn how to control the screaming power of a Super Cyclone, how to tame it into a tight, altitude-grabbing spiral. They had figured out what it took to get that instant transition from climb to glide without losing fifty feet of precious altitude, what it took to make a five-pound airplane hang like a feather on the very edge of a stall, soaring the lightest bubble for ever and ever and ever . . . .

Like the expert rubber modelers they had so recently elbowed out of the mainstream, these new, hotshot gas jockeys had squandered the best years of their youth in developing their hobby into an art and a craft and a science. Why should they abandon all this hard-won skill and cunning for a brick on a string that went *vroom, vroom, vroom*?

Double U - Double U - Two

This was the essence of their argument, and they were still repeating it to one another—punctuated with vigorous nods and the occasional good-natured poke in the ribs—when a terrible thing happened. One Sunday morning the warplanes of Hideki Tojo fell out of the dawn sky over Oahu, and America came home from church to find itself right in the middle of act two of the Second World War.

In less than six months, that first-ever generation of gas model experts were, almost to a man, in harsh woolen uniforms and scattered willy-nilly across three continents, with matters on their minds far more compelling than *downthrust* and *washout* and *center of lateral area.*

The Great Plane Robbery

If World War II was a setback for aeromodeling in general, it was nothing short of a disaster for freeflight. Four years later, when all those expert gas jockeys came trickling home, they found their world changed forever. Opening their old boyhood closets to take a peek at their boyhood pastimes, they discovered yet another meaning to the phrase *the high cost of war.*

For starters, their precious dog-eared collections of *Flying Aces* and *Air Trails* and *MAN* were gone—mom had donated them, early in the war, to the local paper drive. And if that wasn't bad enough, a blatant robbery had occurred, as well.

Their entire hobby was missing!

144

Sometime during their absence, the science of freeflight gas, which they had entrusted so lovingly to their kid brothers in 1942, had been stolen outright, by person or persons unknown. Stolen, and (in the best traditions of car thievery) stripped down and reassembled so cleverly that it was now virtually unrecognizable. Only the prewar engines, the Elves and Ohlssons and high-revving little Bantam .19s, looked and smelled and sounded familiar. The models themselves were changed utterly.

Got the World on a String

The model airplanes of 1946, the model airplanes a million kid brothers were now flying, bore almost no resemblance to prewar designs. They had shrunken to a third of their 1941 size. Gone were the old stick-and-tissue structures with their lithe, translucent, bird-like beauty. These new postwar models were mostly solid wood—little more than powered boomerangs—stubby chunks of balsa and hardwood with no more wing area than a pullet, no more grace than a shake shingle. Unflyable, unaerodynamic, unaesthetic little creations, these "ukies"—much closer to the shelf models of the early thirties than the huge *Bombshells* and *Zippers* and *Sailplanes* of pre-Pearl Harbor days.

Furthermore, these new models didn't really *fly*. They just swung around in circles, like yo-yos, on the end of a string.

Varoom-varoom-varoom.

Inevitable

Challenged about this, the kid brothers could only shrug. It wasn't their fault. Could they help it if their idea of a *model airplane* had been molded by the half-million solid-scale Wartime Identification Models they'd been recruited, back in '42, to build for the U.S. Navy?

Could they help it if four years of gas rationing had made trips out into open freeflight country a nearly forgotten dream?

Could they help it if all the people who understood *downthrust* and *washout* and *center of lateral area* had gone off to war, leaving them with a generation of gray-haired shop teachers who were well-meaning—and often excellent wood-carvers—but aerodynamic illiterates?

And finally, could they help it if the world of their imaginations had been stocked, over the past four years, not with the tube-and-fabric *Robins* and *Corbens* and *Taylorcrafts* that inspired the thirties freeflighters, but with *Corsairs* and *Helldivers* and *Liberators* from two hundred weekly Pathe´ newsreels?

Under such circumstances, U-Control was almost inevitable.

Their Name is Legion

How many of these newfangled controlline modelers, these crazy circle burners, were there after the war? Statistics—never very reliable in the world of aeromodeling—disagree widely about the size of the movement. The *Saturday Evening Post,* in November, 1950, reported that "about 80%" of all model flying was on lines, a figure almost certainly overinflated, and yet indicative of the high visibility of this newest branch of the hobby. Every empty lot, every city park, every unused ball diamond seemed to buzz with little planes on wires. All you had to do was stop, look and listen: U-Control was everywhere.

Perhaps the best barometer of the times was Bernie Winston's four-story mailorder house down on West 22nd Street in New York—America's Hobby Center, Inc. AHC had been advertising in the mags ever since the company was founded in 1931; by the late forties they virtually dominated the front two or three pages of every national modeling magazine. AHC catalogs, printed on that same cheap and fragrant pulp the mags themselves used, were stuffed to the margins with every kit and engine and modeling accessory available in these United States.

So what can we learn from America's Hobby Center about controlline popularity? Just this: Their 1951 catalog lists fifty different gas-powered freeflight kits . . . and more than *two hundred* controlliners.

Half a Million Ringmasters

There can be no doubt that, in the long decade between World War II and Sputnik I, control line was the fastest growing branch of the hobby. In a 1966 interview, Ed Manulkin of Sterling Models claimed that the Sterling *Ringmaster,* introduced fourteen years earlier, had by then sold over half a million—making it, in his words, "very possibly the single most popular model airplane kit of all time."

(Figures are cheap. Barney Snyder of Modelcraft claimed his *Pacific Ace* rubber model was over a million by 1948. And certainly the Ringmaster's half-million has since been surpassed by a number of R/C kits—notably Goldberg's *Falcon* series. But to the starving kitmakers of 1966, half a million sales in *any* branch of the hobby except plastics must have seemed like an impossible dream.)

Nats entries, curiously enough, never reflected this postwar stampede to controlline. Even though everyone agrees that sport flying and contest flying are vastly different worlds, the Nats figures—and they appeared in every magazine—serve to temper some of the wilder estimates of U-Control's popularity. At windy Olathe in '46, only 12.5% of the entrants flew ukies. At the first Dallas Nationals, in 1950, speed and stunt (still the only wire events) amounted to just 18% of total registrations, while free flight gas totaled a whopping 40%. (Glider, rubber and indoor gobbled up the remaining 42%.) The '54 Chicago Nats drew 66% free flight and R/C, 28% control line—percentages that were repeated the following year in Los Angeles, where U-Control, supposedly, was king.

Yet the ads in the model press were dominated by U-Control. In a typical issue of *Model Airplane News* during the late fifties, controlline planes and accessories were featured in 46% of the ad space; R/C was next with 22%; and free flight amounted to a mere 14%. (A reader survey in that same issue put U/C Scale tops in popularity, U/C Stunt second, and R/C third. Free flight, presumably, came fourth.)

So U-Control was already carrying the magazines on its back, dollar-wise, by the late fifties. And it would continue to do so for almost another decade, until R/C finally came into its own and began the long climb toward its current dominance of the hobby. (As late as 1967, Glenn Sigafoose claimed that 60% of the Sig balsa he sold to scratchbuilders went into U/C models. Thirty percent went to R/C, he said, and the remaining 10% to freeflight.)

The conclusion seems plain: Without two wires and a bellcrank, the aeromodeling hobby would have died long before radio control came to its rescue.

But Nevilles E. Walker of Portland, Oregon—jealous guardian of the U-Control patent, and beyond question the greatest promoter of aeromodeling in American history—didn't live to see any of this. He died in the spring of 1958, just a few days before his fifty-fourth birthday.

Died, many of his admirers felt, of a broken heart.

Prototype

Jim Walker's entire life was dedicated to the hobby. He was, by any standard, a modeling madman. He was not merely one of us—he was the prototype for all of us. A feature story in the '54 *Air Trails Annual* labeled him "America's Number One Modeler," and few people at the time would have disagreed. In his heyday, which was the long decade following World War II, Walker spent more time on the road than he did at home in Portland. He traveled by station wagon, by convertible, and later in a sleek, limited-edition Buick Skylark that pulled one of Wally Byam's high-dollar Airstream camping trailers.

Walker never competed in controlline events. But he would arrive at a contest, and, when things got dull, pull out a *Fireball* and do the most amazing and unimaginable freestyle stunts: stand it on its tail in a full stall, then, by manipulating the two-speed ignition, back it down slowly, tail swinging like a pendulum, until a straight pin protruding from the rear of the fuselage popped a balloon—his famous "sabre dance."

He could put on a one-man, three-plane team race, flying a Fireball in each hand, with the third one attached to a flashy white man-from-Mars helmet on his head and controlled pneumatically by a bulb held between his teeth. By 1957, the year before his death, Walker had figured out how to fly a fourth model from his belt: four Fireballs at once. *Vroom . . . vroom . . . vroom!* It made for one hell of a show, and the crowds—modelers and non-modelers alike—loved it.

And that crazy-looking man from Mars helmet he wore wasn't all flamboyance. It held a voice mike and transmitter that allowed Walker to describe for the crowd exactly what he was doing during his Fireball demos—be his own pitchman. After the sabre dance and balloon bust, an assistant would step out and snatch the plane right out of the air, with the open-throated Ohlsson .23 still growling menacingly and Jim, controls firmly in hand, heckling him through the mike from out in mid-circle. Or else the assistant would crank up and launch, at Walker's signal, a second Fireball, this one with a crepe ribbon draped loosely over one wing. Then came the *streamer exchange,* in which this ribbon was deftly transferred to the wing of the other model, and then just as deftly returned—all without any 'cuts,' as combat fliers would later call them.

When 1/2-A engines hit the scene around 1950, Jim quickly came out with the two-and-a-half-ounce, all balsa *Firebaby*—by far the best ukie trainer ever designed for that engine class. Almost too light to be damaged in a crash, the Firebaby was a slip-together profile job with pre-dyed parts in the tradition of the A-J rubber band and glider models. Walker could stunt two Firebabies at once, two little screaming streaks of red in the air—all the while explaining, through his radio helmet, the secrets of formation flying without throttle control.

If the day happened to be calm, he would bring out a Fireball on a U-Reely handle and crank out an incredible 150 feet of line, so that the model was flying in football-field circles about his head, giving an illusion of free flight that harkened back to those first 1940 ads. Then he'd reel in to normal length, fifty to seventy feet, and demolish a few helper-launched balsa gliders. Or else drop some white-flour 'bombs' on ground-based models.

The man was a tireless ham. He could entertain a crowd with nothing more than a handful of dime gliders—bursting balloons, juggling three gliders in the air at once, clipping the ash off a helper's cigarette while making William Tell jokes. And when the

149

field permitted, he often finished off his act with an R/C demo, doing consecutive loops, rolls, and Immelmans—old-hat stunts today, but absolute magic in the early fifties.

People loved Jim's Fireballs and his gliders, but they went simply wild for that big trike-geared radioplane of his. Not one American in ten thousand had seen a 'remote controlled' model in those days—and no more than one in 100,000 had ever attempted to fly one.

Genius of Flight

This was the public side of America's Number One Modeler— the smiling, loveable genius of flight who gave away his kits by the hundreds, at contests and flying demonstrations and shopping centers and anywhere else he could gather an air-minded crowd. (Any kid who could start and fly one of Jim's *Firebabies* always got to take it home, engine and all.) This was the man—tall, lean, bronzed and striking, part Lindbergh, part Barnum—who could charm *Time* and *Newsweek* and *Saturday Evening Post* reporters into calling him "Jimmy" and repeating some of his propaganda lines verbatim: "American Junior makes 75,000 gliders a day . . . turns out more aircraft than all the rest of the world combined."

This was the man who, because the Nats were too far away, sponsored and ran his own three-day Northwest Championships up in Portland, with paid timers, food sold at cost, official flying from 8 a.m. to 7 p.m. (longer by request) and *a trip around the world* for first prize.

This was the man who, when a crowd of manufacturers failed to respond to Ed Lidgard's plea for help in sending the '51 Wakefield team to England, jumped up from his seat and wrote Ed a check for $3,000.00—the equivalent of nearly thirty grand today. (Has anybody given thirty grand to an FAI team lately?)

Pied Piper

Ten years after Walker's death, Bill Winter still remembered him as "a cosmic force of a man." Winter admired not only Walker's energy, but his generosity, as well—and most of all, his vision. A constant flow of products and ideas emanated from Jim's brain. When the fifties Nationals began to get too big for the

Navy, Walker argued against limiting entries. "Encourage *more* entries," he said, "and board the contestants in private homes—it'll be good for public relations."

He sponsored contests in which skilled fliers could win points by teaching non-modeling spectators to fly. He dreamed, in the fifties, of simple, cheap R/C systems that the youngest child could operate. For kids who couldn't afford an engine, he published plans for "whip-powered" ukies, to be jerked about with a Victor Stanzel-like fishing pole. He built Fireballs that did rolls, and rubber models that did touch-and-gos. He designed low-speed props and pressure tanks and fuel regulators and little windup helicopters that reversed direction when they hit something. "For me," Bill Winter wrote fondly, "Jim Walker was a pied piper who led us to bright places."

Perfectionist

There was another side to the man, of course—a private side that never appeared in the magazine articles. Walker was a relentless perfectionist. He pushed himself, and everyone around him, to the limit. He was impatient and short-tempered; the smallest mistake could bring on a violent tongue-lashing, followed later by a guilty gift. Not an easy man to work for, he rode his employees constantly about quality: *No American Junior model was ever to leave the factory flawed. No plane of his was ever to disappoint a child.* He had constant problems with family members who owned part of the company—non-modelers who cared more about profits than Jim did.

Jim Walker loved aeromodeling above almost anything else in life, and he had little tolerance for anyone whose dreams fell short of his own. From the early forties, when U-Control first brought him to prominence, to the day of his death, Walker flew and talked and dreamed (and, incidentally, smoked) nonstop. Today we'd label him a "Type A" personality—most likely to succeed, most likely to get a heart attack in the process. It was, in fact, a series of strokes that killed him.

But not before he had suffered a head-on collision—with the future.

The Plastic Era

Leroy Cox of Los Angeles was, like Walker, a manufacturer who plied his trade in that gray area between toys and models. Cox, too, was something of a perfectionist. Back in 1947 he began marketing, under the Thimble Drome label, a nifty little scale model race car of cast aluminum, a .19-powered machine that sold for a modest (considering its quality) four bucks without engine, twenty bucks with. As time went on, he added other cars and engines to his line.

Although he was a skilled machinist, Cox at first contracted for his engines. But by 1951 he was building his own. Car engines led naturally to plane engines, and in early '52 the L.M. Cox Manufacturing Company entered the fast-growing 1/2-A market with the first of their high-powered, high-quality reed-valve motors, the Space Bug .049. The Space Bug wasn't cheap and it wasn't light—but it was a powerhouse. It and its tankless cousin the Thermal Hopper immediately began to dominate 1/2-A competition.

Success is wonderful—even success in a minor field like aeromodeling. But Leroy Cox wasn't satisfied. He wanted a bigger market for his engines. And he soon found it, right under his nose.

Two brothers named McRoskey, both former L.A. area modelers, had introduced, back in 1949, a little all-plastic, ready to fly U-Control model they called the WenMac *Aeromite*. Heavy and crude and homely, the Aeromite was nevertheless an astounding success, selling at the rate of 5,000 units a week by 1952. Marketing, not aerodynamics, was its secret. The McRoskeys had wisely decided to bypass the traditional model shops and go straight for America's vast and growing toy market—where they struck gold.

Leroy Cox cast a critical eye upon the Aeromite. It wasn't the least bit realistic. It was a molded imitation of a *model* airplane rather than a full-scale machine. Cox decided he could do better.

And, to a degree, he did. In July of '53 he introduced the *TD-1*, a racy, semi-scale midwinger featuring a red plastic body, a clear canopy, and a lovely, fully-symmetrical wing created from two thin shells of extruded aluminum. The TD-1 sold for almost twice the Aeromite's $9.95, but it had a hotter engine (the Space Bug) and a lot more wing area. It flew circles around its little competitor, despite the fact that, at ten ounces, it was still too heavy for a half-A controlline model airplane.

Did You Say 'Model Airplane'?

But then, neither the Cox TD-1 nor the WenMac Aeromite was, in any real sense, a model airplane. Both were toys, pure and simple—mass-produced toys, designed and packaged and targeted toward a mass market. Leroy Cox, to his credit, had no illusions about this; he repeatedly referred to his products as *powered toys*.

Cox had seen the handwriting on the wall. The stick-and-tissue era of modeling was drawing to a close, just as the tube-and-fabric era had in full-scale. From a business standpoint, balsa was out. Plastics were the wave of the future—and not just in display models, but in ready-to-fly powered models, as well.

The Aeromite and the TD-1 were harbingers of this trend, and Jim Walker hated everything about it. Plastic models, even well designed plastic models, were all promise and no performance. They might look beautiful, they might look exactly like 'real' planes— but they could never be made to dance with the air in the same way a balsa model did. Plastic was too heavy, too opaque. It was all surface image; it had no depth, no character—and certainly none of the grace, none of the litheness of balsa. Even at the end of a string.

And both the Aeromite and the TD-1 flew at the end of a string—a pair of strings, in fact, that terminated in curiously familiar-looking bellcranks. Both models used exact copies of the Walker "U-Control" system described in Patent #2292416. The difference was this: the McRoskeys were licensed by American Junior. L.M. Cox Manufacturing was not.

In September of 1953, a United States Marshal appeared on Cox's doorstep with what the law calls a *complaint*: American Junior was bringing suit against L.M. Cox for two counts of patent infringement, and one of unfair competition.

153

A-J Aircraft vs. L.M. Cox

American patent law gives the creator of a new product or process seventeen years to get rich—seventeen years to capitalize on the invention before it becomes public property. Walker's seventeen years began on August 11, 1942, the date U-Control was officially granted its Letters Patent. The grant would have expired naturally on that same date in 1959.

Because the mills of justice grind slowly, the Walker-Cox suit didn't come to trial until March of 1955. By then Cox was marketing a second ready-to-fly plastic ukie, called the *TD-3*. The TD-3 was smaller and lighter and cheaper and uglier than the TD-1, and it was aimed directly at the market carved out by WenMac's *Aeromite*—a market that was, to some extent, shared by Walker's all-balsa *Firebaby*. Because the TD-3 was down around six ounces, it flew a little better than the TD-1, though it was still no match, performance-wise, for the 2.5-ounce Firebaby.

The TD-3's control system was a duplicate of the TD-1's: another flagrant violation of the Walker patent. Incensed, American Junior petitioned the court for triple damages—the maximum penalty the law allows for patent violations.

Judge for the trial was the Honorable James M. Carter, a Los Angeles magistrate of no small experience in patent law—and a man whose son, as it turned out, had once owned and flown a Stanzel *Shark*. So Judge Carter was not totally unfamiliar with the world of model airplanes.

The plaintiff's case was clearcut: The defendant had violated the U-Control patent repeatedly. In addition, the defendant was engaged in the manufacture of a device called the "Skylon Reel," a copy-in-principle of Walker's "U-Reely" handle, which was protected by a second U.S. patent. Finally, the defendant continued to print on its boxes the phrase *All you do is control it*, which American Junior felt was an attempt to confuse the public and capitalize on the prestigious and copyrighted phrase "U-Control."

Exhibit A

The defendant's case was nearly as clearcut. It rested on a number of exhibits. The principle one, Exhibit A, was a huge, high-winged model aircraft created by an Oregon watchmaker named Oba St. Clair and demonstrated—according to sworn testimony of both the watchmaker and his wife—to one Nevilles E. Walker, better known as Jim, in the fall of 1937.

It was the defense's contention that this model, which was called "Miss Shirley" in honor of the watchmaker's daughter, was built and flown some three years before Walker applied for the U-Control patent. Although Miss Shirley and its control system were never patented, plans for the plane were drawn up by a patent draftsman in July of '37, and advertised for sale in the January 1938 issue of *Model Airplane News*. Defense had even managed to locate, back in Illinois, one of the 1938 buyers.

Patent law says that anything that has been public knowledge for a year or more is unpatentable. Clearly, Miss Shirley and her control system were public knowledge by 1938. At this point only one question remains: *What was the nature of Miss Shirley's control system?* Was it substantially the same as Walker's two lines and a bellcrank? Or was it something else?

The 64 Dollar Question

This is the question that I couldn't put out of my mind as I read and reread the two-part article Dale Kirn and Charles Mackey wrote for *Model Builder* back in 1981—the article that presented Oba St. Clair as the true father of control line. Unfortunately, Kirn and Mackey never address the issue of Miss Shirley's control system. But then, they weren't writing a legal brief. Their intent was clear: they simply wanted to pay tribute to the aging Oba St. Clair—to give him belated credit for his part in the development of U-Control.

But what exactly <u>was</u> St. Clair's part in U-Control? Did Jim Walker copy elements of Patent 2292416 from *Miss Shirley*? (Walker swore, in court, that he couldn't recall ever seeing the plane—claimed he didn't remember the 1937 interview attested to by both St. Clair and his wife.)

The model shown in the Kirn/Mackey article—the original *Miss Shirley*—is being flown on four strings. Not wires, strings. Not two, four. The control handle in the photos looks something like a TV antenna with about four feet of mast still attached. The pilot cradles this mast, fishpole style, and manipulates a joystick that pivots the arms of the antenna as if they were two huge U-Control handles.

The four control strings attach to the tips of these arms. But where do they go from there? What do they attach to on the model? *What, exactly, do they control?* (Always we get back to the key question.)

The *Model Builder* piece claims that *Miss Shirley* had elevator, motor, rudder and aileron control. But how they worked, no one seems to remember. Dale Kirn took photos of the model in 1965; Leroy Cox was just then getting around—after a decade—to returning "Exhibit A" to St. Clair. By then the plane was nearly thirty years old. Who knows how much of its original hardware remained? Who knows whether it had bellcranks inside of it, or curved tubes, or even some kind of sliding pushrod system like Schwab's *Controlled Lightning*?

Judge Carter—He Knows

The answer lies tucked away in the trial transcripts, and the trial transcripts lie tucked away deep in the frigid interior of the National Archives, down in Laguna Niguel, California—that giant pyramid built by Lockheed Aircraft just off the 405 Freeway below Los Angeles. I spent a long, cold summer day reading through those transcripts—nearly 500 pages—and xeroxing them. Only the transcripts themselves are preserved. Exhibits, unfortunately, are never retained by the courts; they have to be imagined, by a careful reading of the transcripts.

One of the defense exhibits, in addition to the *Miss Shirley* model, was a copy of those 1937 plans advertised in *Model Airplane News*.

Referring to these plans in his "Findings of Fact," Judge Carter practically draws us a picture of *Miss Shirley's* internal workings. The plane, it seems, had not one but four bellcranks, mounted in pairs. The first two, minus their pushrod arms, were out on the left wingtip. One of these controlled the ailerons (and, with full deflection, the motor speed.) The second one controlled the elevator.

Throughout the trial, the two wingtip bellcranks are referred to as *levers*, to distinguish them from the second set of bellcranks, which were inside the fuselage. Each of these were connected by wires, parallelogram fashion, to one of the 'levers,' and it is these internal bellcranks that functioned—and looked—exactly like the one in the Walker patent. The bellcrank that controlled the elevator was joined, by pushrod, to a single elevator horn: pull on one side and you get "up," pull on the other and you get "down."

Clearly, the elevator-control bellcrank inside Miss Shirley anticipated exactly the system described in patent number 2292416. But what about those funny "levers" out on the wingtip?

The St. Clair levers, Judge Carter ruled, served precisely the same function as Walker's patented wingtip guides: they stabilized the plane in roll mode while transferring the control forces to the internal bellcranks. By that light, Oba St. Clair had anticipated the Walker patent on every significant claim.

Jim Walker didn't have a leg to stand on.

Whether or not he had copied the U-Control idea from St. Clair was irrelevant to the question at bar. The plain fact was, *two wires and a bellcrank* were public knowledge at least three years before Jim Walker applied for his patent.

U.S. Patent 2292416—the most famous patent in all of modeling history—was totally null and void.

Similar arguments quickly demolished the validity of the U-Reely patent, as well. And then the judge (perhaps, as Walker's lawyers contended, without sufficient evidence) struck down the "U-Control" copyright, on the grounds that Walker had failed to maintain control over his licensees, so that the trademark was no longer a guarantee of quality, and hence had no commercial value.

Jim Walker lost on all three counts. American Junior was assessed Cox's court costs and lawyer fees, and left the field in utter defeat. No attempt was ever made to appeal any of the three decisions.

"Father of Control Line Flying"

Ironically, it appears from the court record that Oba St. Clair had no more claim on *two wires and a bellcrank* than Jim Walker did. Throughout the trial there are repeated references to "Sampson 2061953," a patent dated November 24, 1936 that describes the wire-control of a model airplane.

In his "Memorandum of Decision," Judge Carter gives us a glimpse of this Sampson patent: "Sampson taught the use of a pair of continuous flexible lines running to the bellcrank in the fuselage to operate a pushrod attached to the horn of the elevator," the judge writes. "Had Sampson guided his lines through guides on the left wing, his patent would have contained every element in [Walker's] '416."

And then, just two paragraphs later: "It is obvious, and certainly not invention, to know that the tether would have to be attached to, or through or near the wingtip nearest the holder of the tether line. Any school boy would know you could not attach the line alone to the tail or to the nose."

Here, then, was a patent claim for a similar controlline system that anticipated St. Clair's 1937 drawings by nearly a year.

Yet Kirn and Mackey write that the judge, presumably sometime after the trial, "sent a letter to Oba St. Clair naming Oba as 'the father of control line flying.'"

Why Oba St. Clair? What about the mysterious Sampson? What about Leo Weiss back at M.I.T., with his electric elevators? What about F.B. Thomas, the Britisher who flew round-the-pole models with elevator control in 1929? What about the thousands of youngsters of the twenties and thirties with their "whip control" solid models?

I leave it to you to select your own Father of Control Line Flying. For myself, I try to steer clear of paternity suits.

158

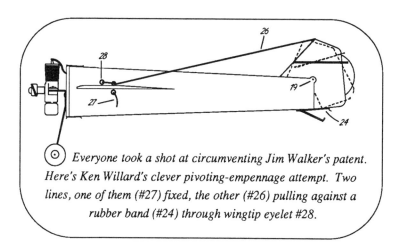

Everyone took a shot at circumventing Jim Walker's patent. Here's Ken Willard's clever pivoting-empennage attempt. Two lines, one of them (#27) fixed, the other (#26) pulling against a rubber band (#24) through wingtip eyelet #28.

Roll Call: Ukies

The twelve years between V-J Day and Sputnik were the golden age of U-Control. Dozens of small kitting operations and literally hundreds of models came and went during this time; to ressurect them all would take a book. Some of the very earliest were the 'goats'—converted freeflights like Consolidated's *Bay Ridge Mike*—but the best ones were designed specifically for this new field. Here are a few of the ones I remember:

Rick's *Dilly, Dinky, Yo-Yo, Box Car* and *Box Car Chief*—the F-B *Viking* and *Vampire*—ConSOLIDated's *Guided Star* stunt and *Hell Razor* for speed—the Master Modelcraft *Wing Dingus* (both mono and bipe)—Scientific's *Trail Blazer* and *Little Mustang* and *Kingpin*—the Enterprise *Tuckette* and *Knock-Out* and *New Era*—the Trixter *Barnstormer* and *Invert Jr*—Testor's *Freshman-Sophomore-Junior-Senior* profile series, with their 2-piece hardwood wheels—Hal deBolt's *Bipe* and *Stuntwagon*—the *Pee Wee Pup* (75¢ in 1951!) and *Pee Wee Pursuit* by Joy Products—Sterling's *Maverick* and (of course) *Ringmaster*—Megow's *Sky Streak, Bantam Special, Tyro* and *Flying Circus*—the Cleveland *Sharpie* and twin boom *Streamliner* and flying wings (*Whatizit, Nose Cone*)—the *Zing* and *Trainee* by Goldberg—Capitol's *"400"* and staggerwing *Beechcraft*—the Comet *Whizzer*—Palmer's *Smoothie* and the pollywog-airfoiled *Chief*, both by Veco—Bill Skipper's symmetrical-foiled 1947 *Akro-Bat*—the Bunting Brothers (of Philly) and their *Buzz Bomb, Yak-21* and *Baka Bomb* profile models—the *Joker, Jiggers, Jeepers* and *Jester*, all from Crescent Model Shop in Los Angeles—Berkeley's *Bat, Bee* and *Bug*—the *Duraplane*, the *Aero Puppet*, the *Presto-Liner*, the *Tyro*—ConSOLIDated's *Super Cinch* and *Baby Cinch* . . . . and where do we stop?

159

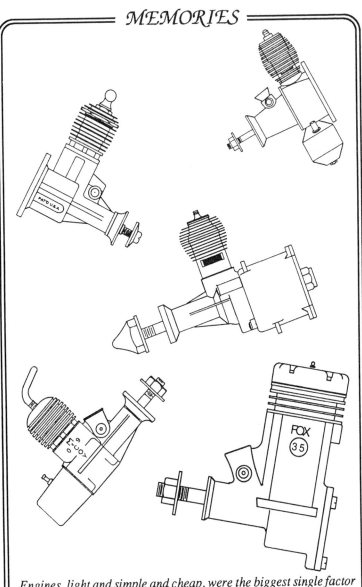

Engines, light and simple and cheap, were the biggest single factor in creating the postwar modeling renaissance. From 1946 to 1960, they seemed to rain from the skies: diesels and glows of every size and shape and type—some designed just for free flight, some for U-Control, some exclusively for radio control. Top to bottom: K&B Infant .02, Herkimer Cub, Space Bug, McCoy Diesel, Fox .35.

Chapter Seven

THE POSTWAR
DECADE:
MODELING'S RENAISSANCE

*As one gets older, the actual fun of model building diminishes
and flying seems to count for more . . . .*
—*Flying Aces Magazine,* April 1941

August 15, 1945: V-J Day. The long war was finally over, and
the troops would be coming home! Deep August in America:
watermelon and sweet corn season, and all across the country the
last heat of summer lay heavy on the fields. Fall would soon
arrive, with its calm, cool mornings and long, golden afternoons—
the most beautiful flying weather of the year!

But all across the country, practically nobody was flying.

It was a tenuous time, a watershed time for aeromodeling, that
long-ago autumn of 1945. The hobby, like the country as a whole,
was in shreds and tatters. The stick-and-tissue, nickle-and-dime
Depression years already seemed like ancient history—like a fairy-
tale childhood that never really happened. Bill Barnes and Jimmie
Allen were faded memories; Randolph Hearst's fabled Junior
Birdmen were long since defunct. The AMA, such as it was, was
penniless, and the country's two million model builders were
scattered to the winds.

Most of the clubs had been gutted early in the war, chiefly by the Army Air Corps. Model builders were quick to volunteer, easy to train, made the very best pilots and navigators and mechanics. (What free flighter of 1945 could look at a *Bay Ridge Mike* or a *Topper* without remembering Scotty Murray of the Brooklyn Sky Scrapers, who joined the RAF in '39 and went down in a Spitfire over Malta even before the U.S. entered the war?)

Balsa, the heartwood of modeling, had disappeared right after Pearl Harbor. Every stick of it went into life preservers, and Germany's U-boats cut off any possibility of new shipments. As a consequence, dealers shelves were uniformly bare in that fall of '45. Or worse than bare: cluttered with those awful cardboard-and-pine wartime kits that nobody, but *nobody*, would touch.

Engines? Forget it. Of the two-hundred-odd prewar American motors, only one—Bernie Winston's G.H.Q.—was still in production. "WE HAVE ENGINES!" the G.H.Q. ads shouted to anyone desperate enough listen; "Over 100,000 Now in Actual Daily Use!" (Picture a hundred thousand modelers flipping, flipping, endlessly flipping those hundred thousand GHQs . . . .)

Low Point

No balsa—no motors—no fliers. From every outward appearance, it was the low point of U.S. modeling history. If the sport had simply rolled over and died during that weary, disjointed autumn of 1945, few people outside the hobby would have been surprised.

But America's model builders weren't ready to give up their old passion. Far from it. War or peace, good times or bad, the spirit of the air age . . . the sweet dream of flight . . . was still very much alive in their hearts. But it had no outlet. What was needed was a good old-fashioned Nationals: a blowout, a celebration, a whooping, shouting, back-slapping reunion of all those old familiar faces.

One engine can be a lonely sound. What people craved was the roar of a dozen engines—a hundred! Enough noise to let everybody know that the Clan was alive and well, that it had survived the war and was ready for the peace—*ready to go flying again!*

It was an air-minded newspaper back east—the Philadelphia *Daily Record*—that first tapped into this hidden need. Not long after V-J Day the *Record* innocently announced plans for a one-day 'flying circus,' to be held on Sunday, October 6, in the Strawberry Mansion meadows of Philadelphia's Fairmount Park . . . .

Flying Circus

Not just a contest, gentlemen—this would be a *flying circus!* The very name was alluring, romantic! And modelers, who spend more time dreaming than building, more time building than flying, are suckers for romance. All over America, hundreds of them began packing their automobiles:

"Contest ain't till next Sunday, buddy—what's the big rush?"

"You kiddin? Gotta get to Philly on Saturday so we can get a couple planes built!"

Californians came, and people from Utah and Colorado. Texans rolled in, and Oklahomans, and a handful of fliers from the wheat fields of Nebraska. Every state east of the Mississippi was represented. A tent city sprang up on the park's baseball field. By Saturday morning some eight hundred contestants and fifty thousand spectators were on hand—all for a one-day event!

At eight o'clock sharp the Flying Circus began. Free flights screamed up into the low overcast, paused, fell like soft rain on both banks of the Schuylkill River. (A good omen: surprisingly few went in the drink.) Little controlline speedsters, both monoplanes and bipes, broke record after record after record. For ten marvelous hours, pandemonium reigned.

When the dust finally settled and the scores were announced and a Navy metalsmith named Harold deBolt had hauled away the three-foot-tall Grand Award trophy, two dozen weary contest officials looked at each other in stunned amazement. Eight hundred fliers on thirty days' notice! Where had all these people—all this wild enthusiasm—come from?

Pent-up Modeling Energy

In his book of reminiscences, *Tales of an Ancient Modeler*, Norm Rosenstock describes how the dream of flight—augmented by a 25¢ catalog from Clinton DeSoto's Radio Control Headquarters in

New Jersey—had carried him through Okinawa and brought him home to the States with three years of pent-up modeling energy. (Result: one of the first hand-held transmitters for R/C, as well as half a dozen original-design radioplanes, including the *Electron*, published in December 1950 *Flying Models*.)

The troop ships of 1945 must have been bursting with people like Norm Rosenstock, because right on the heels of the war, the model airplane hobby, instead of rolling over and dying, went into a long renaissance—a true rebirth, a golden age of energy and invention that lasted more than a decade, from war's end until deep into the Eisenhower fifties.

Era of Numbers, Age of Abundance

Golden age, I realize, is a pretty subjective term at best. The temptation of every historian is to apply it to his own childhood, whenever that might have occurred. To label the postwar years a golden age, then, needs some explaining. After all, writers in the past have traditionally lumped modeling's heyday with that of full-scale aviation, assigning both to the late thirties.

And certainly the thirties was, for aeromodeling, the era of numbers.

Take 1937, for example. In that year alone, Megow produced 14,000 tubes cement each and every working day. Kitmaker Joe Ott, with nearly 600 employees, hit daily highs—*daily* highs—of 46,000 kits. Birdman membership peaked in '37 at something near two-thirds of a million, and Boston's venerable Junior Aviation League was mailing weekly newsletters to nearly 5000 active modelers. That was the year the Jimmie Allen magazine *Air Battles* printed 1,750,000 copies a month, while the Chicago *Times* Air Cadets claimed 30,000 members and was still growing . . . .

For sheer numbers, the late thirties are unbeatable.

But *golden age* arguments can be made for the postwar years, as well. If the 1930s was the era of numbers, then the postwar decade became, for American aeromodeling, the age of abundance.

Hobby Shops Everywhere

In the modeling field, war industry made the shift back to peacetime production with surprising speed. Within months after V-J Day, every one of those empty dealers' shelves were bulging once more—piled high with brand new balsawood kits. Many of the old familiar names were back: Comet, Cleveland, Berkeley, Modelcraft, Jasco, Guillow, Scientific, Megow. But they were almost buried among the dozens of strange new labels: Consolidated, Eagle, Enterprise, Joy, Monogram, Sterling, Top Flite, Cox, Dmeco, Testors, Sullivan, Mercury, Veco, Dare, North American . . . just to name a few.

With the manufacturers' pipeline flowing once again, every drugstore and dime store and candy shop reopened its little one-aisle model department, almost reflexively. But beginning in 1946, a new phenomenon arose. The specialized *hobby shop*, which had been confined, before the war, almost entirely to the major cities, suddenly came into its own.

All across the country, in big towns and small, everywhere you looked you found some hopeful soul tacking up a HOBBY AND MODELING SUPPLIES sign. Little garage-and-storefront shops mostly, started on a shoestring by returning GI's—young men long on combat experience but short on job skills, hoping to parlay their old pastime into a modest living for themselves and their growing families.

How could so many new hobby dealers expect to prosper in a nickel and dime industry like model airplanes? They couldn't. These postwar dealers weren't hanging their hopes on the ten-cent kits of 1939, but on yet another postwar phenomenon—the ten-dollar gasoline engine of 1946.

We Have Engines!

For the model engine industry—just like the kitmakers—moved quickly into high gear at war's end. During the thirties, gas engines had remained expensive and comparatively scarce. With the war they disappeared entirely. But in late '45 restrictions on steel and aluminum were removed, and scores of idle machine shops leaped into the model motor market.

165

Within months, engine technology and engine production far outstripped the wildest of prewar dreams. Back in the late thirties, old Major Moseley out in Los Angeles had boasted of turning out 200 Baby Cyclones a day; by mid-1947, another California firm, the brand-new partnership of Irv Ohlsson and Harry Rice, was quietly shipping nearly *four times* that number.

As engine production soared, of course, engine prices plummeted—while quality, so often unconnected to either, bounced about like a rubber ball.

During the late forties, it wasn't unusual for a dozen new motors to hit the market in the same month, some of them good, some of them so-so, some of them plain awful: everything from the Buzz (.19, .29, .35 or miniature CO_2—take your choice for just $4.95!) to Leon Shulman's ball-bearing Drone Diesel at a whopping $21.50 and worth it. Engine collectors have identified nearly 200 manufacturers from the year 1946 alone.

The skyrocketing popularity of controlline speed events, along with a parallel boom in tether-car racing, constantly challenged the best of these postwar engine makers to higher and higher performance. New metals, new porting, new methods of carburetion were needed—and found, almost daily. Competition between manufacturers was fierce, and very few survived their first year in business. By 1950, the market had winnowed out most of these newcomers, and you could once again rattle off America's top engine makers in a single breath: Anderson, Atwood, Forster, K&B, Herkimer, McCoy, Ohlsson.

Fueling Around

But engines were only half of the postwar performance picture. No motor was any better than the fuel in its tank. Enter the forties 'homebrew' artist—by the thousand. For a time, fuel mixing seemed to be everybody's specialty. Compared to engine making, fuel mixing was easy—an amateur science. It took little knowledge and even less machinery: a measuring cup and a few canning jars put you in business. Secret formulas were passed about like bootleg liquor, like cheat-notes in a classroom. Basement chemists had themselves a field day.

Before the war, your standard ignition fuel had been a simple mixture of white gas and SAE #70 oil, in ratios that varied all the way from a super-safe two to one up to a scorching nine or ten to one. Before the war, everybody mixed their own fuel, and thought nothing of it—just as everybody in the fifties mixed their own two-cycle lawnmower gas.

Most prewar fliers tended to stay in the safety range of three or four parts gasoline to one part oil. No need to pay extra for ethyl (leaded) gas—regular worked just fine. Although Gordon Codding likes to tell of a guy at the old Rosecrans & Western site in Los Angeles who used leaded gas exclusively—and pulled amazing performance out of his fleet of 'slag' engines. When the lead deposits inside got exactly thick enough, those cheap-alloy pistons and cylinders would mate perfectly for a few brief runs, putting out tremendous power!

After the war, the same craving for speed that drove engine designers drove the homebrew artists as well. Everybody wanted more RPM. Methanol and other alcohols began to creep into the picture, replacing gasoline as the major fuel ingredient. Alcohol-based brews were more expensive, of course—but vastly more efficient, too. Alcohol needs only nine parts air for combustion, while gasoline takes fifteen. The word spread quickly: alcohol was hot, gas was not. These "hot" fuels (they were mentioned in *Air Trails* as early as June of '39) soon became the norm for serious postwar competition fliers.

"Hot Fuel Proof"

Like a dummy, I grew up thinking that the phrase *hot fuel* referred to the stuff that sprayed out of the exhaust ports of my little O.K. Cubs, on those rare occasions when I could get the damn things to run. Not so. Exhausted fuel might be hot to the touch, but chemically it's fairly benign—mostly just unburned castor oil, plus whatever it was that old Nils Testor added to those yellow cans of Testor's 39 to make it smell like Shinola.

167

"Hot" fuel, back in the forties, simply meant alcohol-based rather than gasoline-based. Unburned alcohol isn't benign. Unlike gasoline, it attacks plastic gas tanks and nitrate dope finishes—melts 'em right down. Alcohol fuels called for the use of butyrate dope and other supposedly "hot fuel proof" finishes.

A wonderful old phrase, *hot fuel proof.* It rang like a church bell down through the Eisenhower years. It was a part of every modeler's vocabulary—even though, like so many advertising slogans, it was almost totally untrue. No finish, prior to the invention of two-part epoxies, was ever any more than hot fuel *resistant,* at best. But *hot fuel proof* still appears on many dope containers, Aero Gloss in particular—a forty-five-year-old legacy of the postwar switch from gasoline to alcohol.

Ignitionless Ignition

Thanks to all those back-yard experimenters, all those amateur chemists of the forties, the "hot" fuels just kept getting hotter and hotter. This led, during the spring of 1947, to a brief few months of "ignitionless" ignition engines. If your mix happened to be just right (Ben Shereshaw discovered this, and Art Hasselbach of ConSOLIDated, and Ray Arden, among others) certain engines would keep running *even after the plug wire was removed.*

Wha-a-a-t?

That's right—no spark needed! This meant you could package most of the ignition mess (coil, condenser, switch, batteries) separate from your airplane, and use it only for starting. *Mirabile dictu!* Think of the weight savings! Think of the battery savings!

The secret was in the brew, and the secret was soon out: a mix of 35% white gas, 25% castor oil, 20% nitro-ethane, 10% ether and 10% turpentine would do the trick. (The ether and turpentine had sneaked in via the diesel movement. This was the brief heyday of the *Drone* and the *Mite* and the *Micro*, all American-made diesels, as well as the Swiss *Dymo* and the English-built *Mills*.)

It soon became clear that these ignitionless systems worked even better if you filed the electrode of your spark plug thin—so thin that it would glow from mere combustion heat, and then keep glowing after the spark was removed. Just the way a Dynajet continued to fire from its own cherry redness . . . .

Glow Little Glow Plug, Glimmer, Glimmer

From here it was only a short jump to the platinum-hearted "incandescent" glow plug itself. Ray Arden handed out the first samples at the '47 Minneapolis Nats; his ads broke in September of that year. 'Incandescent' engines ran best on the very newest of the hot fuels: three parts methanol, two parts castor, and three parts of a brand-new additive from the race-car circuit called *nitromethane.* (Consult your abacus and you'll find that this amounts to a 37.5% mixture of nitro—more nitro than almost any fuel on today's market. No wonder a Dooling .61 on glow was said to put out 32% more power than the same engine on ignition!)

Arden's 1947 glow plug revolutionized the engine industry overnight. By 1950, half a dozen manufacturers were supplying these magical little devices to virtually every engine-builder still on his feet. The twenty-year tradition of spark ignition died quick and hard. Only a few specialized spark motors remained in production into the fifties—the 1935 Forster .99 was still available in small quantities for the R/C crowd as late as 1957—but no new sparkers were being designed. The glow plug, simple and light and efficient, was king. Not until the Old Timer revival of the seventies did anyone ever again seriously extol the virtues of spark plug and batteries and coil.

Paperweights

The immediate effect of the glow-plug revolution was to shrink the size of model airplanes in virtually every category: freeflight, R/C, and controlline as well. Overnight, model airplane engines shed half their weight while taking a walloping jump in power. Who needed that old spark-ignition sixty, when a new thirty-five had almost as much zip? In fact, who needed those big engines at all? With 'hot' fuels costing five to ten times as much as

169

the old gas-and-oil mix, it wasn't even good economics to convert those big guzzlers to glow.

Put 'em away, throw 'em away, give 'em away—use 'em for paperweights!

One of the first victims of the glow plug revolution was the young and growing "barn door" school of ukie stunt, based on fifty to sixty inch planes powered with Orwick .60's and Fox .59's and the occasional .99 Forster. The barn doors were quickly replaced by smaller .29 to .35 sized machines. The little three-foot glow jobs seemed to perform every bit as well as the old ignition monsters, even in the wind. And they were cheaper to build, too—plus a LOT less work to fly. (A single, uninterrupted, twenty-minute tug-of-war with a screaming Orwick was about all the exercise most guys needed in a day.)

Freeflighters responded to the glow plug by moving away from the "C" and "D" Gas events, with their sixty to hundred inch spans, and courting the smaller A and B engine classes. *New Rulers* and *Playboy Seniors* and C-sized *Bombshells* gave way to *Hogans* and *Fubars* and *Kiwis*—plus the occasional resurrected *Zipper*, powered now with a Torp .29 instead of an Orwick .60.

But the most significant result of the glow plug revolution happened not at the top of the engine size category, but all the way down at the very bottom.

Bring on the Midgets

When Arden introduced the glowplug in the summer of '47, his own .09 was the only 'small' engine in most people's heads. True, the prewar Atom .09 was still on the market, and a few people were flying those little .09 Mite Diesels, produced over in Jersey by a sometimes-editor of model mags named Walt Schroder. But to most folk, the Arden was the only .09, and .09 was as small as engines got—unless you counted those miniature CO_2 jobs, which nobody did.

It took a little over a year for the glow plug to change all that. By Christmas of 1948, the west coast team of Lud Kading and Johnny Brodbeck—K&B—were shipping their first production run of an engine that was just one-fifth the displacement of the Arden: the K&B Infant Torpedo .02. Including its optional underslung gas tank, the Infant Torpedo was almost exactly the size of your thumb. "A watchfob," people sneered when they first saw the Infant. "A tie-tack! A tie-tack with a propeller!"

Was it a powerhouse, this K&B .02? Well—no. But that was actually a plus. There weren't any gas kits for engines that size, anyway, but since it was so gutless, and weighed a mere ounce, you could slip it into just about any small rubber job. And dealers' shelves, in December of '48, were full of small rubber jobs.

At first the other engine manufacturers dismissed the K&B Infant as a novelty. But it sold like crazy right from day one, and within a year it had three companions in the under-.09 class: the O.K. Cub .049, the Baby Spitfire .045, and a slightly larger K&B model of .035 displacement.

Half-A

By the time 1950 rolled around, these midget engines—they kept multiplying like rabbits—had their very own AMA contest classification: "Half-A." The word had spread like prairie fire: *little engines are fun!* They opened up a whole new world of apartment-sized models—scaled down versions of those C and D monsters that most people could only build in their heads. With a 1/2-A, you could build a 30" *Zipper*, a 20" *Madman*: models of models!

Half-A engines were so small and harmless they could be flown indoors, in gyms and armories and basements, using either U-Control or just a simple tether. (Guys at the '49 Nats went nuts sticking Cubs onto Jim Walker dime gliders and racing them round-the-pole in the Navy work hangar: greasy little blue streaks going *e-e-e-o-w, e-e-e-o-w, e-e-e-o-w*, all night long.)

Half-A engines gave free flight an instant shot in the arm: within twelve months after the first Infant .02 hit the market, the most popular event in every major contest had become 1/2-A FF gas. In March of '51, June Dyer, secretary of the newly-formed Northern California Free Flight Council, reported that 1/2-A

171

entries, during the NCFFC's 1950 contest season, had exceeded all other categories by a margin of four to one.

The magazines jumped on the small engine fad—partly because they could print 1/2-A plans full-size, but mostly because their readers just loved these little models—couldn't get enough of 'em.

Editors loved them, too. Small, cheap motors dovetailed perfectly with the "typical-reader" myth of the fifties magazine editors—the myth that painted America's model builders as bright, creative, twelve-to-fifteen-year-olds, kids who financed their hobby on a two-bit weekly allowance plus the occasional lawnmowing job. (By 1950, junior membership in the AMA had already fallen below 25%, never to rise again. But such figures ran counter to the myth, and were seldom mentioned.)

Fly-For-Fun

The glow plug and the 1/2-A engine go far in explaining another phenomenon of the postwar renaissance: the wild explosion of fly-for-fun models published in the magazines during the late forties and fifties.

This was the era of Roy Clough's freeflight and controlline flying saucers and his curious, lifting-body *Martian Space Ship*; of Paul Del Gatto's deltas and Donald Broggini's flying wings; of Don McGovern's long, skinny seaplanes and Parnell Schoenky's helicopters and Earl Cayton's bat-shaped ukies and bird-shaped chuck gliders. It was a time of autogyros, both free and tethered—a time of ornithopters and engine-powered boomerangs—a time of Jetex canards and pusher freeflights and balloon-powered stick-and-tissue rocket ships.

Every magazine, during this period, carried four to five construction articles per issue, and a high percentage of these models were—in the beatnik jargon of the day—"far out." There were controlliners with a second engine mounted on the wingtip and pulling outward at 45°, to allow flight on 200-foot lines. There were 'captive' free flights with bridle strings (walk them in the park just like you would your dog!) and escapement-controlled models *sans* radios, that went puttering about overhead dragging a pair of thread-thin control wires behind them, just like the German 'guided bombs' of early WW II.

During the postwar renaissance, biplanes and triplanes and quadraplanes all had their day once again, almost as if 1910 had returned by popular demand. Swept wings, of course, were commonplace—some sweeping back and others forward. During the fifties, nothing seemed too radical to try. And if it flew at all, then the very next step was to photograph it and publish it in your favorite mag.

This free-ranging creativity is pretty much gone from today's magazines. It disappeared in the sixties and seventies, as radio control came to dominate the hobby. Radio—even sport radio—has always been conservative, a much more "serious" pursuit than either freeflight or controlline. Not necessarily more adult, just more serious. (*R/C Modeler* still gets a letter or two every week, saying, in so many words, "Cut out the humor already!")

And that's too bad. I miss the weird, unpredictable, jokey, fly-for-fun designs of the postwar period. I miss the designers like Clough and McLarty and Musciano and Strader who didn't take themselves or their hobby too seriously—designers with nothing to prove, and no contests to win, and (seemingly) all the time and imagination in the world . . . .

Fly to Win

Not that the fly-to-win boys were asleep during these postwar years. Far from it. But your serious competitor in any modeling field is, of necessity, a pretty narrow-minded guy: his eye is fixed on certain well-defined performance goals, and his thinking tends to run down straight and narrow paths. Following any breakthrough, competition designs quickly fall into a rut. Still, there were lots of competition breakthroughs during the postwar years—fully 75% of today's vast array of contest categories originated then.

Take controlline, for example. This was the era in which ukie stunt men first discovered flaps, and coupled them to their elevators for tighter loops. It was the era that gave us team racing and rat racing and combat and Navy carrier. It was the era of the Dynajet and Monoline speed, of Walker's U-Reely and J. Robert Smurthwaithe's third-line control—of six-engined B-36 scale jobs and little flying wings (*Wow, Half Fast, VooDoo, Arrow, Dar-Wing*) that turned on a dime and gave you back 8¢ change.

Freeflight, during this period, finally dropped the ancient and venerable cross-section rule, its final tie to fullscale aviation. The cross-section formula (length squared over 100) had for years dictated that a 30" long fuselage, for example, must have at least nine square inches of cross-section (30 x 30 ÷ 100.)

This rule, dreamed up by the English Wakefield committee in 1927, was the only reason Goldberg's *Zipper* and Struck's *New Ruler* had those graceful teardrop lines—the only reason a *Buzzard Bombshell* could, with luck, sometimes glide as well as a Cleveland *Playboy*. Way back in the thirties, Charlie Grant had told the guys to make their fuselages deep. The cross-section rule said to make them wide, as well.

Now cross-section was dead, and the first "pencil bombers"— flying sticks—began to appear. The year was 1948, and the new ruling split freeflight once again into two scowling, fist-shaking camps. Thousands denounced the functional ugliness of the pencil bombers. Not even Paul Gilliam's graceful-but-deadly *Civy Boys* pleased their eye. Give them the old-time realism (realism?) of the *New Ruler* and the *Bombshell*, or give them death! (Shades of 1910: it was the flyer-versus-racer controversy all over again.)

But in modeling, nothing good ever dies. By way of countering this rulebook blow to 'realism,' Pan American Airways stepped forward with a brand-new competition event—payload. (They preferred, for obvious reasons, to see it spelled *PAA-load.*)

Payload models were an interesting design challenge. The object was to carry a fairly hefty dummy "passenger" aloft for a max, and then get him back down in one piece. Later, a variation called Clipper Cargo was added, for all-out weightlifting. The prize money—up to $500 for Nats winners—was tempting, and both events were enormously popular. Never mind that the philosophy behind these tasks ("modelers can teach the fullscale boys a thing or two") was twenty years out of date. They were a brand-new challenge, and, like every well-thought-out event, they were fun. By 1955, Pan Am claimed to be sponsoring some 5000 PAA and Clipper contestants worldwide each year.

When the airline finally dropped out of the picture in 1961, the AMA kept both events in its rulebook. You'll find them there today, scaled down from their original .30 cubic inch engine size to a miniscule .025. (And proving once again that models of models are always popular with modelers.)

Sponsors

Pan American Airlines—may she rest in peace—was just one of many "outside" supporters that made the postwar era a golden age for model building. The Navy, which began its permanent Nats sponsorship in '48, was another. And so, to a lesser degree, was the Air Force; during the fifties it ran an annual eliminations program that sent teams to every Nationals. There was also the National Exchange Clubs, and the Salvation Army and the Boys Clubs of America and the American Legion and the Boy Scouts and a dozen newspapers like the Philadelphia *Record* (that first Flying Circus became, for a few happy years, an annual affair.)

But two other major sponsors stand out in the postwar renaissance story. Both left an indelible mark on the era. These two were the Plymouth Motor Corporation in Detroit, and the New York *Daily Mirror*.

The Plymouth Internationals

"The most elite of all model-plane meets," the *Saturday Evening Post* called it—an annual late-summer bash, limited to 500 contestants, that took place in Detroit every year, starting in 1947. For all-out image, those very first Plymouth meets were tops. Unlike the AMA Nats, which has always been *come one, come all,* the Plymouth made every contestant earn his right to be there, through a system of state and local eliminations. They wanted— and got—only the cream of the competitors.

175

All 21 floors of the Hotel Fort Shelby, home of those now-mythical prewar Nationals, were booked for the meet. Every flier was issued a white pith helmet and every member of the press a sky-blue one—thus beginning the fifties hat fad, when pith helmets decorated with wings and engines and windsocks and flashing beacons became *de rigueur* at contests everywhere.

Plymouth Motor Corporation footed the bill for the Internats 100%, prodded along by the Aero Club of Michigan. The venerable Mr. Merrill Hamberg—that same Detroit shop teacher who had unplugged the dike of modeling enthusiasm back in 1927—acted as CD. Freeflight events were flown on Selfridge Field, while the controlliners took over the huge athletic fields on Belle Isle, out in the Detroit River, turning the place into a flag-and-bunting spectacle that more than one onlooker compared to the movie *Ivinhoe*. Plymouth dealers in every state plus Canada and Mexico sent their state winners from each age class to Detroit—hence the 'internationals' tag.

Chevy, Plymouth's direct rival, had struck gold in its sponsorship of the annual Soap Box Derby competitions, and Plymouth hoped to mimic that success with its model-plane Internats. For that reason, after the first year or two, the company began to slant its rules in favor of youth. This was its downfall. By 1950 the Plymouth meet had totally eliminated fliers over 21—almost the entire air age generation—and the handwriting was on the wall.

Despite a growing network of dealer-sponsored clubs, dubbed The Plymouth Aviation League, interest in the Internats began to taper off around 1950. Who knows why? Maybe Chevy's simple downhill races made better newspaper copy than Plymouth's complex 50-event model plane contests. Maybe hotrods were 'in' and airplanes were on the way out. Maybe television . . . .

Whatever the reasons, the kids drifted away, and the only people who really cared about the Plymouth were barred by age. 1953 was Plymouth's final year of sponsorship. When the bunting came down that August at Belle Isle, it came down forever. The last midnight engine had roared in the Fort Shelby's airshaft, and the last glue had been smeared on the hotel's elevator buttons and doorknobs. In Detroit at least, an era was over.

It might have been just too sad to bear, except that another contest, equally famous, was still going strong—gaining momentum, even—back east in that *other* traditional modeling stronghold, the city of New York.

The Mirror Meet

Picture a model airplane contest on Long Island that begins at 6 a.m. and draws *two hundred thousand* spectators in a single day— the largest crowd, according to the cops, to attend any sporting event in New York state that year.

Picture an even one thousand contestants flying in sixteen events, competing for ten thousand dollars worth of prizes that include not just the usual hobby supplies, but motorbikes and television sets and (at the very top, fresh off the assembly line) a full-scale, eighty-five-horse *Ercoupe*!

The year is 1950, and the site is Grumman Airfield in Bethpage, NY. It's the fifth annual "Mirror Model Flying Fair"—the biggest, richest, gaudiest, noisiest one-day model meet in the history of the planet.

Shaw's Junior Birdmen may be dead, but the Hearst newspapers, in 1950, haven't completely abandoned American modeling—and won't for another ten years. Chief sponsor of this fabulous contest is the New York *Daily Mirror*, at the time the country's largest-circulation daily. *Mirror* publisher Charles McCabe, another of modeling's Friends in High Places, is an old hand at promoting the sport—he was sponsoring model contests out in Denver under the Scripps-Howard banner well before World War II.

It was McCabe who called every shot for the Mirror Meets, and he made some great calls. Entries were limited to the first 1000 who applied. All timers and officials were *paid* for their services—and required to attend a dress rehearsal. Only gas-powered events were flown. (Sorry, Mr. Shaw—but remember what killed your Birdmen!)

177

The Mirror rules recognized only two age classes, below and above 18—a bit of wisdom that even today's AMA hasn't caught up with. (Coddling young competitors has never yet promoted aeromodeling. The bright ones are offended by it, and the dull ones aren't listening, because modeling simply doesn't attract many dull ones.) At the Mirror Meet, "professional" modelers, defined as people who made their living in the hobby industry, were welcome to compete for the glory and the plaques, but all the cash and merchandise prizes went straight to the top amateurs.

Substitute Nats

For modelers along the eastern seaboard, "the Mirror" was something to look forward to all winter—a kind of substitute Nationals. (Some years, in fact, it drew more entries in one day than the Nats did in five.) A majority of the Mirror contestants flew in two or more of the three categories (FF, R/C, U/C.) And not just because of the grand prizes, either. People flew multiple events at the Mirror because they flew multiple events at home every weekend. The meet, which ran annually from 1946 to 1960, managed to span those magical postwar years before modeling had entirely fragmented into specialties. (Example: of the 200 R/C entries in 1955, 180 were registered in one or more of the freeflight and controlline events, as well.)

The first Mirror Meet was held in '46, at Bethpage. When Grumman dropped its sponsorship in 1952, the venue was switched to Floyd Bennett Field in Brooklyn without skipping a beat. The end finally came in 1960, during modeling's post-Sputnik doldrums.

By that time, the magazines had quit covering the Mirror. Contests—even first-rate contests—were no longer big news. Entries had been dropping off for two or three years; latecomers no longer had to line up at 1 a.m. with 300 other people, hoping to claim a 'no show' place and fly with the elect. Other contests— other pastimes—were beginning to divert the Clan's attention.

The hobby was shrinking, no longer on the upswing as it had been during those magical postwar years. You could see it in the mags: first *Flying Models* and then *Air Trails* (or whatever they called it that month) cut back to every-other-month publication.

Only *MAN* stayed monthly, and it was down to sixty pages by 1960.

Plastics were on the rise. Jets and rockets and space stations (and cars—America was, barring the Edsel, *crazy* about cars) seemed ideally suited for modeling in plastic: just click 'em together, and paint 'em, and then set 'em on the shelf and go buy another. By the end of the decade, a single plastics company, Revell, was grossing $10 million a year—at a time when the entire balsa industry combined was lucky to hit $30 million.

Aeromodeling seemed to be going into an eclipse. First Jim Walker died, then Paul DelGatto and then Cal Smith—three of the most prolific creators of the postwar period. The only bright spot in the picture was R/C: there the juices were still flowing, there the energy level was high. But R/C in 1960 was small—far too small to carry the rest of the hobby on its back. Its time hadn't yet come. Even the best radio equipment was still bulky and expensive and eight to ten years away from the kind of buy-it-and-fly-it convenience that it has today.

What was happening to the hobby? Editors wrung their hands and trotted out all the old arguments: we don't do enough for the juniors, prefabrication is killing everybody's incentive, jobbers won't stock handlaunch gliders any more. The plain fact was, the two oldest branches of the hobby, freeflight and controlline, were shrinking. Not dying, mind you, just shrinking, under the combined pressures of TV and urban sprawl, toward the small specialty interests that they are today. The great burst of aeromodeling energy that had shaped the forties and fifties was finally spent.

The postwar renaissance was over.

Roll Call: Fuels

Before the war people mixed their own. Not until the postwar renaissance was it common to buy model fuel in cans. The most famous renaissance fuel was the mythical *Blast*, used by *MAN*'s intrepid cartoon character, Conrad Conrod. According to Bob Godden, Conrad's creator, *Blast* was "blended and compounded of the finest available mixture of atomic slag and used hog disinfectant, by Standback & Duck Laboratories of Chicago, Illinois." In the early sixties Duke Fox borrowed the name—but not the formula—for one of his own racing fuels.

Besides *Blast*, there was Francisco Laboratories' *Powermist* in the green can and *Spitfire* in the brown can, as well as their *Blue Blazer* and *Nitrol*. There was Spitzy *Nitromic*, and Midwest's *Nitro XX* and *Piston Power*. There was Ranger *Dyna Glow*, and Sportco *Super Glow* and *Super Atomic*, and Tiger *Air Blaze*, and *Reggie Pink*.

Then there was Consolidated's *Liquid Dynamite,* one of the transition fuels between ignition and glow—and George Cooley's *White Magic* (for ignition) and *Octolene* (glow), both by California Chemical. There was *Drone Diesel Fuel* and *Red Devil Nitrated Glow Fuel*—and one called *Hi-Fire,* by Technical Model Products of Pittsburgh. There was *Testor's 39* and *X-99*, and Veco *Power Fuel 1*, and O&R's *Cheminol AA* in the red-and-white can. And *Exol Racing Fuel*, and *Rever Glo-Fuel*, from Jersey City. O & R made *Hellz Fyre*, and Pactra brewed its *Power Fuel* 'with Lubex 27.' And don't forget the specialized speed fuels: *This is It, Hop Up, Zoom*— plus the Super Chief line from Oklahoma City: *Midnite, Siccem 66* and *Pandemonium*. Fox made *40/40, Missile Mist, Duke's Fuel* and *Superfuel,* while George Aldrich turned out *Magnum.*

And finally, there was K&B *Supersonic* and *Cox Blue Label*—the only two fuels from Conrad Conrod's day that you can still find on your dealer's shelf.

Chapter Eight

THE NAVY NATS

Gathering of the Clan, Part Two

"There is a definite tie-in between air power and model aviation. The boys who fly the model airplanes today will become our aircraft designers and technicians tomorrow."
— Rear Adm. T.F. Combs, Chief, Navy Bureau of Aeronautics

"The Nats is a state of mind. Some are up, some unfortunately are down, depending on the people, the weather, the quality of the planning, the officials, the base personnel, and all sorts of little nebulous things." — 'Wild' Bill Netzeband

"The Nats? It proves we are still here." — Bill Winter

Wichita, 1946

After the war, it took the AMA—broke as usual, and running on its customary handful of volunteers—until Labor Day of 1946 to get the first postwar Nationals together. This was the fifteenth Gathering of the Clan, and the only Nats ever covered by *Life* magazine (two full pages in the 15 September issue.) Twelve hundred contestants from every point of the compass drove forever and a day to get to Wichita, way out in south-central Kansas—dead in the middle of the 48 states, and just about as far from anywhere in America as you could get without a compass.

Stunt and speed were the only official controlline events at the Wichita Nats, but the *Life* photographer, with a reporter's nose for what's hot, caught five guys in one circle trying to clip each other's streamers with identical Ercoupe-looking ukies. *Life* labeled the scene a 'dogfight'—but it clearly contained the seeds of both combat and team racing, two events that were still five years in the future.

The Boeing and Beech ramps at the Wichita Airport—half a mile of steel-reinforced concrete—provided the bottom line for U-Control and R/C activity, and wiped out enough of those fragile old prewar engines to break a collector's heart. Freeflight got a softer deal, seven miles east at Rawdon Field. Rise-off-water events were flown at a third site called Crestview Lake, while indoor took place in an auditorium downtown.

Cigar-chomping old Charlie Grant was there, in his fifties now and feisty as ever. The pylon models, he declared flatly, just didn't fly as well as "the others"—meaning the deep-bellied cabin jobs. Pylons won everything in sight, of course, but Charlie's heart was still with the *Buccaneers* and *Bombshells,* and he stayed away from the scoreboards.

"Out of the Wind Belt"

It rained and it blew at Wichita, but the reporters, not wishing to bite anybody's hand, downplayed the weather. The town, after all, had taken on this Nats at the last minute, after Chicago canceled out. Still, the mags couldn't resist one marvelous, deadpan quote from a local: *"It has never blown like this before—we're out of the wind belt, you know."*

(For years Wichita had a quonset-hut hobby shop out at the edge of town called The Hobby Bowl. It was surrounded by some of the most popular U-Control circles in the entire state. Reason: the shop sat at the bottom of a shallow depression—a bowl—that tempered somewhat the relentless Kansas wind.)

1947: Minnesota

Memory is kinder than most people suppose, and for this reason almost nobody remembers the '47 Nationals. Held about 40 miles northwest of Minneapolis under American Legion sponsorship, it drew less than eight hundred people. Even so, there were too many contestants, and far too many events, for the site and the manpower. CD Frank Nekimken's family was involved in a car wreck just before the contest, and things went downhill from there. "A fiasco," Bill Winter recalled years later—and Winter is a kind man.

People slept in tents and bathed in the Mississippi and fought flies and mosquitoes and ticks and heat. Tempers flared. The only cool head at the entire meet was on the shoulders of Los Angeles stunt flier J.C. 'Madman' Yates, who was out there day after day, putting his big Orwick .60 machine through smooth, effortless patterns on 80' lines. Soft-spoken, easy going, totally relaxed, Yates was in his prime at Minneapolis, making stunt look like something anybody could do—even with a 90-mph *Madman*. "How do you do it, J.C.?" everybody wanted to know. "I just steer it around," Yates would answer with a shrug.

When the dust settled, however, it was not Yates but a young New Jersey state employee named Bob Tucker who took home the hardware. Flying a little Lee Shulman design called the *Hot Rock,* powered by one of Shulman's Drone diesels, Tucker had slipped past the laid-back Californian unawares. Keith Storey, another ukie flier from L.A., had better luck. He wrapped a huge teardrop cowl around his exposed cylinder heads and broke three national speed records, changing the shape of go-fast airplanes forever. (Hal deBolt went straight home and designed his *Speedwagon* series.)

Minneapolis was a Nats for testing the rules. Dick Korda showed up with a CO_2 version of his *Powerhouse* pylon design and entered it in outdoor rubber, causing a near riot. Then Chet Lanzo threatened to fly his R/C job in FF and "steer the thing into thermals." There was nothing in the bare-bones AMA Rulebook of 1947 to bar either of these entries. (The next year CO_2 got its own event—exactly as Korda intended—but two decades went by before R/C became enough of a threat to ban its use in freeflight.)

The '47 statistics: 149 people flew indoor rubber, 246 outdoor; 125 entered controlline, while 572 flew FF gas. Another Los Angeles flier, indoor expert Frank Cummings, won the National Champion cup, and then everybody went home to bathe and recover.

First Priority

The Minnesota experience made it clear that the first priority of the eleven-year-old Academy of Model Aeronautics (dues: fifty cents a year for rubber fliers, a buck for gas) was to somehow put the Nationals on a more stable footing. The annual bash had become far more than just a contest—it was now the symbol of American aeromodeling, the mirror that the sport saw itself reflected in. For every clan member who attended a Nats, another hundred stayed home and waited eagerly for those first magazine reports.

In 1947, Plymouth Motor Company's four-day 'Internats' had far outclassed the AMA meet; a December *Air Trails* article unabashedly labeled the Plymouth "the highlight of '47." And it was probably no coincidence that the AMA's first serious rival, northern California's "Western Associated Modelers," was founded not long after that disastrous Minnesota Nationals.

If the AMA hoped to stay in the saddle of this runaway hobby, the National Model Airplane Championships simply *had* to get better.

And it did—the very next year at Olathe.

1948: The First Navy Nats

Olathe, Kansas (there's that windy sound again) lies eighteen miles below Kansas City, just minutes from the Missouri border. In 1948 the town had an aggressive young Chamber of Commerce and a youth-minded American Legion post. But its biggest asset was its immense Naval Air Station—idling along, at the time, on a light and flexible postwar schedule. If the Navy could be talked into offering the use of its airbase for a flying site, the Olathe C of C and the local Legionaires were willing to tackle a Nationals.

With very little persuasion, the Navy agreed. After all, it was already co-sponsoring some twenty regional contests a year in different parts of the country—including the Philadelphia *Record's* now-aannual Flying Circus. Why not go for the Big One?

Of all the military services, the United States Navy had always been the most supportive of aeromodeling. It was the Secretary of the Navy who, right after Pearl Harbor, had given America's schoolchildren the task of whittling out those 500,000 solid-pine identification models for use by pilots and gunners and civilian spotters. And it was the Navy Bureau of Aeronautics that supplied the three-view drawings for every one of these models.

When the war was over, the Navy continued its courtship of America's modelers. In 1946, the woodworking shops on all thirty-five Naval Air Stations were thrown open to civilian hobbyists, free of charge, as a way of promoting both model aviation and Navy recruitment. Young men who built and flew model aircraft, the Navy knew, have a natural grasp of aerodynamics; they fit into aviation production and support positions with a minimum of training. Also, there was one ringing statistic that nobody could dispute: *Ninety percent of all WW II naval aviators had once built model airplanes.*

And so the Navy readily agreed to provide the flying site for the '48 Nationals. But ultimately it did much more. It undertook to house every contestant, as well: a thousand bunks in the Station's on-base gym (a gym complete with the largest swimming pool in the whole sticky, sweaty midwest!) Navy chow was provided at cost— and the first of those marvelous Navy work hangars with a quarter-mile of bench space, where repairs could be made, engines tuned, and night-before-the-event models slapped together by those sleepless, bleary-eyed maniacs (*"Forget the dope, man, it's only gotta make three officials!"*) that major contests always attract.

Perhaps most important of all, the Navy provided *manpower*— manpower for timing and retrieving and crowd control and first aid and all the hundred hidden and indispensable duties needed to run a national meet. In later years, estimates would show that it took nearly 25,000 man-hours to set up and break down a Nats, plus an additional 50,000 during the week of the contest. And the Navy did this, no strings attached—first at Olathe in '48, and then year after year after year for the next quarter of a century.

Five Days of Madness

'48 Olathe began on August 3 and ran for five days. Engines screamed day and night. Bull sessions went on around the clock and hardly any of the 900 contestants slept—or wanted to. People caught catnaps in processing lines, in chow lines, between combat matches. Old friends spent days chasing each other without ever crossing paths. Everything happened at once, and nobody could possibly see it all. This was the first modern Nats held on a single site, with FF, U/C and R/C all within walking distance: a hundred and twenty hours of glorious, unmuffled, two-cycle chaos.

Pan American Airways sponsored its first "PAA-load" event that year, with a $500 winner-take-all first prize. The rules were simple: .20-.29 engines, ROG with two 8-ounce dummies in the cabin, a 20-second engine run, and unlimited flight time. Herb Kothe of Omaha pocketed the $500—two months' salary in 1948—and made a nice little speech about how the PAA event was a good idea "because it provides a contest for realistic models." (Herb's ship had polyhedral, see-through covering, an exposed engine and a 40% stab.)

Jet speed was added to the controlline lineup, and Les MacBrayer and Keith Storey, a couple of members of the First All Speed Team (FAST) from Los Angeles, demonstrated a new west-coast fad called team racing. Ukie scale jobs, with huge, ugly ignition engines protruding like warts out of their cowls, were immensely popular. In a Sunday show, Jim Walker flew three Fireballs at once on two-speed McCoy .29s—a performance that *Model Airplane News* said "outshone the Blue Angels in modelers' eyes."

Everyone was pleased with the '48 Nats—so pleased that the Navy soon announced plans for permanent sponsorship of the affair. And so began twenty-five years of support for the Big Meet—support that was valued, by 1967, at well over $10,000 annually. If the Nationals were the only yardstick, then the Golden Age of model aviation began at Olathe, Kansas in August of '48 and lasted through the final Navy Nats at Chicago in 1972.

1949: Olathe Again

The town of Olathe—population 5,062—hadn't had enough of the Clan yet, and agreed to host the Nationals again the following year. This time well over 1200 fliers showed up, making it very possibly the biggest Nationals up to that time (though not the biggest *contest*: the first Mirror Meet, in '46, drew 1544 entries, after which the newspaper clamped on its thousand-entry lid.)

'Second Olathe' ran for six days instead of five, and included every one of the amenities (swimming pool, bunk hall, food at cost) that had made the '48 meet so nearly perfect. This year, the highlight of U-Control was watching a group of Little Rock speed fliers, under Kingfish Sadler, help each other out. Whenever one of them was called to fly, the entire contingent would respond *en masse*—rolling out lines, setting up pit supplies, keeping back the crowd—and they took home over a dozen trophies for their efforts.

On C Gas day, the Kansas skies split wide open. But the free flighters ignored the pouring rain and went right on cranking 'em up and turning 'em loose—then spent the rest of the contest ragging the ukie boys, who had shut down and run for cover with the first raindrops. In all, 26 events were flown: 11 FF, 8 controlline, 3 glider and 3 indoor rubber. (And—oh, yes—one radio control event, where less than twenty models got airborne during the entire week. R/C in 1949 was still the pampered baby of the modeling family.)

1950: Dallas

After two straight years, Olathe was ready for a rest. So the Nats took a 500-mile hike south, to Dallas Naval Air Station. This was July of 1950—right in the middle of the big Navy/Marine call-up for the Korean War. Every other NAS in America was caught up in the official paranoia, with doubled security and gates sealed to the public. (Communists, in 1950, were under every rock.) Attendance at Dallas dropped to around nine hundred—a reasonable size, many people felt, for a Nationals.

Only a handful of New Yorkers came, including a lanky young balsa butcher named Donald McGovern, assigned to cover the meet for *Flying Models*. McGovern instantly fell under the spell of 37-year-old Johnny Clemens, the boisterous, Stetson-clad Contest Director. Clemens was a character: he wore fancy boots and told tall tales and talked as though everyone else were deaf, and McGovern filed a glowing report, dead certain that he'd met his first "real, live Texan." (He hadn't. Like most professional Texans, Clemens was a Yankee—born in Indiana.)

It rained at Dallas—every single morning. And not your heaven-sent cooling summer shower, either. This was July in east Texas, and it rained *hot water*, stewing the contestants in their own juices. Everything sagged: tissue, engines, spirits. Bedtime brought no relief—the sheets clung to you like raw oysters.

"Worst weather in Nats history!" everybody went around saying, Wichita already forgotten. The skies would clear by 11 a.m., but then came the fabulous Dallas wind. It blows day and night in Dallas—always has, always will. Fliers who live there, like the fliers in Kansas, learn to cope with it. People who drive a couple thousand miles hope for better. At Dallas, they seldom get it.

R/C was a blowout. The average windspeed was 20, while the typical airspeed of a single-channel model, in 1950, was around 25. This makes for slow progress toward that first turnpoint, 500 feet upwind. If your engine falls off a hundred rpm, it's all over, bud.

There were some firsts and some lasts at the '50 Nationals: the first Navy Carrier event, the first 1/2-A freeflight and 1/2-A PAA-load, the first Navy Bomb Drop event in R/C; the last CO_2 event; and the retiring, after sixteen years, of the once-prestigious Moffett Trophy for outdoor rubber.

Free flighter Bill Lovins remembers the '50 Nats for the sight of Paul Gilliam and the Texas Eagles club smashing their screaming, zero-zero *Civy Boys* into the tarmac, one after another—a carnival of catastrophe that led Bill Winter, in a 'MAN at Work' column, to mourn all those wasted engines during a time of war shortages.

1951: Dallas Redux

The next Nationals was a touch-and-go affair. The Korean War was by then in full swing, and as late as April the Navy still hadn't announced a definite site. The dates were fixed—July 23-29—but no location. The July issue of *MAN* (out the first week of June) finally carried the scoop: it was to be hot, windy Dallas once more.

And hot it was in '51, with the thermometer above 100° all week. This was the year the wind blew from the northwest, straight towards the huge and curiously-named (for flat country) "Mountain Creek Lake." The lake borders the whole eastern edge of NAS Dallas; a twenty-second engine run and a ten-minute max were guaranteed to get you right out in the middle. (One lucky model hooked a boomer, failed to D/T, and managed to overshoot Mountain Creek completely, fetching down some 73 miles away.)

Indoor, in '51, hit its all-time low. Held in a Fort Worth coliseum, it had more trophies than contestants: ten junior, four senior, and twelve open fliers in all. But towline glider, for some reason, blossomed. So did ROW freeflight, flown off a perfect little man-made pond on the air station ("Outa one pond into another," guys quipped, watching their ships disappear over the lake.)

Radio drew only two dozen entries, about half of which managed to stagger into the air. Gene Foxworthy, who had won the event in 1950 and drove down from Indianapolis planning to win it again, got pressed into the Event Director's job at the last minute. Since a Nats CD can't fly in his own event, Foxworthy had to stand aside while Jim Walker (whose engine fell out in the middle of one official) took the honors.

In U/C stunt, a young Texas lad named George Aldrich put a design he called the *Nobler* through a near-perfect 400-point flight, only to lose 10% of his score to a faulty engine shut-off, dropping him from first to third in Senior. (Guillow *Barnstormers* took both senior and open.) Navy Carrier, now in its second season, was popular with the spectators, but not yet with the contestants.

1952: The First California Nats

Los Alamitos Naval Air Station, down in the orange groves below Los Angeles, was the site of the 21st Nationals, held during the last week of July. It was the first west coast Nats ever, and it came perilously close to going the way of the Minneapolis affair: c.d. John Bollinger, the man who had put the whole show together, died unexpectedly just before opening day. But Bollinger's organization was first rate, and the rest of his team picked up the ball with a heavy heart but a sure hand. It was a great contest.

The weather in the L.A. basin is fairly predictable: calm mornings and breezy afternoons, with the drift dependably down-runway, day after day. Violet Hoyt cleaned the boys out in jet speed, and George Aldrich, his engine cutoff working, outflew everybody in stunt. Carrier, popular from day one at the Plymouth and Mirror meets, finally got off the ground at 'Los Al.'

This was the year that gas replaced rubber in FF flying scale— and the year Joe Foster did an incredible 1:13 in indoor handlaunch glider, over in the blimp hangar at Santa Ana. (Foster won the Nats Champ trophy, as well.) The lucky ROW fliers had their best takeoff pond yet: 100' x 200', with the water right at ground level—no high banks to plow into.

Radio, like most of the other events, was west-coast dominated, with nearly a third of the fliers using Rockwell reed sets made up in San Francisco. Everyone had these huge ground-based transmitters that put out enough microwave energy to fry an egg—or a sperm. Some fliers were reporting *three-mile* ground checks. Alex Schneider of San Francisco won, flying his famous uglified Capitol *Cub* . . . with Rockwell reeds, of course.

1953: Willow Grove, PA

From Los Alamitos in '52, the Nats took a flying leap to the east coast. The '53 affair, billed as "the first eastern Nats in twenty years," marked the beginning of a regular rotation cycle for the big meet. From Willow Grove it would move to NAS Glenview, just above Chicago; from there to Los Al again, then back to Willow Grove via Dallas—a slow, four-pointed, counter-clockwise spin that continued unbroken for the next fifteen years.

The idea was that no U.S. modeler should be more than 500 miles from a Nationals, every four years. The four sites were chosen jointly by the meet's two primary sponsors, the U.S. Navy and the National Exchange Clubs, based on the availability of Navy and Exchange facilities in the respective areas.

Each of the four Navy bases were reserve training stations, where the weekend warriors of the Naval Reserve came for their fourteen days of active duty each year. To squeeze a week of modeling madness into this system, then, meant choosing a 'fifth-weekend' month—invariably July. That's how the annual Gathering of the Clan became locked into a regular time-frame as well as a dependable system of rotation. If the Nats was in Dallas this July, then you could be sure it would be in Willow Grove the next.

People like being able to plan ahead. They still won't have their ships finished and test-flown in time, but at least they can put in early for their vacation dates. It was this regularity of schedule that gave the 1950s Nationals their near-mythic status—the prestige that made them, finally, too popular for their own good. And the Willow Grove bash in '53 was the beginning of that fabulous cycle.

190

Thirty-two events were flown at Willow Grove, including indoor, 50 miles east at Lakehurst, NJ. Matty Sullivan of Sullivan Products was overall CD. Radio finally came into its own at Willow Grove—event director Hal deBolt claimed almost 200 pre-entries, over 75 of whom actually got a model into the air.

Aldrich won Senior Stunt again; *Ringmasters* dominated combat; and the ukie crowd was knocked silly by a little .19-powered *Aeronca* crop duster in Open Scale. Its builder, Tom Dean of Corpus Christi, TX, had imitated every detail, visible or not, of the full-scale craft—right down to the steel-tube structure and the internal control system. Even the wheel brakes and wind-driven dust hopper worked. Tom Dean's Aeronca set the standard for future controlline scale competition. No longer would crude, solid-wood fuselages and uncowled engines have a chance. From now on, doors had to open, controls work, instrument panels gleam with authenticity.

Barnstormer designer Lou Andrews, a regular winner in east coast stunt circles, didn't even sign up for U-Control this year. He was too busy demonstrating a homely, potbellied R/C model he called the *Trixter Beam,* soon to be kitted by Guillow. Like deBolt before him, Andrews had become yet another defector to radio. (Get too near one of those five-watt R/C transmitters of the fifties and it fried the freeflight and U-Control nodes of your brain.)

Clipper Cargo and PAA Rubber and FF Helicopter all made their debut this year on Willow Grove's 4000-foot runways, in accordance with the now-ancient tradition of always adding new events but seldom dropping old ones. Total body count topped 1200 once again, just like Chicago in '41, Wichita in '46 and Olathe in '49. So this Nats, too, was labeled by the mags as the "biggest ever."

1954: Glenview NAS

At Chicago the following year the facts finally caught up with the reporters' rhetoric: 1600 people, with over 6000 model airplanes, showed up to fly. For the first time since Chicago in '41, it was indisputably 'the biggest Nats ever.'

By now the number of events had jumped to 38—bad news. But the worst news was yet to come. Registration was on Wednesday, with only two events scheduled for that day: Clipper Cargo and A-B PAA-load. Since the contest was over on Sunday, that left only four days to fly the other 36 events. And flying always stopped early on Saturday and Sunday for the Blue Angels public air show— the 'commercial' that helped justify the Navy's sponsorship. So the usual five days flying would be squeezed into less than four.

The bad news went on: the runways were to remain operational during the meet—meaning aircraft would be arriving and leaving constantly. This eliminated freeflight from the base. It was moved to Chicagoland Airport, ten miles north ("A postage stamp surrounded by corn," as *MAN* described it.) R/C got the same shuffle—until the fliers took a look at Chicagoland's dirt runways and revolted. Result: they got a paved runway on base, and lived to regret it. Their first six flights were shot down by Navy radar.

Even after the radar was decommissioned, interference continued to plague the R/Cers. A few signals may have come from off base (this was the era of the great 'diathermy' scare) but most of the trouble came from their own pits. Proof? Whenever interference was shouted over the PA system, the stray signal usually stopped.

Incredible as it sounds today, this was a 200-man R/C contest with 190 fliers on a single frequency—27.255—and *no transmitter impound!* Two hundred people on their honor not to flip a switch, on either transmitter or receiver. (Many of the receivers of 1954 were so large and powerful that they generated low-power output signals of their own—a receiver could shoot you down just as quickly as a transmitter.) Small wonder that only 72 of the 200 people registered actually flew during the meet.

The R/C boys felt mistreated at Glenview, and it made them sulky. There was even talk—the first ever—of splitting radio off from the regular Nats. If they had bothered to check with some of those other 1400 modelers at the meet (especially the free flighters, who suffered from understaffing as well as a lousy field) they'd have found that just about everybody got the same deal that year. NAS Glenview wasn't 100% behind the 1954 Nationals.

Under such conditions, U-Control stole the show. Compared to FF and R/C, circle burners take very little space, and their antics are always more interesting to non-modelers, including the hundreds of base personnel who put in the overtime that made the Nationals happen.

Combat saw the first *Half Fast* flying wings out of Missouri. Shirley Austin used one to chew the entire ribbon off two of her opponents—the only "kills" recorded during the meet. The redoubtable George Aldrich, booted up into Open class at last, came third in Stunt. (Another Texan, Beaumont hobby shop owner Don Still, took first that year with an immaculate semi-scale *Stuka*.)

Speed times, despite the heat and humidity, were high, and the newly-legalized Monoline system, flown by Dale Kirn and 'Atlanta' Bob Elliot, pulled a couple of respectable thirds.

When it was all over, a NACA aerodynamicist named Woody Blanchard had won the National Championship for the second time in a row. It was no fluke—by 1961 this quiet Virginian had carried off the huge Exchange Club trophy an astounding *five* times in nine straight Nationals. No one else ever came close to Woody's record. (To become National Champ, you had to place high in nine pre-chosen events that were divided among freeflight, controlline and indoor—an almost herculean task at a Nats like Glenview, where the events were so widely scattered.)

1955: Los Alamitos Again

West Coast Nats always set records for non-attendance, and '55 was no exception: only 855 fliers showed, including 75 from the east, 200 midwesterners, and a handful from Mexico and Canada. With former Brooklynite Sal Taibi as CD, the 24th Nationals opened for business on 18 July, the very same day that a cartoonist named Disney opened his new theme park in Anaheim, a few miles north. It (the Nats, I mean) ran for seven straight days.

What this year's Los Al fliers lacked in numbers, they made up in quality. More records fell at this Nationals than ever before. In controlline, Stanzel's Monoline came into its own, and speed times took a solid 10-mph leap. The brand-new Texas team of Jim Clem, Sam Beasley and Dale Kirn pushed a Thermal Hopper .049 through the magical 100-mph barrier in 1/2-A, and then went on to win B Speed, Jet speed and Proto as well.

In freeflight, vertical takeoff was the newest wrinkle—one guy even VTOed off the water, using balloons! Senior Champion Don Alberts put up an astounding six straight 6-minute maxes in 1/2-A, flying a club design called the *Privy Boy* (*MAN* published it later, chastening the name to *SWAT*, for Albert's club, the South West Aero Team.) The first of Ron St. Jean's *Ramrods* appeared, and finished in the money in nearly every category. C.O. Wright, that grand old man from windy Topeka, hoisted nearly 42 ounces with a Space Bug .049 for a new record in Clipper Cargo.

Radio, divided now into single and multi, pulled 75 entries. Among the "country clubbers," as the multi boys were beginning to be called, reed sets took everything in sight. Single channel was dominated by Bonner's new 'compound' escapements, and a 17-year-old named Ed Friend, flying his first-ever contest, beat out all the old-timers with a perfect spot landing on the final day.

Only indoor lagged. Despite the use of the Santa Ana blimp hangar, times were little better than they had been at St. Louis in '35, and attendance was poor. Once again there was talk of dropping this oldest of modeling categories from the Nats schedule. As late as 1947, someone pointed out, indoor had been more popular than U-Control. But by 1955 it seemed to have run its course. (Fortunately it wasn't dropped. It rebounded, and six years later Microfilm Stick became a recognized world championship event.)

1956: Dallas NAS—The 25th Nats

Not everyone who went to Dallas in '56 appreciated the fact that they were attending the Silver Anniversary Nats—including even some of those who carried home silver (instead of the usual gold) trophies. Still, it was a great contest—only a little bigger than 'Los Al' the year before, with six flying days and everything but indoor held right on base.

The customary twenty-mph Dallas wind tapered off as the week progressed, although the chimney smoke at nearby Trinity Cement Works was seldom less than horizontal. Official temperatures hovered once again around 100, and once again hundreds of sweaty out-of-staters swore on their rulebooks that this was their "last ever" Dallas Nats.

Ramrods and *Kiwis* and *Spacers* dominated free flight. At times the lift was fantastic—one towliner, launched from a 164-foot line, disappeared straight overhead in a minute and forty-five seconds. Local hams pitched in to help recover lost models, and for once the damned wind didn't blow toward the damned lake.

The R/Cers, fast becoming a clan within the Clan, adopted the nearby Belmont Motel as their unofficial headquarters, and went around waving newfangled colored antenna flags at one another (red for 27 mc, yellow for 29, green for 50-54.) Eighty-two fliers put in officials, and for the first time everyone suffered through the same flight line—no more short lines for those clever enough to pass their ham license tests and get off 27 megs. (Screams of misery, howls of protest!)

A young Californian named Jerry Nelson cleaned up in Jr-Sr rudder-only, copping more points than even the open winner. Howard Bonner won multi, flying CG reeds in a *Smog Hog*. Dale Root of Oakland came second with a Babcock three-channel, and Walt Good was third flying his new two-tone simultaneous propo system, stuffed into a blind *Rudderbug* he called the *WAG*.

As for U-Control—well, Dallas was home territory for speed's hottest team, the Clem-Beasley-Kirn trio from Mesquite, so the AMA promptly appointed all three of them CD's. Nevertheless, their designs dominated the go-fast circles, and—heat or no heat—eight records were shattered that year. (Bob Lauderdale broke 170 for a new record in C, *without winning a trophy*. The judges had failed to record one of his flights.)

In scale, this was the year of Captain Richard Moorhead's magnificent B-36, with its six Torpedo .19s and four Jetex 150s. The blast of those Torps alone pushed Tom Dean's Aeronca crop duster into second place. Aldrich finally topped old master Bob Palmer in open stunt (though a senior, Bill Cummings of Dallas, wound up with the Jim Walker high-point trophy.)

1957: Willow Grove

The Nats planners fully expected to be mobbed at Philly, so this was the first Nationals in history with a cutoff date for registration. It didn't help. "The second battle of Willow Grove," as Bill Winter labeled it afterwards, drew 1521 contestants (960 open, 273 senior, 288 junior.) Over 5,000 models in 38 events. Even R/C was becoming unmanageable: a record 207 of the 350 pre-entries were actually processed to fly.

Over at Lakehurst, where indoor was held, Californian Lee Hines twice tossed a *Sweepette* toward the rafters, and twice the little ship avoided the floor for an amazing minute and seventeen seconds. Joe Bilgri of San Jose broke 32 minutes in mike, and indoor enthusiasm was finally on the rebound.

In freeflight, *Ramrods* took six first places, making the same two points over and over: first, that ten to twenty degrees of downthrust was no handicap, and second, that Willow Grove NAS, with a crosswind, is simply too small a site for a major free flight contest. By the end of the week, almost every local landowner had been alienated, and one farmer had begun patrolling his property by shotgun from the roof of his barn.

Star of an otherwise ho-hum controlline show was a young Mesquite, Texas speed flier named Hardy Lewis. A protege of Clem-Beasley-Kirn, Lewis won 1/2-A, A, B, C and Proto, giving him a clean sweep of every junior speed event except jet. Aldrich took open stunt again, and Tom Dean's Aeronca duster bounced back to the top in scale.

Radio control had by now become a Nats within a Nats, and this fact did not go unnoticed by the freeflight and ukie fliers. Three new R/C classes—pylon, scale and intermediate—were added this year, robbing precious manpower from non-radio events. When pylon drew only 20 entries, intermediate 21 and scale 12, the freeflight boys (who had seen their popular B and C gas events combined to save manpower) pitched a fit. Each of these events traditionally drew two hundred or more entries, and the free flighters, quite rightly, felt cheated.

Yet it was R/C, and not freeflight or controlline, that made the giant strides in '57. Bob Dunham and Hal deBolt finished 1-2 in multi, flying aileron-equipped models that forever relegated rudder-motor-elevator ships to the field of sport flying. (True, Walt Good came third *without* ailerons—but Walt was simply too expert to count!) Everyone seemed to be using home-brew wheel brakes: jerk a string to make something or other rub against a tire.

But the really big R/C leap of 1957 was in control boxes, and the meet's outstanding control box—the box of the future—belonged to Hal deBolt. His eight-channel reed set was rewired so that all the primary controls were on a single stick, just like the joystick in a full-scale aircraft (and just like the intermediate fliers, with their 'beep-boxes' and galloping ghost rigs, had been using for years.) No more unnatural blipping of individual toggle switches to get aileron and rudder and elevator and such—now you simply moved one stick for everything but throttle.

But deBolt's single stick was five years ahead of its time; it never caught on with most reed fliers. The joystick systems that we take for granted today had to await the development of 'feedback' proportional gear in the sixties before they finally came into widespread use. And by then, multi fliers were so accustomed to playing those toggle switches like an organ that they had to re-learn flying almost from scratch.

1958: Glenview

With 2000 bunks in a single hangar, and an estimated 200 transistor radios playing Sheb Wooley's "Purple People Eater," the twenty-seventh Nationals got under way on 21 July for a seven-day run. It drew just over 1400 entries, down a bit from '57. This, combined with pre-registration, made for more flying time for all.

Open stunt turned into a fiasco. A marvelous new qualifying system that looked great on paper managed to eliminate nearly every one of the nation's top open fliers before the contest was half over. Juniors and seniors, fortunately, were spared this noble experiment, so that senior Art Palowski was able to take the Walker trophy for the second year in a row. Speed times weren't super, despite the almost universal use of Monoline and metal pans and pen-bladder tanks. (How long since you've owned a pen with a bladder, eh?)

Free flighter Hank Cole of the Oakland Cloud Dusters entered a ship with a variable-camber airfoil: the flaps dropped when the engine quit. (Jim Walker had suggested auto-surfaces for freeflights in a February 1944 *Air Trails*.) High thrust line jobs appeared in numbers, though few of them made it to the top; *Satellites* and *Ramrods* and their imitators took most of the hardware. Paul Gilliam, trying to cover the whole meet for *MAN*, noted that, as usual, the winners in FF were "the marathon runners who could scale an eight-foot fence, dash into the woods, climb a tree, and get back to the field before the event closed." B and C were combined again this year, and 230 fliers registered their disgruntlement. The free flighters, like the radio men, were beginning to agitate for a Nationals of their own.

Low-wing *Astro Hogs* took the top four multi-R/C places. Only four of the ten scale entries got airborne; winner was Bill Bertrand's Jetco *PT-19*. Pylon, still flown one ship at a time, hadn't yet become a spectator event; the winning speed was 31 mph.

1959: Los Alamitos

In '59 it was back to the orange groves once more. The turnout this year was well under 800, tying Minneapolis for the title of smallest postwar Nats. Junior figures were up, though, thanks to the presence of 50 "Air Youth" champions—one winner per state—from a program sponsored by the Hobby Industry Association's new Model Aeronautics division. One of these state winners, Michigan's Sherwin Maslowe, took the Senior national title, while Junior and Open were taken by Billy and Bob "*Satellite*" Hunter, the tireless father-son freeflight team from Sun Valley, CA.

New FF power-loading rules wiped the slate clean this year, so a lot of records were posted, mostly by Californians, who hated the rules change but still dominated the meet. The weather was perfect—class A day saw 23 models in a single thermal! *Satellites* were the plane to beat, although a handful of *Zippers*, a couple of *Sailplanes* and even one *Buccaneer* made their appearance for old times' sake. Diehard rubber man Jim Cahill showed up, after years of inactivity, with an FAI gassie that sported a high thrustline and fiberglass-rod fuselage—a giant technological leap from his stick-and-tissue *Clodhopper* of 1938.

A brand-new Clipper Cargo event for .02 drew an encouraging 58 entries, and more original designs than any other event. PAA in general had the biggest turnout ever. New rules, based on total flying weight rather than cargo alone, had eliminated the flimsy 1200-square-inch monsters of the past. Good old C.O. Wright, nearing retirement age and perched calmly on his wooden launching stool, took second in the .049 and third in the .020 Clipper events.

Old hand Bob Palmer won open stunt with one of his *Thunderbirds*, but it was 17-year-old Bill Werwage who took the Walker hi-point trophy, flying his *Ares*. A curly-haired Texan, Riley Wooten of Lubbock, came out on top in combat, while Bill Wisniewski's home-brew engines set two new records in speed. In the junior speed circles a new name appeared: Dubby Jett of Seagoville, Texas. (He's today's '91-'92 R/C Pylon World Champ.)

For the first time, the radio events at Los Alamitos weren't called due to the afternoon winds. Radio control had finally come of age; by 1959 even the Californians had learned to fly in the wind. And it was Californians who stole the show. Milt Boone's *Chargers* finished 1, 2 and 4 in single channel, and Jerry Nelson designs took first and second in pylon. In fact, five of the six R/C events were won by west coasters—including Bob Dunham's third straight win in multi.

Intermediate, the tinkerers' event, drew only ten fliers, thus beginning its long slide into oblivion. Here, too, a Californian won—a fellow named Ken Willard. (A Seattle dentist and future world champion, Ralph Brooke, came fourth.)

1960: Dallas NAS

Proof that the wind doesn't always blow at Dallas: half-A freeflights on Wednesday were racking up *twenty-minute* fourth flights, floating far out over Mountain Creek Lake before swinging around and coming home again, never out of sight of the timers. The next morning came a gullywasher that blew down tents and closed the field until the mud had dried (as Bill Netzeband put it) "enough to prevent disappearing into." Afterwards, the sun came out and it was calm for the second straight day—a local record!

Nordic glider was beginning to mature by 1960. For years, towline entries had been mostly afterthoughts—a freeflight wing and Wakefield stab hastily attached to a balsa stick the night before the event. This year, most of the top planes were carefully crafted to win. Bucky Servaites of Dayton flew a DelGatto *Gull* to first in senior A-1, while Warren Kurth won open with his own *Jetstream*. Dave Edmonson of Minneapolis took senior A-2 with an *Inch-Worm*, while *Nor-Easters* won open and came second in senior.

This was the Nationals where Duke Fox and Bill James went around the work hangar handing out Berkeley *Interceptors*—flying wing combat models—and offering a free engine to the fastest builder. (Berkeley was bankrupt in '60, and Duke was trying hard to rescue the company by combining it with his own.) The winner finished his model, including one coat of dope, in exactly 42 minutes. And this in the days of Testor's cement!

1961: Willow Grove

Nationals number thirty. An eastern Nats always draws a lot of entries (1548 this time, nearly 25% of them in radio) and calls for extra planning. This year they tried processing models the night before each event, so that flying could begin earlier—at 6 am, in some cases. Sounds good, but it cramped the style of the build-'em-the-night-before crowd, and generated a record number of hell-in-a-handbasket editorials. Even C.O. Wright complained.

In controlline, Cleveland's Bill Werwage bounced back at the last minute to take senior stunt away from last year's winner, Artie Meyers; *'Ruffy'* Lou McFarland won open and the Walker hi-point with his latest design, the *Shark*. A wild bunch of Texans—Billy Durr, Larry Grogan, Fred Carter, Dub Jett, Jerry Small, Ed Rankin, Leland and Donny Morton—just about walked off with the speed events, until the rain started on Saturday and washed them away. (Some of these Texans claimed they never saw rain before—"but my grandfather has.") While they were hamming it up for the easterners, open flier Bob Lauderdale of Alabama sneaked past them to win A and C speed.

Free flight was predominantly hi-thrust by '61, and the Goldberg *Vikings* that had cleaned house at Dallas in '60 did so again. One Viking was spotted coming down dethermalized at 7:10 in the evening, following a noon launch—over seven hours up there in the storm-laden Pennsylvania air! Another Viking, flown by Carl Goldberg's son Bob, tied junior champ Dennis Bronco for first in A free flight, each with a perfect 15 minutes. Drift was mostly down the runways this year, and retrieving was good.

But freeflight ended on a sad note: Pan American announced that this would be their final year of contest sponsorship. Cargo and payload, as the events' creator Dallas Sherman explained, simply didn't draw enough kids. The airline's formal goodbye, issued a few months later, said it all with a painful succinctness:

> *"Today's space age has rendered doubtful the future effectiveness of PAA's program to stimulate small-fry interest in aeronautics."*

Damn, but the truth hurts! Thousands of modelers read this and winced—hoping against hope that the Navy wasn't listening.

These were the lean, post-Sputnik years in modeling, when event sponsorship at the Nats all but disappeared. The AMA itself, by 1961, was underwriting 90% of the trophies, as one by one both full-scale and modeling companies withdrew their support.

But there was good news, too. We still had the Navy's Admiral Pirie on our side. Smiling, white-bearded, trig-looking R. B. Pirie, Deputy Chief of Naval Operations, was by now the man almost single-handedly responsible for the Navy's continued support of the Nationals. And there he was at Willow Grove, handing out the trophies and grinning like a kid at the beauty queens (Miss America was there that year, sucker—and where were *you?*)

1962: Chicago

The Glenview gates swing open on Monday morning and a thousand guys go racing for bench space in the work hangar. Immediately an engine starts, and the roar continues unabated for seven straight days.

That's Glenview.

Total registration was almost 1500, for 35 events. R/C was immense—691 flights recorded, with multi leading single and intermediate by three to one. Kazmirski won, with his *Taurus*, while Chet Lanzo flew a copy of his 1937 winner. Twin-engined jobs took the top three places in scale, and for the first time somebody disconnected the elevator on a multi ship to enter it in intermediate class. (Soon the rush would be on!)

Too windy, said the ukie fliers—and *cold*, too, can you believe it! (Fifty-five degrees, with 20 mph winds on Wednesday morning. Other days were calm and warm.) Nevertheless, stunt masters McFarland and Werwage came through once again, and combat saw some of the toughest competition ever, with everybody using 90 to 100 mph flying wings with little stabilator tails. Hi Johnson's screaming .35 Combat Specials powered almost all of the top placers this year.

Bill and Betty Bell wowed everybody with their little Honda step-through motorcycle for retrieving models. This, and a brief but spectacular flight by the Illinois Model Aero Club's 50th-anniversiary *Bleriot* (built from 1912 plans!) kept freeflight from being ho-hum. Only one *Satellite* placed—the field belonged to *Vikings* and *Ramrods* and *Spacers* and *Stardusters*. Wednesday's wind gobbled 1/2-A's by the mouthful: 52 crashes were recorded. Sunday saw the return of C Gas, won by Al Vela and his beautiful elliptical-winged *Mexi-Boy*.

The list of winners at Chicago included most of the top fliers of the era. In indoor, under the 85 foot ceiling of the Madison Street Armory, there was Otto Heithecker, Bob Larsh, Shaye (wife of John) Diebolt, Jan (brother of Bucky) Servaites, David (son of Walt) Erbach, Bob Champine, Charlie Sotich, and Dick Kowalski. Outdoors, it was Glenn Lee, Lee Taylor, Steve and Faust Parker, Keith Hoover, Bill Hartill, Bob Sifleet, Ray Van De Walker, Jim (son of Norm) Skarzynski, Terry Edmonds, Sal Taibi, Larry Miller, John Gard. In controlline: Warren Kurth, Dub Jett, Bob Violett, Riley Wooten.

For the fifteenth straight year Johnny Brodbeck of K&B ran his on-site engine "hospital"—repairing, free of charge, not only K&Bs but anything you brought in. And following the close of this Nats, the U. S. Navy (miracle of miracles!) signed on for *twelve more years* of sponsorship!

1963: Los Alamitos

The 32nd Nationals got underway on Monday 29 July with over a thousand contestants—average age slightly over thirty. (The Air Youth program that had temporarily boosted junior attendance was now defunct.) Competition was California-tough, as usual—fifteen national records fell during the week.

Indoors at Santa Ana, engine designer Bill Atwood and freeflight scale man Ed Stoll finished 1-2 in both paper stick and FAI microfilm. Lee Hines flew just under 1:18 to win open handlaunch, and the long-dormant Frank Cummings pushed a cabin mike job to 25:43. Two flights of over 40 minutes were recorded in stick, and the mike boys began to dream their fifty-minute dreams.

Back at Los Al, the R/C event was far too big, with a lot of griping about the "bunch of controlline guys" headed by ukie speed expert Les MacBrayer who were roped in at the last minute to run it. (Few people seemed to realize that MacBrayer and his FAST club had switched from controlline to radio four years earlier, in 1959.) R/C Scale, won by Iowa's Maxey Hester, was down 75% from Chicago. Lou Proctor, who had won solid scale at the '29 AMLA Nats, unveiled his first *Antic*, powered by a Morton M-5.

Interference was a big problem on all five 27 mc frequencies—much of it caused by FF chase crews using walkie talkies, a strictly illegal practice on a Naval air station. Everybody's transmitters were impounded this year, and that seemed to be the only thing that people found no complaint with. Reeds still outnumbered proportional rigs, and both rudder and intermediate classes showed every sign of dying. The hero of the contest was Granger Williams, who trashed his beautiful Nieuport bipe on Tuesday, rebuilt it flawlessly for a Thursday qualifying flight, then went on to place third with it in scale.

In controlline speed, Steve Mueller took four junior firsts flying with his leg in a cast, while Bill Wisniewski (open) and Dub Jett (senior) each won three events. Reformed R/Cer Don Yearout took both half-A speed and open scale, while a couple of cool combat fliers, Carl Berryman and Howard Henry, finished 1-2 in open after a beautiful, ballet-like match. Stunt went to Bob Gialdini (open), Steve Harris (senior) and Gerry Cipra.

Free flighter Reid Simpson led the Air Force team to first place in a field that was tight and tough. In every FF event, the first three maxes were mere eliminations this year—it was that unlimited fourth flight that separated out the real air-pickers. Manuel Andrade's unlimited rubber model drifted out for seven minutes, then a lucky wind shift brought it back for another eight, easily winning the event. Northern Californians dominated freeflight, led by overall Nats Champ John Lenderman.

1964: the Final Dallas Nats

AMA "greeters," Texans all, met every car at the gate with a big howdy—and the thirty-third Nationals was under way. (*R/C Modeler*, that slick new girly mag from California, decided for reasons all its own to label this meet the 41st.) With less than 600 entries, it was easily the smallest Nats since the mid-thirties. A lot of people, apparently, had remembered their vows to avoid Dallas in July. (The AMA and the Navy took the hint—this was the final Dallas Nationals.)

Nevertheless, '64 was a great show—especially for the ukie crowd. Speed times were high, with old hands Phillip Bussell, Jim Summersett, John Newton, and Dub Jett leading the pack. Jett won five senior speed events, enough to make him senior National Champion, while Bussell took the open and Grand Champ trophies. Young Danny Wakerley took both A and C junior. The only big names missing were Bill Wisniewski and Glenn Lee, who were on their way to the World Champs in Budapest (where Wisniewski won, using one of the first-ever Schnuerle-ported model engines.)

Free flight had a weak turnout, but absolutely first-rate retrieving. Yellow Navy panel trucks cruised the neighborhoods north of the base, scanning the skies with binoculars and returning many models before the on-foot chasers could scale the station fence. George Xenakis took open Wakefield away from Frank Parmenter on a tight flyoff following five straight maxes—both flying low-wing models (they failed to start a trend.) On Tuesday night a group of Old Timer fliers got together to eat and swap lies and view Charlie Grant's recently-found 16mm film of the '38 Nats. Seventy-three people jammed the banquet room, which was wallpapered with old freeflight plans rounded up by John Pond.

In indoor, Lee Hines was using a vile-smelling Eastman Kodak product called *cyanoacrylate* to repair his broken toys—instantly.

Radio, slowly inching its way toward dominance of the big meet, got a whole flock of new awards this year: things like Best Single Flight, Highest Total Point, Scale Flight Achievement, and Best Two-Flight average. Less than a fourth of the models flown were kits. Another third were magazine designs, while originals came to over 40%. Four flight lines kept the sky crowded, and a record 1200 flights were scored during the week. Class I (rudder and engine) was tight, with only five points between second and fifth places. Oklahoman Tom Williams won, flying a modified deBolt *Jenny*. Proportional radios dominated Class III, won by Cliff Weirick. Maxey Hester took scale, and Dale Nutter pylon (pushed hard by Austin Leftwich, who won the following year.)

1965: Willow Grove

R/C in '65 was the biggest yet: 195 different ships put in official flights. This was the year that proportional finally overwhelmed reeds—74% to 26%. (Reeds, however, were still more reliable than propo.) Foam and fiberglass were making their first appearances. Walt Schroder's son John flew an ARF model by Woodcraft—one of the first—while Len Purdy of Cobb Hobby previewed his Lanier plastic ARF prototypes. But stick-and-fabric was still the norm, with over 80% of the R/C models finished in butyrate. Monokote was a year away, and epoxies just coming in.

Iowan Claude McCullough, jinxed for years, finally won R/C scale, while Cliff Weirick took pattern again. Pylon, despite the five new superhet frequencies, was still flown one boring delta at a time—but an unofficial late-evening Goodyear race, using semi-scale airplanes, pointed the way to the future. For the first time, R/C awards were given out separately from the regular Nats award ceremony—clearly indicating that modeling's retarded child had finally reached adolescence, and was already starting to turn its back on its parents.

Over in the ukie circles, the first Nats rat races got off to a chaotic start. Winners were John McCollum in open, Thomas Stucker in senior and Kathy Banisch in junior. Phil Bussell, last year's National Champ, pushed the C speed mark up to 179.93 with his screaming Rossi, and Charlie Legg of Council Bluffs turned

111.07 in 1/2-A. On Friday, Dawn Cosmillo topped the boys in junior stunt, while Lew McFarland ran out of gas in the middle of an overhead eight, losing open to Bob Gialdini.

Despite the use of the near-mythical Lakehurst airship hangar number six, indoor times in general weren't high in '65, although Tom Finch of Santa Monica did break forty minutes late in the day to win open stick. But the star of indoor was fourteen-year-old Randall Richmond of Bensenville, Illinois, who won all four junior events, including glider, where he racked up a two-flight total of almost two minutes and nine seconds. (He went on to win outdoor handlaunch glider as well.)

Freeflight had a good turnout in '65, with lots of juniors and seniors competing for a change, and plenty of Navy timers to go around. Not much new technology, though: *Stardusters*, *Vikings*, *Ramrods* and *Spacers* VTOed their way into the winners' lists right along with the usual hybrids and originals. ROW was dropped this year—"too much effort for the results," said the AMA—while 50 contestants entered John Pond's unofficial old timer event on Sunday, guaranteeing that it would soon be added to the rulebook.

1966: Glenview

War in Vietnam, and an eclipsed Nationals. Monday was snipped off the '66 schedule entirely, and indoor was flown on Tuesday, so outdoor events didn't begin until Wednesday morning—with the usual flying-stops-at-one rule on the weekend. 1184 contestants showed up.

Free flighter Bob Sifleet won his third National Champ crown this year—was he out to beat Woody Blanchard's record five wins? (He didn't.) Right behind Bob was Texas speed king Dub Jett, picking up the senior National Championship for the third straight year, while Randy Richmond, son of indoor expert Jim Richmond, took the junior crown. In fact, this was a year of hot-performing kids: Walt Erbach's son Dave cleaned up in indoor rubber; Arthur (son of Bruno) Markiewicz won junior indoor handlaunch as well as outdoor rocket; Susan (daughter of Warren) Weisenbach took junior Nordic A-1; Richard (Ed's son) Dolby won junior unlimited rubber and Gary (out of Frank) Heeb topped junior Wakefield.

206

B gas (A had been cut) was a *Starduster* contest—though Canadian Ron Higgs finally won it with a *Nig Nog*. ("A" was flown unofficially one evening, drawing 80 entries.) The FAI events were flown without rounds, and so became a game of timer-roulette. Freeflight design was about equally split between high and low thrust designs. Wakefield, reduced now to 40 grams of rubber, was hotly contested in '66, with John McGillivray, Catherine Monts and Gary Heeb topping open-senior-junior.

Riley Wooten's stabilator wings (*Voodoo, Demon, Sneaker*) dominated the combat circles, and Wooten himself won open with a new foam-core design. No surprises in stunt, where senior winner Gerry Cipra (*Nobler*) finished only four points behind open champ Bob Geiske (*Nobler*) in the flyoff for the Walker trophy.

R/C saw a new name at the top: James Whitley and his *Daddy Rabbit* took first in Class III, which was fast becoming only class that mattered. Twenty-one reed sets and one single-channel pulse box shared the impound with 140 proportional rigs. AMA pylon, still in the delta rut and suffering from low interest, was on its last legs; goodyear would become official the following year.

Indoor was flown in a stockyards-district amphitheater with an 80-foot ceiling. Times were low—only Robert Watson of nearby Morton Grove broke a minute in handlaunch. Randy Richmond almost swept junior again, with wins in mike, paper stick and cabin, plus a second in glider, while senior Dave Erbach won all three rubber events.

1967: Los Alamitos

Almost 900 peopled showed, three-fourths of them (as usual) from California. The dates were July 25-30, and this was the first Nationals to use data processing, with printouts telling everyone (not just the top five) where they stood. ABC-TV's Wide World of Sports covered the action, airing Navy Carrier, R/C Goodyear, FAI Team Racing, and a few speed runs. Bill Hunter returned to the fold as senior champ, while Air force flier Reid Simpson took the Grand Champ trophy and speedy Dan Wakerley won junior.

Now that the new 72-mc bands were open and four planes could safely be put in the air at once, goodyear pylon was the hit of the meet with contestants and spectators alike, eclipsing even Class III pattern. (Especially when the second-place contestant, AMA President Cliff Weirick, tried a victory roll and augured in spectacularly, with the ABC-TV cameras rolling!) For the first time, the Navy pilot judges were dropped in favor of civilian ones in R/C pattern—to the satisfaction of all.

Indoor was flown once again at the airdock on El Toro Marine Base, Santa Ana, where a model lost in the rafters during the 1963 Nats was retrieved and returned to its owner. Lee Hines tossed another *Sweepette* to another 1:18 in handlaunch—indicating that this event had hit some kind of performance wall.

Junior and senior participation in U-Control was sparse, except in the new 1/2-A proto speed event. Wrist thongs weren't yet mandatory, and guys were still letting go of handles when they got in trouble—hoping, apparently, that the plane would hit somebody soft instead of crashing. The Theobald-Wisniewski team was out-piped in FAI speed by Don Yearout, but bounced back to win both B and C. Young Dan Wakerley, flying his dad's Rattler engines, finished first in every junior event except 1/2-A proto. Combat, with its 110-mph planes, was poorly attended: only ten juniors, eight seniors and 25 open fliers.

Free flight retrieval—thanks to the Navy—was second to none, both on-base and off. This was the year of Vic Cunnyngham's *Galaxy.* Every freeflight event except helicopter and the brand-new Coupe d'Hiver class had a hundred or more entries—1/2-A was over 200. The usual five people entered helicopter, which was won for the fifth time by the heli king who had succeeded Parnell Shoenky, Dr. Lee Taylor of Denver. Open flier Bill Mette of Oakland set a new C Gas record—over 58 minutes!

1968: Olathe

To celebrate twenty years of Navy sponsorship . . . and bypass the Dallas heat . . . Olathe hosted the '68 Nationals, just as it had in 1948. Another eclipsed meet, it ran Monday through Thursday, following a two-day open-base airshow. Lots of juniors and seniors flew—nearly 40% of the 1037 entrants were under 21—and the magazines went out of their way to point this out, hoping the Navy was listening.

Because Navy support was weakening. Despite their 1962 pledge to sponsor twelve more Nats, there was now an obvious need to win the Navy's favor year-by-year. Base manpower was being withdrawn. AMA members had to assume more responsibility for manning the '68 meet than any previous Navy Nats. (Indoor, for example, was run 100% by AMA volunteers.)

It was another windy contest—15-20 knots with gusts to 30 all four days—proving once more that Kansas is no place to fly model airplanes. (This didn't keep the Academy, in its corporate wisdom, from trying to purchase a piece of the state as a permanent Nats site during the mid-seventies.)

Despite the wind, Tom Meyers of Corpus Christi won freeflight scale for the second time with his beautiful little diesel-powered Loening amphibian. Rear-fin designs pushed high thrust models out of the limelight, and young Gary Heeb flew his dad's rubber design, the *Stratowake*, to the meet's high time of almost twenty-eight minutes. The highlight of freeflight, though, was the newly-formed National Free Flight Society's first symposium: 175 people attended.

Radio saw some big changes at Olathe: the event was finally relieved of Class I (rudder only) and Class II (intermediate.) Pylon now meant "Goodyear Pylon," alias "Formula One"—scale racers flying in four-plane heats. Of the 58 Goodyear entries, 20 finally qualified to race; Granger Williams won.

Granger also took first in scale with his time-tested Nieuport bipe, out-flying Dave Platt's magnificent 1/8 scale Douglas *Dauntless* with its carefully chipped and weathered paint scheme— the first R/C model ever to be awarded maximum scale points by the judges. Bill Bertrand flew a quarter-scale Fokker *D-VII*, and pattern went to radio manufacturer Phil Kraft and his *Kwik-Fli* for the second year in a row.

Twenty-one U-Control events in four days makes for a busy field. Juniors outraced everyone for the lowest elapsed times in Rat, Tim Zimmer of Dayton finishing 140 laps in 5:41.2—almost six seconds ahead of the best open time. Stunt brought out some beautiful models—many of which the wind demolished. Texan Bob Gieseke, just back from a U.S. team win in Helsinki, took a hotly-contested first in open, plus the Walker trophy. In speed, the big news was Charlie Legg's 119.32 in 1/2-A.

1969: Willow Grove

The 38th National Model Airplane Championships, held at Willow Grove on 14-20 July, ended on the day Neil Armstrong (an old ukie flier from the Plymouth meets of the early fifties) stepped onto the moon. There was no K&B engine repair shop this year—a bad omen. And sure enough, '69 turned out to be the last east coast Nationals until Chicopee in 1983.

Fifteen year old Mark Kerr will remember this Willow Grove forever. He took firsts in indoor handlaunch glider, 1/2-A Gas, C Gas, FAI Power, A/2 Nordic, plus thirds in FAI U/C speed, A and B Gas, to become Junior National Champion. Gary Myers, with firsts in both B and C Gas, won the Senior Championship, and Bucky Servaites took his first Open and Grand Champ trophies.

Indoors, Ron Plotzke of Mt. Clemens, MI did 42:53 for the highest mike time ever recorded at a Nats—only 49 seconds short of the then-current record. Jim Richmond upped the paper stick record to 26:56, while a junior, Ron Ganser, walked away with all three rubber events. *Sweepettes* were still the plane to beat in indoor handlaunch, winning both senior and open.

Larry Leonard was the hero of this year's R/C show, taking both pattern and Formula One. Hal deBolt bounced back into winners' circle once again with a Formula II win, and Maxey Hester took scale with a beautiful Zlin *Akrobat*.

1970: Glenview

It was late spring before Navy support for the 40th Nationals was assured: the site would be Chicago, only 150 Navy personnel would be provided, and the AMA would be expected to do the rest.

Nearly twelve hundred fliers showed up, with some 200 mechanics in tow. On-base housing was by now only a memory—people roosted in tents and campers and nearby motels, just as they had in the years before Navy sponsorship. The weather was typical Chicago—one day it was so calm that every freeflight landed on base, while on other days engine runs and maxes had to be reduced. Ukie scale was nearly wiped out by the wind.

The U-Control events were well attended. In stunt, Keith Trostle of Dayton slipped past Al 'Bearcat' Rabe for a first in open, plus the Walker trophy. For the fourth straight year, Dr. Linton Keith of Santa Clara, CA took open scale with his magnificent Avro *Lancaster* bomber: moving gun turrets, opening bomb bay doors, and an absolutely flawless finish. C speed times this year exceeded even jet speed—tops was 189.40 by the team of Jack Frye and Jerry Roselle.

Freeflight, as usual, drew the most entries: over 300 in both 1/2-A and handlaunch glider, 200+ in Nordic and A gas, over a hundred each in six of the other FF events. Free flighter Marty Thompson won five firsts on his way to the Junior National Championship, while Bucky Servaites took the open and grand champ trophies for the second time in a row. A brand-new rubber event, Coupe D'Hiver, was added.

Indoors, Chicago Aeronut Jim Richmond proved unbeatable under his own hometown ceiling—he won all three rubber events, setting a new cabin record. Jan Servaites, brother of the Grand Champion, won both stick and paper stick in the senior division.

Retracts were the hot item in R/C—eight of the top ten pattern fliers used them. 1963 winner Jim Kirtland won D Expert (radio was now divided into A, B, C, and D pattern, plus Formula I and II and scale.) Almost every big-name R/Cer of the era was in the winners list: Doc Edwards, Phil Kraft, Jim Whitley, Larry Leonard, Ron Chidgey, Jim Martin, Tony Bonnetti, Don Lowe, Al Oddino, Doug Spreng, Cliff Weirick, Dave Brown, Jerry Worth, Austin Leftwich, Bud Nosen, Bill Bertrand, John Roth.

1971: Glenview Again

The 40th Nationals drew 1264 fliers and over 400 "mechanics." These registered helpers, many of them little more than on-field spectators, by now outnumbered the contest officials—which, in '71, amounted to 110 AMA personnel and 150 sailors.

Bucky Servaites won the grand and open championships again, Bryan Pardue took junior and Brian Webster senior. Vicious winds on Sunday, the final day, wiped out C gas jobs left and right. A full-scale J-3 Cub appeared, covered from head to toe in Top Flite's new Super Monokote—with the FAA's blessing. Maxey Hester won R/C scale again, this time with a Ryan *STA Special*, while Ken Drummond's giant B-36 (six pusher engines!) made its second Nats appearance. Ron Chidgey won C pattern expert.

Tireless Texas freeflighter Dick "Fast Richard" Mathis, who once entered U/C stunt at a Dallas Nats and nearly qualified, finally won outdoor handlaunch glider this year, flying his *Flash*. Dave Rounsaville came out on top in the screaming FAI gas event.

1972: Glenview—the Last Navy Nats

In March the Navy said *no way* . . . and then relented at the last minute, opening Glenview for one final blowout, July 24-30. It was the last Navy Nationals, a full seven days of flying—and the AMA was responsible for manning every minute of it. Even the skeleton crew of 150 sailors, provided for the past three years, was refused. NO base personnel would be permitted lend a hand during the contest unless their time was paid for out of AMA funds—something the AMA could ill afford.

It was a big contest: over 1400 fliers and 600 mechanics. A hundred and fifty AMA volunteers, flown in from all over the country, worked double shifts to put on the entire show. The Navy supplied the field, the garbage pick-up, the first aid, the meals and housing and transportation for AMA personnel—and no more. For the first time since 1948, the two miles of snow fence needed for crowd control was erected and torn down by civilians—just one of the dozens of tasks the Navy had shouldered over the years.

Outdoor flying began early Wednesday in a chill, fall-like rain. By the weekend it was July again, but not before freeflight scale (Thursday a.m.) had been blown completely off the field. Without the usual 60 Navy timers, 1972 became the first-ever "fly one-time one" Nats for the free flight boys. And the system worked great. Except for a lack of Navy helmets, it was like a time-warp back to the fifties, with Taibi *Stardusters* screaming into the sky everywhere you looked, especially on B gas day. In Unlimited Rubber, George Perryman put up eight straight maxes in a bid for the Mulvihill

212

Trophy, which had been eluding him for years . . . only to hear that Phil Klintworth of Detroit had put up nine.

The 1972 R/C event was overshadowed by the upcoming Masters Tournament scheduled for September in Huntsville, where the '73 World Champ team was to be selected. As a further distraction, the now-traditional pattern/scale/pylon events were invaded this year by two as-yet unofficial classes: helicopter and glider. A handful of choppers were demonstrated on site, by people like Dave Gray, Ernie Huber and Nate Rambo. But the glider guys turned out in force— 131 of them competing in a three-day bash at Miller Meadow, south of O'Hare Airport. This was actually the third annual "SOAR Nationals," a locally-sponsored contest that would outdraw the official Nats soaring events every year until its death in 1976. Chet Lanzo was there in '72, and why not? He'd been flogging R/C gliders since the 1940s.

In controlline stunt, 'bridesmaid' Al Rabe finally took the top honors with his beautiful *Bearcat*, while fellow Texan Bill Rutherford came third flying a semi-scale *Mustang*. Half-A speed times, because of the weather, were low: senior Brian Pardue's 102 topped the field. Combat was tough—some of the best matches yet at a Nats. Mike Wheeler won open and J. Russ Green took senior. Ukie competition ended on Sunday with J.E. Albritton winning FAI speed—and then it was time to roll up those snow fences and go home.

Having carried the Nationals so elegantly on its shoulders for over two decades, the Navy did a great job of setting it down, as well. Beginning around 1968, Navy support tapered off a little more each year, and AMA volunteers were forced, bit by bit, to take up the slack. By 1972 the clan was almost weaned of its dependency, and the first non-Navy Nats—at Whitman Field, Oshkosh, in '73— was the better for it. Still, Oshkosh was something of a downer, and every Nationals since has followed Bill Netzeband's dictum from the beginning of this chapter: *"Some are up, some*

213

unfortunately are down, depending on the people, the weather . . .
and all sorts of little nebulous things."

e pluribus unum

Since the great days of Navy sponsorship, the Nationals has lost much of its prestige, become merely one among many important annual contests in American aeromodeling. This has happened not through any fault of the AMA, but simply because the hobby has, over the past twenty years, continued to fragment more and more into special-interest groups.

The United States Free Flight Championships, held every year since 1971 under National Free Flight Society sponsorship, has long been the premier annual contest for outdoor gas and rubber events. Bill Bennett's Tournament of Champions, despite (or perhaps because of) its invitational nature, is THE prestige pattern event in R/C— just as Byron Godbertson's annual scale rally out in Iowa draws the cream of the WW II radio buffs. For scale rubber fliers, it's the Flying Aces Club "Nationals," a moveable feast held every second year since 1980. Even indoor has its own championships, now. In fact, of all the major divisions of the sport, only the controlline crowd still looks forward to the AMA Nationals as its biggest annual bash.

From the perspective of 1992, it would appear that the annual AMA Nationals—so long the mirror of modeldom in America— may well have outlived its purpose. The next decade may well see its demise.

A Footnote: History Rewritten

Don't try counting backwards from this year's Nats to, say, the 40th Nationals, held at Glenview in 1971—the result will only confuse you. That's because, back in the fall of 1975, under pressure from Bert (Peru, Indiana) Pond and Minneapolis model historian Jim Noonan, the AMA arbitrarily decided to rewrite Nationals history—from the very beginning.

According to the AMA's new orthodoxy, the 1928 AMLA Nats was not really the first Nationals, after all. The first Nationals, it seems, took place in 1923, at the National Air Races in St. Louis. This was a fifteen to twenty-man contest—promoted entirely by the IMAC group, and sanctioned by the newly-formed National Aeronautics Association as a mere sidelight to the full-scale Air Races—in which the Mulvihill rubber cup was first offered.

The Mulvihill was contested for again in '24, '25 and '26. In 1927 no national outdoor meet was sanctioned, and Bernard Mulvihill's big trophy—won in '26 by Jack Loughner of Detroit—disappeared for a time. The following year began the AMLA Nats series described in Chapter Five.

Why should the AMA suddenly decide, almost half a century later, to count these four contests as five, and incorporate them into Nationals history? Just to dethrone Carl Goldberg, who was at that time the only person to have attended every Nats? Not likely. Part of the impetus came from the fact that the '76 Nats were scheduled for Dayton, and the AMA saw a chance to celebrate a "50th Anniversary Nationals" in the nation's bicentennial year in the home town of the Wright brothers.

Why Fifty?

But why stop at fifty? With a little more imagination they might have declared the Dayton Nats to be the seventy-fifth or even the hundredth Nats, instead. After all, they totally ignored those three Villard Trophy Nationals held just before and after World War I. And the Junior Birdman Nats, and the Playground Nats, and the American Legion Nats—and all the Junior Air Races, as well. Surely, with a little more research, they could have worked up a nice round hundred contests, and declared them every one to be Nationals!

Traditionally, the problem with writing history is where to begin. When it comes to rewriting history, it seems, the problem is where to stop.

215

Roll Call: Famous Radioplanes

1937: Chet Lanzo's 84" R/C Stick won the '37 Nats almost by default. The Brown Junior powered ship was the only one to take off and land in one piece!

1949: Walt Good's original 6' Rudderbug set the design trend for the entire single-channel decade that followed.

1952: The most popular R/C kits of the fifties were Hal deBolt's LIVE WIRE series. They introduced controlline prefabrication to the R/C field.

1964: The most copied R/C design in history is Phil Kraft's Ugly Stik—proving that H.L. Mencken was right when he said, "Nobody ever went broke underestimating the taste of the American public."

Chapter Nine

CONTROL BY RADIO

*I had been carefully watching R/C for some years, feeling that sooner
or later it would be the answer to my controlline dreams.*
> — Harold 'Pappy' deBolt, recalling the early '50s

*"The Screamin' Demons of Long Island, Inc., a free-flight club of long
standing, is now devoting a major portion of their time and efforts to
radio control . . . ."*
> — R/C Modeler Magazine, 1964

"Isn't R/C the ultimate in modeling?"
> — AMA Executive Director John Worth, 1964

Everyone knows that freeflight is by far the oldest of the three
main branches of aeromodeling.   But it always comes as a surprise
to recall that the second oldest is not controlline, as most people
would guess, but radio control. R/C was born in the mid-thirties,
some five to six years before Walker's U-Control patent. The first
radio flights—tentative and shaky—followed right on the heels of
the gasoline engine itself.

Rules "Impossible"

Radio control was still little more than a rumor when the
NAA wrote it into the schedule of events for the 1936 Nationals at
Detroit. Nobody showed. Undaunted, they put it back on the menu
the following year. Three months before the '37 event, someone
finally queried *Air Trails* about rules, and the editors had to admit
that, as far as they knew, there weren't any. "So little has been

demonstrated in the way of radio-controlled gas models," they explained, "that definite rules are impossible."

That pretty well summed up the R/C picture before 1939. Even though winners were announced in both '37 and '38, it was actually 1939 before the first successful R/C flight was recorded at a Nationals (success, then as now, meaning *up and around and back home in one piece.*)

Then came World War II, and the federal government, in a fit of paranoia, banned all private radio transmission. R/C progress, already snail-slow, ground to a dead halt. As late as 1948, three years into the postwar Nationals schedule, the radio control event drew a paltry fourteen entries.

Drop R/C?

Any other Nats event that showed so little popularity would have been summarily dropped from the schedule. But the question of dropping radio never arose. R/C was somehow not quite like other events, and everyone felt this instinctively. If model building is the endless pursuit of airy dreams—the perfect model, the perfect flight—then surely 'remote control' ought to be useful in that pursuit. The perfect model, after all, never crashes, and the perfect flight always lands right back at your feet. And weren't these the very goals that radio aspired to?

Every free flighter of the thirties had experienced the feeling of helplessness and anger that comes from watching four pounds of silk and dreams come hurdling out of the sky in a death spiral, doomed to destruction—and all because of some slight misadjustment, some random twitch of the uncertain air. At such a time, the same thought occurs to us all: *If only I could reach out and tweak in some opposite rudder* .... Radio control lived in everyone's heart long before it became a practical reality.

Until the early fifties, though, only a handful of America's two million modelers had the necessary combination of skill and ready money to pursue the R/C dream. But almost everyone seemed willing to cheer it along from the sidelines. Had it come to a vote—and it never did—very few would have favored dropping radio from the Nats.

Scientific Modeling

So far from being dropped, in fact, this retarded child of the air age was babied and coddled and nursed along, year after disappointing year—first by the NAA, and then by the young and struggling AMA itself. Not too surprising, really, when you recall that the Academy, until almost 1950, still clung to its 1936 ideal of promoting "scientific" modeling. And what (short of a car bomb) looked more scientific than a coffin-sized fuselage full of tubes and relays and little Burgess batteries in their black-and-white pinstripe suits?

Pioneers, Tinkerers, Consumers

It's convenient to think of the history of radio control in three stages. First came the Pioneer Era, which lasted from the mid-thirties until the opening, around 1950, of the Citizen's Band radio channels. Cheap citizen-band equipment led immediately to the long and profanity-ridden Tinkerer's Decade, when thousands of freeflight and ukie fliers studied the rudiments of electronics (*"With signal off, the grid allows electrons to pass from filament to plate . . ."*) in order to solder up little micarta-board contraptions that would, with luck, make a rudder tab move left or right on command.

The Tinkerer's Decade gave way, during the 1960s, to the current stage—what might be called either the "transistor age" or the "consumer age," depending on your point of view. In any event, beginning around 1965, radios started rapidly shrinking, reliability took a flying leap upward, and the number of possible control functions multiplied far beyond the average flyer's need. By 1970 the wildest dreams of two generations of R/C experimenters could be purchased, all wired up and ready to install, from any hobby shop in the land—no experience, no patience, no radio knowledge necessary. All it took was hard cash and lots of it.

You'll sometimes hear oldtimers bemoan the loss of the tinkerer's decade—that exciting, seat-of-the-pants era when even a rank beginner could stumble onto some new trick, some system of bobby pins and clock springs that would squeeze an extra control function (elevator, motor, brakes) out of a rudder-only rig for mere pennies. Don't be deceived by this nostalgic babble. The transistor age is, by any rational standard, one sweet hell of an improvement over the good old days. Even though it changed the nature of the model airplane hobby forever.

Pioneers, tinkerers, consumers. Let's take a look at these three stages in a little more depth, to see why nobody in their right mind would want to turn back the R/C clock, even if they could.

Pioneers in Pairs

Model building, like most art forms, is a lonely pursuit. But those pre-1950 R/Cers, the true radio pioneers, were seldom totally alone. Almost invariably they came in pairs: one to build the radio equipment and the other to build the plane. The two fields of knowledge, electronics and aerodynamics, were each so new and so challenging that few people had the time or money to master both. During the thirties and forties, before the advent of the Citizens Radio Service, virtually everything took place on the "ham" bands, those frequencies between 50 and 60 megacycles that had been assigned, back in the early days of the century, to radio amateurs— *licensed* radio amateurs. To be legal, it took both a ham and a modeler to get an R/C plane airborne before 1950.

Seven in '35

Al Lewis, writing in the *Christian Science Monitor* for 13 November 1935, estimated that there might be, at that time, as many as seven radio controlled airplanes in the entire United States. An article in *Popular Science Magazine* the following month mentions only one. "To control the movements of a gas model in the air," *Popular Science* notes, "Chester Lanzo of Cleveland, Ohio, is installing a tiny radio outfit." This lone reference to radio control is buried, without further elaboration, in a long feature story on freeflight.

Model airplanes may have been news in the winter of 1935, but radio control obviously wasn't. Small wonder that exactly nobody made it to the Nats the following spring with a radioplane.

220

Over the next year, however, the R/C picture began to brighten, if only a little. Six hopefuls showed up at Detroit for the 1937 Nationals. As if intent on proving that R/Cers were no different from other modelers, they brought with them the customary array of unflown, untested models. The first two of the six crashed on takeoff, from simple tailheaviness—a clear indication that neither had been in the air before the contest.

Lanzo of Cleveland

Then Chester Lanzo of Cleveland—he of the "tiny radio outfit"—stepped forward with his entry. Despite *Popular Science's* description, nothing about the Lanzo model or its radio was tiny, even by 1937 standards. It was a gawky, seven-foot, parasol-winged beast that looked for all the world like a scaled-up ROG rubber job (the Comet *Firefly,* maybe.) Its fuselage, if you could call it that, was a flat crutch: no formers at all, just a couple of basswood sticks with some spreaders between. A brick-shaped box containing two pounds of homemade R/C gear had been strapped to this crutch, almost as an afterthought—strapped right under the big wire birdcage that held the wing in place.

After the customary hour of tinkering and tuning (every minute in the air, in 1937, represented sixty or more minutes on the ground) Lanzo finally informed the judges that he was ready to fly. And just in time, too, for the weather was closing in: a tall, dark thunderhead leaned ominously over the south edge of the field. With its Brown Junior snarling, the big plane lumbered off across the rough ground and rose slowly into the gusty, storm-charged air. Once there, it bounced about nervously, aggravated as much by the turbulence as by the occasional signal from Lanzo's transmitter.

A hundred spectators held their breath as the nine-foot wing banked first left and then right, almost at random. After a little over a minute of this—it seemed like forever—the engine sputtered to a stop and the model turned tail, gliding in for a typical pioneer-era landing: downwind and off-field. A few minutes later the storm broke, and time ran out for the other three contestants. Since only one day had been allotted for R/C, Lanzo was declared the winner.

Two crashes and one disrupted free flight. Not much of a spectator event, this radio control.

The Figure Nine

The following year was even more of a disappointment. Another one-flight show, the '38 radio event was over in a matter of seconds. The day was windy, and the only contestant willing to brave the weather was 21-year-old Walter Good, of Kalamazoo. Walt's *Big Guff* R/C model, scaled up from his highly successful *Guff* free flight, was a veteran of dozens of hops back home. But the turbulent Detroit air was its undoing.

With Walt holding a wingtip to stabilize the takeoff run—a common procedure in the pioneer days—the *Big Guff* lifted off smoothly enough. But just then a weed caught the stab, pitching the nose up violently. As Walt turned and sprinted for the transmitter, which was being manned for him by a non-modeling ham, the wind lifted the Guff up into a hard stall. A touch of rudder at this point might or might not have saved the day, but we'll never know, for Walt was still at full gallop when the model, now beginning its second stall, went right over the top, screamed down the back side of the loop and buried its nose in the planet.

The infamous figure nine! For pioneering this maneuver, the judges awarded Walt and his shattered Big Guff first place. "Not a very satisfying win," he recalled later.

Historic Performance

But the following year, 1939, Walt and the rebuilt Guff were back. This time his twin brother Bill came along, and together they restored their good name, so to speak, by performing every maneuver the judges demanded. With Bill at the controls—the brothers always took turns—they garnered eighty-nine points for a near perfect flight: left and right circles, half-mile goal and return, a figure-eight over the transmitter—plus a spiral dive and a stall for their elective maneuvers. The Guff spent a total of fourteen minutes in the air. When the engine quit it floated downwind gracefully, turned crosswind, turned once more onto final, and touched down gently within a hundred feet of the transmitter. A great cheer went up from everyone in sight.

This, at last, was radio control—the first totally successful flight ever performed under contest pressure in the USA. No one who witnessed the Guff's flight that day ever forgot it. Glider guru Frank Zaic went away cackling like a hen: "Was it under control? Sure was!" he reported. "It was worth coming to the Nationals just to see this historic performance!"

Way to Go

The next year, 1940, the Nats shifted from Detroit to Chicago, and the Good brothers showed up once again: same airplane, same radio, same pair of identical shy smiles. Every year their competitors' models seemed to grow heavier and more complex. This year six of the others sported 'R-E-M': rudder, elevator and motor controls. But the quiet twins from Kalamazoo beat them all handily, using just rudder. By now the *Guff* had an elevator channel installed, though it was always disconnected for contests.

The message, in 1940, seemed clear: *rudder-only was obviously the way to go.*

1941, however, was a different story. That was the year Jim Walker—U-Control Jim Walker—came down from Portland with a big white trike-geared high-winger carrying two receivers and two pulsed proportional actuators. The first actuator controlled the rudder, and the second was for . . . *motor control.* "Motor?" everybody said incredulously. "Why not elevator?" They soon found out. When Walker taxied out to the middle of the runway, paused as if waiting for tower clearance, then proceeded to make the first recorded *proto takeoff,* the judges were simply blown away.

Walker's proportional system was simple but effective: signal on gave one extreme, signal off the other. Blip-blip-blip gave something in between. The Good brothers didn't compete that year, and Walker, with his infinitely variable engine and rudder, won out over a field of a dozen airplanes. Second through seventh places went to models with complex multi-controls; the top rudder-only flier finished eighth.

Now multi began to look like the way to go.

Schism

And so the First Church of Radio Control, a secular Sunday-morning society less than half a dozen years old, had already generated its first schism, with some members firmly in the rudder-only pew and others pursuing the broad path of rudder-motor-elevator. (Nobody had yet tackled ailerons.) In the months following the '41 Nats, the debate raged: Could a first-rate rudder flier *really* do any maneuver a multi-control plane could? If the Goods had been flying, with all their rudder-only experience and finesse, would Walker have won?

It was one of those questions (as they used to say in the nineteenth century) *upon which reasonable men may differ.* And, as it turned out, there was plenty of time for differing. Within six months America was at war, and R/C was once more relegated to the world of daydreams. The next major radio event would not take place until the Wichita Nationals, in 1946—five long years into the future.

Seeds of Progress

Primitive as these prewar contests sound, they contained the seeds of almost all R/C progress for the next two decades. In fact, *the entire future of radio flying, right up to the introduction of digital proportional in the early sixties, was demonstrated at one or the other of those five prewar Nationals.*

For their '38, '39 and '40 wins, the Good brothers had used a single-tube receiver and rubber-driven escapement—two items that became industry standards after World War II.

Leo Weiss—that same bright Leo Weiss whose 1936 electric-servo controlliner had anticipated Walker's U-Control—showed up at the '37 Nats with a three-channel tuned reed system for rudder, elevator and motor control. *Tuned reeds in 1937!* Weiss' radio was the kind of rig that single channel fliers as late as 1965 were still dreaming of owning.

And Jim Walker's 1941 *blip-blip* proportional, popularized after the war by George Trammel and Howard McEntee and others, became one of the primary toys of the Tinkerer's Decade.

Even Lanzo's erratic 1937 rudder control system was portentous. It used a motor-driven servo that cranked the tab continuously through a *right-neutral-left-neutral-right* sequence—a foreshadowing of the "galloping" proportional rigs of the fifties.

The big drawback was that Lanzo's system wasn't exactly what you'd call *selective*. When the transmitter key was depressed, the servo started turning its crank and the rudder began to wag, making for a kind of wobbly straight-ahead flight. This was 'neutral.' To get a turn, Lanzo simply released the key and watched to see what the model did. Wherever the rudder tab landed when the signal stopped was where it stayed until the next signal. So he just kept starting and stopping the servo until the tab landed more or less where he wanted it. Then he left it there until the turn was almost complete before standing on the button to get 'neutral' again.

Walt Good used an actuator similar to Lanzo's that year, although his was rubber driven. Nobody at the '37 Nats had an escapement, for the simple reason that there were no escapements in July of '37. (Ross Hull and the staff of the amateur radio magazine *QST,* whose pet project was an 18' R/C slope glider, were up in the Connecticut hills that very summer inventing the escapement.)

Failsafe

Besides the possibility of a sort of proportional control, Lanzo's "cranked" rudder offered another harbinger of things to come: a built-in failsafe. If the radio signal should be cut off for any reason (plane flies out of range, spectator stumbles over transmitter, snake bites operator) Lanzo's rudder would freeze in some position that wasn't likely to be dead-on neutral, and the model would tilt over into a circle and fly away slowly instead of all at once. Variations on this 'failsafe' idea resurfaced again and again over the next three decades, until sometime in the late sixties, when radios finally began to win the trust of their owners.

Starting Over: 1946

The second world war, which accelerated technology in so many fields, contributed exactly nothing to radio control. When the

225

government finally relaxed its ban on civilian radio transmissions in late '45, R/C modelers picked up just where they'd left off four years earlier—with crude single-tube receivers and even cruder escapements. All the equipment was still limited to the ham bands, where you had to pass stringent theory and code tests to operate legally. These tests, largely irrelevant to R/C, were a major stumbling block to radio control popularity.

A few months after V-J Day, however, some welcome news trickled in from England: U.K. modelers had been granted, simply for the asking, two separate "exam-free" bands for R/C experimentation. The first was in the 27-28 megacycle range, the other up around 460 mc (*cycles* didn't become *hertz* until the '80s.)

The AMA leaders in Washington, full of postwar optimism, assumed that they might expect no less from their own government.

But that was before most of them had ever heard the initials "FCC."

Saying No

The Federal Communications Commission is a New Deal agency—a branch of the Commerce Department established under F.D.R. way back in 1934. One of the FCC's primary jobs is to pretend that it owns the invisible radio spectrum, and dole out slices of same to needy applicants. Ever since the Commission's founding, there have been more applicants than slices—*far* more applicants than slices. So the chief function of the FCC, right from day one, has been to refuse new frequency requests.

Most people don't enjoy saying no. If that's your job, you look for ways to avoid it. For starters, you simply ignore as many of the applicants as you can, for as long as you can. You make the ones who persist climb through snarls of red tape—a snafu of regulations that say "no" for you. The telephone becomes your enemy, the morning mail an irritation. You spend much of your time and energy ducking and dodging and evading applicants.

On a daily basis, this is not very satisfying work. Do it long enough and it will make you defensive—then angry—and finally passive-aggressive. Eventually, unless you are an extraordinary individual, you become a bureaucratic prick.

There were few extraordinary individuals in the Federal Communications Commission of the late 1940s. Not only did the bureau stonewall the AMA's repeated requests for an exam-free R/C frequency like the British had; as soon as they satisfied themselves that such a thing as "radio control" actually existed, they began to send their local pettifoggers to contests (hitting the Nationals in '47, '48 and '51) to threaten and harass the small handful of six-meter amateurs who were attempting to compete in the R/C events.

465 Megacycles

It took three long years of bowing and scraping to this harassment before the almighty Commission finally granted, in June of 1949, a single spot for exam-free R/C use. That spot was at 465 megacycles—a practically worthless region for modeling purposes, due to inadequate receiver technology at the time. To add further insult, the Commission forbade the use of homemade equipment on this spot: all 465 transmitters had to be commercially built, under rigid FCC controls.

Only two companies ever managed to leap all the hurdles the Commission put in the 465-mc road. Vernon MacNabb's Citizen-Ship Radio Corporation of Indianapolis got a single channel transmitter-receiver combo approved in the summer of 1950, just three days before the Dallas Nats—which it promptly won. (It took a last-minute call to MacNabb's congressman to prod Commission bureaucrats into finishing the months-old paperwork.)

The second company, Babcock Radio Engineering of Los Angeles, despite being the largest producer of guided missile equipment during WW II, wasn't able to get their much-touted two-channel 465 set approved until 1956—too little, too late in the rapidly changing R/C market.

Neither of these rigs ever became very popular, partly because of their size and complexity, but mostly due to their cost. Like all first-line, factory-built equipment of the era, both sets carried price tags that were beyond the reach of the average modeler.

Garbage Band

Meanwhile, the AMA continued to petition the tin gods of Washington for another frequency assignment—one that would permit inexpensive, low-power, *homemade* radio sets. After three more years of groveling and pleading, they were thrown a second insulting scrap: R/Cers would be permitted to squeeze in on 27.255 mc, a spot frequency known privately among FCC bureaucrats as "the garbage band." (Everything the Commission couldn't find a place for—from dog training devices to overhead cranes—was dumped onto this frequency.)

Such continual third-rate treatment raised the hackles of thousands of R/Cers and would-be R/Cers throughout the country. But in fairness, it should be noted that the arrogance and disrespect cut both ways. Postwar radio control fliers, long before the opening of 27 megacycles, were notorious for thumbing their nose at the FCC. Rumor had it that Berkeley Models alone sold more of their wooden-cased 50-mc "D-E Aerotrol" transmitters than there were licensed hams *in all of America*—thus quantifying what everyone in the hobby already knew: that the vast majority of six-meter fliers during the forties and fifties were operating illegally.

And 27.255 users proved to be no better. Of an estimated thirty thousand 27-meg transmitters in use by 1954, less than 3,000 were legally licensed. (A magazine campaign the following year helped double this figure, but the FCC was still unimpressed—and rightly so—by such paltry numbers.)

Heroes

Despite the ill-will on all sides, two unblemished heroes emerged from the AMA's six-year battle for the garbage band. One was pioneer R/Cer Walt Good, whose patience and persistence and unfailing gentility as the Academy's spokesman in Washington finally wore down even the hardened bureaucrats of the FCC. (Good himself, it should be noted, had little to gain from the citizen's band. A licensed ham, he flew then—and still flies—on six meters.)

The second hero was an FCC Commissioner by the name of George Sterling. Although not a modeler himself, Sterling was a licensed radio amateur—and beyond question one of aeromodeling's Friends in High Places. Without George Sterling's help, beginning in the spring of '51, it's entirely possible that we would still be squabbling with the FCC's lower bureaucracy for the right to share the garbage band with every babbling idiot who could afford the down payment on a CB rig.

Diathermy

The 27 megacycle spot-frequency (it wasn't yet a band) became legal for R/C use in March of 1952. A part of the ISM band (industrial, scientific and medical), the frequency's biggest users at the time were hospitals.

In those days, every good physical therapy department had its diathermy machine—a kind of huge, spot-focused microwave oven, designed for the selective cooking of human bodies, one organ at a time. These machines generated tremendous radio-frequency power, and were much feared by R/Cers at first. But they proved to be largely bogeys: as long as you didn't fly within a mile or so of a hospital, you were usually safe.

The great danger to radio controlled model airplanes in the mid-fifties, it turned out, wasn't diathermy machines—it was entire cities. That's because in 1954, just two years after opening 27 to modelers, the FCC began handing out licenses on that same spot to towns like Chicago and Evanston and Los Angeles for traffic light operation—using transmitters with up to 500 watts of killing power!

R/Cers were limited to five watts maximum, and ninety percent of them flew on two watts or less. This meant that, given the proper 'skip' conditions up in the ionosphere, the pride and joy of your building board could be spun out of the sky over Houston by a stray signal from a traffic light system in Chicago.

The Tinkerer's Decade Begins

Despite such petty irritations, R/C interest mushroomed after the opening of 27.255. New York radio supply houses with names like Gyro and ESSCO and Lafayette began to fill the model mags with huge, fine-print ads—noisy ads, jammed and overcrowded (just like NYC itself) with every imaginable tube and meter and coil and widget for the radio builder.

In their wake came a host of smaller operations all across the country, companies like John Worth's Control Research of Hampton, Virginia; like Radiomodels up in Baltimore; like Paul and Bobbie Runge's Ace R/C out in Higginsville, Missouri. These smaller outfits, in imitation of their prototypes in New York, sold inexpensive kits as well as completed sets—transmitter, receiver and actuator—for the new 'exam-free' band.

It should be pointed out that a *completed set*, in the fifties, didn't mean a ready-to-fly radio, as it does today. It simply meant that the receiver and transmitter chassis were both pre-wired. The buyer still had to break out the soldering iron and wire each of these units to the appropriate switches, meter jacks, rheostats, power supplies, antennae, control boxes and batteries. (This era wasn't named the Tinkerer's Decade for nothing—the original tinkers were nomadic, semi-skilled solderers of pots and pans.)

Everything Under Control

After the opening of the citizen's band, the model magazines began to do all they could to nurture this growing branch of the hobby. In 1950, *Air Trails* hired freelance writer Howard McEntee to do occasional 'roundups' of R/C information and new products. These roundups finally coalesced, in early '53, into a monthly column, variously called "R/C News and Comment," "McEntee on R/C," and finally "Everything Under Control."

During the fifties, Howard McEntee probably was, as the magazine liked to boast, "the most quoted R/C columnist in America." He designed R/C circuitry, he wrote succinctly and clearly, and he seemed to be privy to every new technical breakthrough, no matter where in the country it happened to occur. (*Does your ground-based transmitter lose range in dry weather? Try pouring a bucket of water on the earth beneath it to increase the antenna loading.*)

Mac's secret was simple: he was a licensed amateur, and every Sunday morning he held court on single sideband, trading info with other hams in an R/C "net" that covered much of the English-speaking world.

McEntee quickly became the guru of this growing branch of the modelplane hobby. Few people suspected that this gentle and soft-spoken man, who had been building rubber models since the early twenties, was actually a newcomer to radio control, and not a pioneer at all. Howard McEntee wrote accurately and well about R/C because he was both a ham and a professional writer—and not because of any wealth of flying experience. Mac had never owned a gas engine, much less a radio model, until 1950.

Lorenz

In November of '53, *Model Airplane News,* a little slower on the uptake, launched its own R/C column, "Radio Control News." It was conducted by one of the genuine pioneers, Ed Lorenz—the designer of Berkeley's popular Aerotrol radios. Like McEntee, Lorenz contributed a number of important circuit designs to the Tinkerer's Decade. His Lorenz two-tube receiver (1952) and MOPA transmitter (1954) were R/C milestones, and very close to my own heart: this was the combination that finally got my heavy, sloppily-built, McCoy-diesel-powered *Mambo* in the air, sometime during the windy summer of '56.

Everyone read Lorenz, just as they did McEntee. Even people with no real interest in R/C (diehard freeflighters, ukie stunt men) would skim through the radio news at least casually. In the fifties most modelers still read their magazines cover-to-cover. The hobby was already diverse, and becoming more so every year, but even the specialists still spoke one another's language to some degree.

Volume Up, Prices Down

Like any other consumer item, R/C units began to drop in price as their sales volume rose during the Tinkerer's Decade. At one point, around 1955, complete single channel radio kits, ordered by mail, could be put in the air for under twenty dollars—something like a day's pay for most adults. These were simple gas-tubers, but they worked. Every year, tubes and relays and batteries got a little smaller, so that airborne weights, once measured in pounds, began at last to be reckoned in ounces. By 1956, the .049 powered single channel model was no longer a freak, and almost every R/C club had its small-plane specialist.

At this point, midway between the 50-mc pioneers and the transistor age to come, there were still only two basic ways of turning a radio signal into a control movement. You either used an *escapement* (simple, light, rubber-driven) or a *proportional actuator*, based on electromagnets. (The *servo*—a sort of motor-driven escapement—came later.)

Escapements were by far the most popular. The first ones were sequential: left-neutral-right-neutral-left was the order of things, and God help you if you forgot what your last control direction was. Then, in early 1952, Howard Bonner of Los Angeles began to market the first selective escapement: one push of the button gave you right, two pushes gave you left. *Every time.* This was a giant step forward, and pumped another ten to fifteen years of life into escapement flying.

But all through the era, single-channel proportional control rapidly gained popularity—systems that fluttered the rudder continuously, offering degrees of left or right in place of the escapement's violent all-or-nothing movement. Ugly and nervous and unaesthetic on the ground, these primitive propo rigs managed to look suave in the air. With tinkering, they could be adjusted so that the plane ignored the rudder's constant dithering and responded only to its *average* position, as determined by the stick movements at the transmitter.

Using little hand-wound electromagnets, proportional could be made almost as light as escapements, although the smoothest control came from heavier and more complex motor-driven actuators. To many, the extra weight and complexity seemed worth it: proportional, with its joystick control box, was unquestionably a more natural way to fly.

But then the button-pushers discovered 'cascaded' escapements, a way of hooking two escapements together so that the second one controlled the elevator. Two controls from one channel! Naturally, the proportional boys had to follow suit.

When they added elevator to their propo systems, however, the flutter in both controls would become more pronounced, causing the plane's tail to gyrate through the air in a kind of screwing motion, something like an early Beech *Bonanza.* This was the infamous "gallop" of galloping ghost rigs. (Compromise, compromise, compromise—everything you did to squeeze more controls out of one channel was a compromise.)

Multi gear was available, of course, and getting better every year: three, five, even seven channel tuned reed sets with names like Rockwood and Schmidt and Bramco. But they were still the size of lunch boxes: huge metal-clad receivers full of vibrating reedbanks, each reed requiring its own separate relay, and each relay prone to dirt and vibration and arcing and crash damage.

These multi sets sold for up to *twenty times* the cost of a single channel rig. Worse yet, they required six or seven feet of wing to carry them, putting them at odds with the postwar trend to smaller engines and lighter models. Little wonder, then, that during the fifties, the Tinkerer's Decade, single channel fliers outnumbered the multi men by nearly a thousand to one.

Rudder versus Multi

With such a lopsided balance between single channel fliers and reed tweakers, it's not surprising that the old prewar schism between rudder-only and multi-control died hard. As late as 1953, a hotshot pilot named Jack Port flew his .19-powered rudder model to a seven-point win over Howard Bonner's big R-E-M machine at the Willow Grove Nationals. It was a real upset victory, and event director Harold deBolt (whose Live Wire R/C kits were all single channel at the time) could hardly contain his glee. "This just proves what I've been telling the boys," deBolt crowed at meet's end, "If you know what you're doing you can still win with rudder control only!" And deBolt seemed to be right—a rudder-only ship had placed third, as well.

But '53 proved to be rudder's last stand at the Nationals. The following year the highest placing rudder-only flier was seventh, and deBolt himself showed up with 5-channel reeds. The multi men had finally learned how to handle those touchy, untrimmable elevators without roller-coastering all over the sky. They were starting to pull extra points out of maneuvers like inverted flight and outside loops—tricks that not even the hottest rudder flier could manage.

The time had come to separate the two classes.

The Challenge of Rudder-Only

The following year, 1955, multi was duly split off from single channel, and a lot of folks expected rudder-only, on both the competitive and sport levels, to simply wither away.

But it didn't. It hung on, in one form or another, for twenty more years. Rudder was cheap and light and simple—a hard combination to ignore, especially for beginners. More important, it was a *genuine aerodynamic challenge*—had been ever since those first R/C flights back in the mid-thirties—and so it offered something for the expert as well.

Right from the start, radio control had taken as its ideal not the flight of birds—that was for rubber and glider and freeflight gas—but the flight of full-scale aircraft. And a full-scale plane, even in a simple maneuver like a turn, uses three-axis controls: rudder, elevator, ailerons.

To imitate a full-scale turn with only a rudder (and do it well, without excessive yaw or slip or loss of altitude) you have to *build the aileron and elevator functions right into the aerodynamics of the model.*

This was a very different world from freeflight.

And yet almost every early radio job was a converted freeflight. That's because freeflights, in those days, were all people knew: *Buccaneers* and *Cavaliers* and ships like Walt Good's scaled-up *Guff.* These designs, most of them straight out of the theories of Charlie Grant, had only one virtue—stability. They knew how to fly on their own, without any help from a too-often unreliable radio.

"Series of Minor Emergencies"

When Bill Winter first tried his hand at R/C, about 1947, he said it felt like you were "knocking the plane out of its flight path every time you squeezed the button." To keep a model nearby, which was all you could ask of radio in those days, you had to continually create "a series of minor emergencies," as Winter put it, which the plane's natural stability was kept busy correcting.

These are apt descriptions, especially when applied to the kits that many people were sticking radios in at the time—kits like Berkeley's popular *Bootstraps*, designed by Henry Struck as a PAA-load model. An old-time cabin free flight with a relatively high thrust line, the *Bootstraps* had a reasonably good force layout for R/C. But oh, that polyhedral wing! Polyhedral on a powered R/C model makes the rudder so twitchy that a full control, held for more than a second or two, can produce an instant barrel roll. And every control, in escapement days, was a full control.

You could cut the rudder throw to nearly nothing, of course, but then you'd be out of luck in the glide. The problem boiled down to this: *too much difference in airspeed between engine-on and engine-off.*

The Rudderbug

One of the best solutions to this dilemma was Walt Good's 72" *Rudderbug*, first published in *Model Airplane News* in May of 1949. A direct descendant of his Nats-winning *Big Guff*, the Rudderbug featured some important new twists. First, its fuselage aft of the wing wasn't square. It came to a steep point on top, just like an A-frame house. This provided a smoother airflow over the fin during the glide, so that the difference between power-on and power-off rudder effect was minimized. (Gene Foxworthy of Indianapolis solved this problem by moving the rudders out to the stab tips in his 1950 Nats-winning *Hoosier Hot-Shot.* Foxworthy thought he was placing them out of the prop's slipstream, but mostly he was just getting them clear of the fuselage wake during glide.)

The second trick up the Rudderbug's sleeve was its ancient, undercambered airfoil—a genuine NACA 6412. Old prewar 'banana' foils like the 6412 had plenty of lift for carrying heavy R/C gear—

and plenty of drag as well, thanks to their deep camber. High drag airfoils tend to equalize climb and glide speeds. Add a trike gear with a huge nosewheel and you've got a terrific built-in headwind.

A Friend in Drag

Not everyone realized it in 1949, but a built-in headwind was just about the best thing that could happen to a single-channel, escapement-controlled model airplane. Drag kept airspeed in check—kept spirals from tightening into death dives, kept stalls from turning into a frustrating series of scallops, kept overpowered models from climbing too high too fast. Drag slowed everything down to realistic speeds—to *thinking* speeds. In the tinkerer's decade, drag was the R/C flier's best friend.

The third trick that separated Good's Rudderbug from earlier designs was its stabilizer placement. The Bug's stab was radically low—way down below the thrust line. All the way down on the bottom of the fuselage, in fact.

Everything else about the Rudderbug was right out of the spiral-stability theories of Charlie Grant. (In fact, Good himself, in his modest way, sometimes refers to the *Guff*, the Rudderbug's predecessor, as "a modified *K-G Gassie*.") But the Bug's stabilizer placement was unique. It was totally out of the wing wash. It was thick and blunt and fully symmetrical. It never stalled, and it never faltered, and it never, *ever* blocked the rudder—even in the steepest glide. It made the Rudderbug just about the finest 'flying platform' for single channel R/C ever designed. Eleven of the twenty contestants at the '49 Olathe Nationals flew Rudderbugs, even though the design had been out for less than three months at the time.

When Harold deBolt began a few years later to create the series of *Live Wire* kits that started most fifties fliers on their R/C careers, he tried his best to improve on the Rudderbug layout, without much luck. He substituted a fat fuselage for the Bug's hard-to-cover undercambered wing, and went back to a two-wheel gear for simplicity. But everything else about the Live Wires—high wing, high thrustline, small fin, low stab—had "Rudderbug" written all over it.

The same is true of Lou Andrew's *Trixter Beam,* Fran McElwee's *Robot,* E.J. Brown's *C.Q.,* as well as the *Esquire* and the *Mambo* and almost every other first-rate design from the rudder-only era. Even Ben Parr's screaming little *Separators* of the late fifties—those fat, heavy, frighteningly overpowered rudder-motor designs that took advantage of the old saw that says "elevator controls airspeed, motor controls altitude"—even those were basically just Rudderbugs with upthrust.

Meanwhile, Back at the Multis:

Multi-channel ships, as it turned out, were less fussy to design than rudder-only models. The more controls you had, the more design latitude you had. With rudder-motor-elevator, for example, you could get away from that boxy, high-wing "Live Wire" look. You could build a bipe, or a shoulder-winger, or even the occasional racy-looking mid-wing. Although the big winners seldom did. Howard Bonner's *Smog Hog,* deBolt's *Equalizer* and *Over-and-Under* and *Live Wire Cruiser*—most of the top R-M-E planes of the mid-fifties were still semi-scale high-wing boxes, exactly like their rudder-only counterparts.

This mold wasn't broken until 1957, when Bonner took his Smog Hog back to Willow Grove to win the Nats, and an L.A. flying buddy named Fred Dunn stayed home to design the *Astro Hog,* America's first really popular aileron-equipped radioplane. The Astro was a low-winger, but a low-winger that anybody could handle. It had *eight degrees* of dihedral in each panel—almost enough to fly it rudder-only! ('Don't try it,' Dunn warned in his April 1958 *MAN* building instructions.)

Ailerons Are Here to Stay

The Astro Hog was an instant success. Everyone who watched its tight axial rolls, its smooth, sustained inverted flight and precise cuban eights, knew immediately that *rudder-motor-elevator* was now a thing of the past as far as competition flying was concerned. The aerobatic ante had been permanently raised; ailerons were here to stay.

With its two-wheel gear and barn-door ailerons and absurd dihedral angle, the Astro Hog (Sig revived the design in 1984) looks positively quaint today. Nevertheless, this stubby little six-footer was, in the fall of 1957, the radioplane of the future. It led directly to the design that everyone—competitor and sport flyer alike—is still flying today: Ed Kazmirski's *Taurus.*

The thick-winged, strip-aileron *Taurus* was like no model airplane before it. It had a steerable trike gear for arrow-straight takeoffs. It had almost no dihedral and almost no decalage and a shockingly rearward balance point—it was trimmed for neutral stability in every axis. Put a Taurus into a turn and you had to take it back out. Put it into a dive, even a shallow dive, and only up-elevator could save it.

Designed to win multi pattern in 1962, Kazmirski's Taurus became the prototype of almost every intermediate-and-up R/C model for the next thirty years. Hanno Prettner and Chip Hyde still fly tuned-pipe Tauruses; Joe Shmozzle at the local dirt strip rips erratic holes in the sky with his *Ugly Stik* version. Almost everyone who flies four channels or more flies a Taurus. If rudder-only found its epitome in the '49 *Rudderbug,* then multi design peaked thirteen years later with Ed Kazmirski's Taurus. The Taurus completed the main trunk of the R/C tree; the next step was to begin separating into branches.

The Urge to Scale

Not surprisingly, the largest and most fertile of these branches has been Scale.

For most modelers, the basic radio dream has always been a modest one: a few touch-and-go's, a graceful puttering about the patch, a loop, a roll, and maybe a spin, then a nice three-point landing at the end. This would have satisfied nine out of ten R/C pilots thirty years ago—and it still does today.

Spins and rolls and touch-and-go's: all these are scale-like maneuvers. And so, when the dreamer envisions his model performing them, it's natural to picture that model looking something like a 'real' airplane. Didn't Walt Good put transparent windows on his *Rudderbug* way back in '49, and didn't deBolt always paint a cabin on his boxy-looking *Live Wires*? The *Astro Hog* has its open cockpit, complete with headrest and windscreen, and even Phil Kraft's *Ugly Stik* has that World War I rudder shape, tempting its builder to Fokker-red Monokote and big, black Maltese crosses.

The urge to scale runs deep in the veins of most aeromodelers—but especially those who are drawn to radio control.

DeSoto's Cub

Clinton DeSoto, a staff member of the ham magazine *QST,* was one of the earliest R/C "scalers." He arrived at the 1938 Nats with fourteen feet of *Taylor Cub,* a bright yellow monster that was authentic in everything but its landing gear. (It had struts and wheels so gargantuan that it looked poised for vertical takeoff!) Inside, the *Cub*'s radio system was a nightmare of complexity. There were four separate receiver-actuator combos on four separate frequencies to achieve up/down and left/right—no motor speed or cutoff. DeSoto didn't attempt to fly his Cub at the Nats, but still it excited everyone. Here was a radioplane that, barring that absurd landing gear, looked "real"—compared to everything else in sight.

Among the thirties R/Cers, DeSoto's Cub stands alone. Nobody else seemed willing to play out their dreams of scale in those rugged pioneer days before World War II. Just getting a successful flight was challenge enough. Realism could wait.

And in the long period following the war—the end of the pioneer era and beginning of the tinkerer's decade—scale fared little better. Only one model of note was published. This was a highly-detailed *Stinson 150* in the October and November 1947 issues of *Air Trails*—six feet of airplane that was clearly too beautiful to trust to the vagaries of rudder-only in those rude times.

Hollinger's J-3

Not until Chuck Hollinger published his two-inch-to-the-foot *J-3 Cub,* in 1955, did R/C scale begin to get off the ground. Berkeley kitted the Cub immediately, and Hollinger followed up the next year with an even bolder model: a 72" Fairchild *PT-19* (which Christine Zaic at Jetco snapped up.) Because of its low wing, the

Fairchild was no off-the-board wonder: it took 8° of right thrust and nearly as much down to make it fly. But fly it did—on rudder-only escapement. (Two years later, a PT-19 fitted with 8-channel reeds won the first Nationals R/C scale event.)

Cal Smith, another master modeler of the era, gave us his stub-nosed *Nieuport Bipe* in 1954, a .60-powered rudder-only model that thousands of R/Cers had the good sense not to tackle—and then a fine clipped-wing Aeronca *Champ* in '56.

If Smith's Nieuport left any doubt that the experts were getting bored with simply boring holes in the sky, *Flying Models* columnist Ted Strader set everyone straight in 1958 by unveiling his surprisingly scale (and frighteningly heavy) .09-powered *Mustang* for rudder/ elevator control—on escapements! The Strader Mustang was one of the first published R/C models to be covered almost entirely in sheet balsa, a trick that U-Control scalers had long been using to duplicate the metal skins of modern aircraft. (Throughout the fifties, only the ukie fliers seemed to notice that tube-and-fabric was dead.)

Toward the end of the decade the first transistors began slipping quietly into R/C circuitry, and those huge multi-channel reed receivers at last began to shrink. Dunn's *Astro Hog* had already shown the world that, with ailerons, anything could be balanced successfully on the wind. The time was ripe for the multi boys to zero in on scale. And they did.

Phil Breitling's 66" *Mustang* (kitted by Sterling), Lanzo's *Arado* bipe, Claude McCullough's finely detailed Fairey *Barracuda*, Maxey Hester's *King Cobra*, Ralph Schellenbaum's *P-47*—the sixties gave us the first flock of no-compromise R/C scale jobs: airplanes with accurate dihedral angles, proper stab and rudder areas, working flaps, retract gears, and out-of-this-world cockpit detail. Progress in scale paralleled exactly progress in radio reliability; by 1970, both had achieved today's plateau.

Since then, scale models have continued to swell in size, reaching 1/5, 1/4 and even 1/3 the wingspans of their man-carrying counterparts. The current AMA weight limit for such monsters is 55 pounds, with fuel, but there's no reason to suppose that this limit won't continue to rise. The Army, after all, flew full-scale Culver *Cadets* as target drones during the forties, so it's just a matter of time before someone with deep pockets (and a fear of heights) stuffs a radio into a full-scale *Mustang* and shows up at the Top Gun or Scale Masters or Tournament of Champions.

Fanjets

Not until the mid-to-late seventies did R/C Scale begin to find other directions than simply bigger. That's when America's first commercial ducted fan system, the Scozzi, hit the market. Bob Violett demonstrated an early Scozzi at Lakehurst during the '74 Aerolympics. It flew, though not too impressively. What people seemed to remember most about Violett's model was its ungodly racket.

Ducted fans (their history goes back to the 1950s experiments of Roy Clough and Wayne Schindler and Bob DeVault in this country, Thomas Purcell and Ray Booth in England) finally matured in the 1980s with the Jet Hangar Turbax, a development of the original Scozzi, and Byron Godberson's Byrojets out in Iowa. Today, most of the guesswork is gone from the field, and any R/Cer who wants to build jet scale can do so without hanging an embarrassing prop on the nose.

Choppers

A second direction scale R/C has taken is into helicopters. Totally high-tech and infinitely challenging, helicopters have become, in just a few short years, a big moneymaker for some hobby shops, a rich advertising source for the magazines, and a top crowd-pleaser for the AMA show teams.

Vertical flight has come a long way since Ken Norris showed up at the 1961 Willow Grove Nationals with his SuperTigre .56-powered, eight-channel Sikorsky S-64. Helicopter was by then an eight-year-old free flight event, but the Norris R/C job was a Nats first; almost a full decade would pass before other R/Cers began to take choppers seriously.

Dieter Schlüter in Germany, and John Burkham and Dave Gray in the U.S. were among the many whose work advanced the sport during the late sixties and early seventies. Schlüter's Bell *Jet*

Ranger (kitted by Kavan, imported by MRC) hit the U.S. market in late '71, followed a few months later by Dave Gray's little fixed-pitch DuBro *Whirly Bird.*

These early models, before the invention of gyro stabilizers, were a real video-game challenge to fly. In 1975 Mark Smith, who designed and piloted all those tricky, unstable styrofoam seagulls for the movie *Johnathan Livingston Seagull,* had this to say about learning to fly helicopter: "All you have to do is forget everything you ever learned about flying . . . ." Four years later, Ernie Huber was teaching the world to fly inverted.

Today, top fliers like Curtiss Youngblood, Wayne Mann, Robert Gorham and Cliff Hiatt make helis look easy—even though they aren't. Contest speeds are pushing the 100 mph mark, and the choppers are getting ever more complex, more high tech, more expensive. It's not a do-it-yourself field. A dozen concerns, worldwide, supply virtually all the components used by 95% of today's heli fliers. As fixed-wing modeler Al Alman noted when he put together his first heli kit, "It was more like the Erector Set I had when I was eight years old . . . you don't build a chopper, you *assemble* it."

In this respect, helicopters may well be the paradigm for the future of the entire aeromodeling movement: fewer and fewer people doing the designing and creating, while more and more are content simply to buy someone else's pre-packaged experience.

Gliders and Old Timers

Two other branches of the R/C tree have flourished since the perfection of radio systems in the late sixties: gliders and old timers. Even though they seldom mix on the flying field, the two have much in common, socially as well as aerodynamically.

Both tend to draw former modelers back to the fold. These are the hobby's prodigal sons—the members of that vast prewar generation who, as children of the Air Age, learned to love making things that fly, but let it all slip during their marriage-and-family years. Retired now, and beyond the need to prove themselves in the eyes of their long-dead daddies, they take naturally to the low-key atmosphere of soaring and old-timer R/C, and for a host of reasons: nostalgia, relaxation, fellowship with kindred spirits, fresh air and sunshine, hand craftsmanship, the endless challenge of the invisible air.

If you're looking for a good argument, try raising the question of which is older, R/C gliding or OT radio. The oldtimers will maintain that radio-assisted freeflight goes back to day one, since ALL early R/C attempts were no more than assisted freeflight. U.S. glider guiders can trace their roots through a gaggle of Los Angeles slopers flying escapement off the Palos Verdes hills in the early fifties, all the way back to Clinton DeSoto's eighteen-foot gull-winged soarer described in the August 1938 issue of *Model Airplane News*. But in truth, neither of these present-day groups really began to come of age until the late sixties.

Old-timer R/C grew directly and naturally out of the OT freeflight movement of the early sixties, promoted on the west coast chiefly by John Pond and Bob Bowen, then by engine collector Tim Dannels in Denver, and later in the east by Joe Beshar, Dick Tanis and Woody Woodman.

When some of these free flighters began to agitate for R/C as a way to return their wandering models to the field after a max, the purists among them screamed bloody murder. But Pond, by now the Daddy Warbucks of the OT movement, was no more eager than the next fellow to spend the better part of his flying day tearing through the underbrush on a Honda 90. Slowly, and with great political finesse, he began to integrate the R/C crowd into the fold (labeling it, at first, "R/C assist.")

Today, though many of the staunchest supporters of the old timer movement fly both freeflight and R/C, competition at meets such as the annual SAM Champs has become so tough that only freeflight specialists do well in freeflight, only R/C specialists do well in R/C. Don't look for names like Don Bekins, Eut Tileston, Larry Davidson, Jack Alten or Walt Geary among the freeflight winners—just as you'll seldom find Don Weitz, Sal Taibi, Walt Bowers, Cliff Silva or Joe Foster among the R/C ranks.

Riding herd over both branches of the old timer movement is SAM, the Society of Antique Modelers, an AMA special interest group founded in 1964. SAM today has chapters in over half the states, a world-wide membership, and more events at its annual championships than the AMA Nationals had during its Navy-sponsored heydays!

Soaring

The full-scale soaring movement in America has never appealed to more than a single-digit percentage of all U.S. pilots—and the same is true of the R/C soaring movement among modelers. Like the old timer movement, soaring first began to blossom during the mid-sixties. By 1966, the year Maynard Hill of the DC/RC club published the first electric glider winch to appear in a U.S. model mag, the Harbor Slope Soaring Society (Costa Mesa, CA) was already three years old, boasting such members as Bob (*L'il T*) Hahn, Dale Willoughby, Dr. Rolf (son of Aimee Semple) McPherson, and SSA Director Bob Chase, who set an 8.5 hour world endurance record for R/C slopers back in 1956. But in the 3,000 lonely miles separating these two glider groups, two hundred other serious soaring addicts would have been hard to find.

In Germany, meanwhile, there was enough interest to support over a dozen commercial glider kits—kits like Shuco-Heigi's *Bergfalke* and *Ali*, Graupner's *Amigo* and *Foka*. Then in '68 came the Graupner *Cirrus,* followed in '70 by the *Cumulus*, and these were the two kits that got U.S. soaring off the ground.

Sales of these German kits encouraged a few hardy souls—Mark Smith, Lee Renaud, Roland and Bob Boucher, Dwight Hartman—to enter the glider market with designs of their own. (Like to play who-was-first? Try Frank Zaic's *Thermic 100*, advertised for R/C in the Air Trails *Annual*, February 1954. And toward the end of the fifties, Pactra Chemical—the Aero Gloss dope people—produced their 100" *Zeus* sailplane; then Duke Fox, in 1961-2, kitted a few of his 12-foot *Buzzards*. After that came the Jetco *Imperial R/C 100* and Hahn's *Li'l T* by Midwest, both in '68.)

By the beginning of the seventies, U.S. glider interest was starting to blossom. *Flying Models* was already publishing some of the best of the gigantic east-coast floaters, while *R/C Modeler* and Bill Northrop's newly-founded *Model Builder* began to push the more compact western designs. (*MAN* had by then lost sight of the big picture, and was becoming as slow as *American Modeler* at spotting new trends.)

The annual SOAR Nats, sponsored by Chicago's Silent Order of Aeromodeling by Radio, started its six-year run in 1970, while out on the west coast the first League of Silent Flight tournaments began. Soaring crept into the AMA rulebook, and from there into the Nats schedule. Over the years it has continued its quiet growth, until today it accounts for somewhere between five and ten percent of all R/C flying in America.

Electric Power

The latest twist in R/C is electric power, another idea pioneered in Germany, chiefly by the late Fred Militky of Graupner. Almost every branch of radio control—soaring, old timer, pattern, fanjet, seaplane and even helicopter—has been invaded during the past two decades by the electric motor and its accompanying battery pack.

Heavy and gutless at first, electric units have seen constant refinement over the years until today they are no longer gutless— merely heavy. The challenge they provide is to build light but strong, and the fraternity of modelers that has grown up around electric flying is small but dedicated. Reading the electric columns of the 90s is like reading the R/C columns of the early fifties—the writing is still warm and personal, with lots of names mentioned, lots of plugs for local and regional contests, and plenty of friendly chit-chat to lighten up the customary tips-and-technology format. There's an air of pioneering excitement still about electric flying— and pioneers, I keep noticing, have all the fun.

Roll Call: Magazines

Almost unnoticed in the shadow of the 'big' model magazines, dozens small mags have come and gone over the years. Statistics tell us that only one new business in ten lives to see its first anniversary, and model airplane publications are certainly no exception.

Who remembers the Boston-based *International Modeling Journal*, edited—for two issues—by Bruno Marchi and Bill Tyler during the mid-thirties? The single issue of *Model Aeronautics* that Frank Zaic put out in April of 1937? *Air World*, the brief follow-on to *Flying Aces*, which went belly-up in '47? *Model Aircraft Builder*, started (and ended) by Irv Polk in 1936? *Western Modeler*, edited by stunt man Jim Saftig during 1948 and 1949? *Model Craftsman*, a boat-plane-train-steam engine mag that started in 1935 (and became today's *Railroad Model Craftsman* in 1940?)

How about *Model Fun*, the short-lived 'Bobby Benson' (of the B-Bar-B Ranch) radio tie-in, launched in 1955 by *Flying Models*? Howard Puckett's *West Coast Model News*, a mini-magazine that John Pond says lasted thirty years? *Junior American Modeler*, that became *Sport Modeler* that died with its parent, *American Aircraft Modeler*, in 1975? Dale Willoughby's short-lived *Zephyr*, that grew out of the Harbor Slope Soaring Society's newsletter in 1964? *R/C Sportsman* of Reno, Nevada, that began as a tabloid newspaper and graduated to an 8.5 x 11 slick before it disappeared in 1982?

Who recalls the manufacturers' mags: *Cleveland Modelmaking News and Practical Hobbies*, published briefly in 1933? *Arpiem*, the hints-and-kinks mag published for three or four issues in 1938 by Bill Brown's Junior Motors Corporation? The *Sig Air-Modeler*, edited by Larry and Dotty Conover from mid-'66 to mid-'67? Or Ace R/C's marvelous *Grid Leaks*—1957 to 1966?

All these magazines and more have come and gone during American aeromodeling's eight decades. Some paid the bills for a while; a few even turned a small profit. But most—like so many business ventures within the hobby—were simply labors of love. And any love that's all labor is doomed from the start.

Chapter Ten

THE MAGAZINES

The Ties that Bind

*We anticipate that you, Model Aircraft Engineers, will advance
model flying to a point where models will stay aloft for hours.
Eventually, we believe, you will be able to control your model
while in the air and direct its course.*

> —editorial, Volume One Number One,
> *Model Aircraft Engineering,* April 1934

*Population goes up, circulations down—the trend now
for twenty years.*

> —Bill Winter in *American Modeler,*
> November 1967

*"Largest and most widely read model aviation publication
in the world!"*

> —*R/C Modeler* claim, October 1966

'Model Books'

The aeromodeling magazines of my childhood—*Model Airplane
News, Flying Models, Air Trails*—were elevated, in my private
vocabulary, to the status of books: I spoke (and still speak) of my
collection of model books, of some design that appeared in the
model books about 1955 . . . .

Yes, I know the difference between a book and a magazine. But
even as a kid, I also sensed a difference between *MAN* and, say, *The*

Saturday Evening Post—both of which came into our house on a regular basis. I read both from cover to cover. But only one of the two would be saved for rereading later—saved for future reference. The *Post,* as everyone knew, was just a magazine, something to be read and chucked. But *MAN,* like a good book, was forever.

Today I don't own a single 'real' book (hard cover, cloth binding, dust jacket) from my childhood. But I do have half a dozen *MAN's* from that period—yellowed pulp-paper mags with their Joe Kotula cover illustrations of Sopwith *Pups* and Douglas *Skyrays* and bright-red Fokker *Triplanes*—always in full, cloud-rending flight. Open any of them to page six, to the America's Hobby Center ad, and you'll find an order blank carefully pencilled in with childish dreams—O.K. Cub .039 engines, Berkeley *Zilch* stunters, *Kiwi* freeflights. Like most kids, my reach exceeded my grasp, and I filled in far more order blanks than I ever had the money to mail.

Just Imagine!

And filling in those order blanks was an important aspect of the hobby for every child of the Air Age. All that anticipation, all that dreaming was a cheap and bottomless source of delight. The aeromodeling hobby is nothing if not a field of dreams. We modelers dream over our building boards. We dream at the office. We dream at the hobby counter, and during church, and at the funerals of our wives' best friends. And—just as with any art form—most of the energy resides in the dream. A 1930 ad for the long-defunct Sunrise Model Airplane Supply of Cedarhurst, NY, says it all:

> *Just imagine taking this four-foot Model Glider out into the open, for the first time, and a few minutes later, seeing its long and tapered wing and shining silver fuselage tacking and turning and flowing with and against the wind, 400 or 500 and even 600 feet above the earth. Yes sir! Just imagine!*

It was the magazines of our childhood that helped us imagine—that filled the newsreels of our mind with gossamer dreams of flight.

And they still do.

Whipping Boys

Next to the AMA itself, the model mags are probably the Clan's favorite whipping boys. They provide us every month with something to gripe about: *RCM* is all advertising. *Flying Models* is too East Coast. *Model Aviation* tries to cover too many fields. *Model Builder* is getting overrun with R/C. And *Model Airplane News*, good old *Model Airplane News* . . . just isn't what it used to be.

But we continue to buy the mags every month—continue to buy them, and continue to gripe. Take them away and we'd be without a mirror, without any clear image of ourselves and our shared obsession. Take away the mags and the Clan would fragment even further, scattering into smaller and smaller specialty groups, less and less aware of one another, less and less able to speak each other's language, less and less clannish. Finally it would cease to exist altogether.

Roots in the Thirties

Today's model magazines, like all of the important elements of the hobby, came into full flower in the 1930s. Before Lindbergh, there wasn't enough interest in aeromodeling to support even one specialized publication on the subject. Before Lindbergh, information was passed among the Clan through two-page sections in the back of full-scale magazines. The hobby was hardly unique in this respect. Golf, ham radio, even baseball didn't get their own publications until the thirties.

Because the thirties was the Decade of the Magazine. The late twenties and early thirties brought cheap electricity to just about everybody and their great-aunt Hilda. At the same time, the Depression was hard at work sawing people's income in half. So what you had, by 1935, was a country full of poor folk, with lots of time on their hands and a 40-watt lightbulb overhead. The inexpensive pulp-paper magazine was the answer to their prayers.

Americans had been readers before the Great Depression, of course. But never in such numbers. And during the thirties their tastes began to change. What America read before the thirties was mostly fiction: dime novels, romance and adventure pulps, sleaze

249

newspapers, fat nineteenth-century gothics. But during the thirties, readers suddenly woke up to the twentieth century. They discovered Fact. They discovered the world of science and technology, and the great information age that was just beginning. *Lawd, Myrtle, them science-fellers are a-findin' out something new ever blessed day!* Books, like trains, suddenly seemed too slow to keep up with this rush of new ideas. Only magazines were quick enough to be "modern."

So magazines proliferated, and among them the three that prewar modelers considered theirs: *Air Trails, Flying Aces,* and *Model Airplane News.* These three, after a few years of fumbling and false starts, became the prototypes of every model magazine since. Let's take a look at them, one at a time.

Air Trails

While *MAN* will always be the first and oldest model mag, the history of Street & Smith's *Air Trails*, despite its late start, probably comes closer to mirroring the ups and downs of the long history of aeromodeling itself.

Air Trails—its last descendent died in 1975—liked to trace its roots back to October of 1928, when the first issue of a fiction magazine called *Air Trails: Stories of Aviation* hit the stands. Intended to capitalize on the post-Lindbergh air mania, that first *Air Trails* was a big disappointment to Street & Smith, the huge New York pulp-fiction house that created it. It never enjoyed more than a fraction of the popularity of Street & Smith's other pulps, particularly their westerns and detectives, some of which sold up to a million copies per issue. So when times got tough in 1930, this first *Air Trails* quietly disappeared.

But America's air mania didn't—and so the title was resurrected in August of 1932. The second *Air Trails* wasn't much different from the first: just a small, digest-sized magazine of adventure fiction. It staggered along for three lean years, averaging around 75,000 copies a month (a circulation figure, incidentally, that some of today's model mags would be delighted with.) Meanwhile,

Street & Smith began sizing up a couple of related fields that seemed to be on the rise: full-scale aviation and model airplanes.

Finally, in October of 1935, *Air Trails* took a giant gamble. It became *Bill Barnes' Air Trails*, a standard size (eight-and-a-half by eleven) magazine of "air fact and air fiction." The first issue featured a sleek, roadable autogyro on the cover—and a modest model-plane section tucked into the back pages.

Bill Barnes' Air Trails. To thousands of today's lifers—charter members of the aeromodeling Clan—those are holy words, evocative of some of the deepest memories of childhood. Adolescence is a bright and impressionable age, a period when child freedom and adult awareness briefly overlap, and the world for a time appears to be our oyster. The fiction we read during this time, like the music we dance to, is forever inscribed on our hearts. For America's Air Age generation, for those sky-minded children who were just pecking their way out of the shell during the heyday of Bill Barnes and Doc Savage and G-8, no other fictional heros can ever take their place.

The Tinsley Era

The new, larger format for Bill Barnes and his friends pleased no one more than a young commercial artist named Frank Tinsley. Tinsley had been illustrating Street & Smith westerns since the late twenties. But saddles and sunsets claimed only half his heart, for Frank Tinsley loved to draw airplanes, as well. He soon became chief illustrator for the new *Bill Barnes*, and there he stayed for nearly twenty years, finally quitting in disgust in 1954, when, in his words, "they converted *Air Trails* into a gadget book."

It was Tinsley who created every one of the famous Bill Barnes aircraft—*Bumblebee, Stormer, Lancer, Charger*—and worked closely on the story plots with the various writers hidden behind the by-line "George L. Eaton," supposed creator of Bill Barnes.

That's right, boys and girls of the Great Depression: *there was no George L. Eaton.* Eaton was a "house" name, and house names, as Tinsley loved to explain, are "a neat device whereby the publisher can fire an objectionable author (one that asks for more money) without changing the regular by-line on the stories."

No George L. Eaton! Another childhood hero bites the dust!

251

The Real George L.

A couple of New York freelancers, Harold 'Monty' Montayne and Chick Verral, are credited with turning out the bulk of the George L. Eaton yarns of the thirties. But the technical genius behind the tales, so often years ahead of air progress at the time, was largely Frank Tinsley's. (The Bill Barnes *Bumblebee*, for example, was a swing-wing with JATO—in 1934! Other Tinsley illustrations foreshadowed Doolittle's Tokyo Raiders as well as the Japanese kamikaze attacks of a war that was still six years in the future.)

Frank Tinsley, who had ridden with the horse cavalry in his youth, and begun his illustrating career in the dime westerns, went on to create the widely syndicated "Captain Yank" comic strip of World War II. Born in 1899, he was still doing work for *Mechanix Illustrated* (ironically, the epitome of all 'gadget books') well into the 1960s.

Adios, Billy Boy

It was Tinsley himself, and not the mythical George L. Eaton, who wrote the final chapter of the Bill Barnes legend. It appeared in the March 1951 issue of *Air Trails*. Our muscular hero, Tinsley says, disappeared on a confidential mapping mission somewhere over the Bering Sea in 1947, and was for a while presumed dead . . . but "recent reports have him very much alive, and a part of the guided missiles program." QED.

That 1951 *Air Trails* article, which featured three-views of most of the Barnes aircraft, was titled "Ahead of His Time: Bill Barnes—Prophet." The real prophet, of course, was Frank Tinsley himself.

Air Fiction, Air Fact . . . and a model or two

Air Trails' model coverage before the Tinsley era had been slim. By mid-summer of '36, however, less than a year into the new and larger format, the magazine was featuring two to three construction articles per issue. In early fall, a stocky young balsa butcher named William Winter—he much preferred plain 'Bill'—came aboard as associate editor at the princely sum of thirty dollars a week, and this event closely coincided with the real beginning of Street & Smith's bid for a piece of the aeromodeling pie.

Bill Barnes soon disappeared from the magazine's title, although adventure fiction by 'George L. Eaton' and others continued to dominate its pages. About this same time, Wakefield winner Gordon Light started his monthly "Model Workshop" column, later rechristened "The Dope Can," and *Air Trails* began a long series of marketing innovations that gave cigar-chewing old Charlie Grant, over at *Model Airplane News*, the fantods.

First came a series of contest-winning model designs, paid for out of Street & Smith's deep pockets. Goldberg's giant *Valkyrie*, then Chet Lanzo's 1937 Nats-winning R/C model, then Dick Korda's famous slab-sider known simply as the *Korda Wakefield* . . . and the list went on. Readers began to look to *Air Trails* for a new trophy-winner almost every month.

Another *Air Trails* innovation was "The Discussion Corner," in which experts were invited to incite one another with pro-and-con essays on such monthly topics as *Is streamlining worth the weight? Are adjustable-pitch props useful on outdoor models? Do twin rudders work better than single ones? Which is best, flatbottomed or undercambered airfoils?* This was the height of the design-it-yourself era, when just about everyone who called himself a model builder was prepared to argue such questions till dawn.

When times got dull, the *AT* crew would toss in a direct frontal assault: *Is Grant's "center of lateral area" argument pure malarkey?* (They didn't put it this bluntly, of course. Their question was, "What do you consider to be the best location for the thrust line relative to the profile view of the model?")

Free Plugs

Then, in 1938, came an entirely new wrinkle: the product review. *Air Trails* seems to have been the first model airplane magazine to discover that their readers weren't offended by ads, but were actually hungry for the information ads contained. The average reader, they found, made little distinction between advertising and editorial content. It was a profound discovery, and it put *Air Trails* years ahead of its time.

Paid advertising, which gobbles up thirty to forty percent of every issue, had always been considered—by editorial staffs, at least—as a kind of necessary evil, a mildly embarrassing way of paying the bills. The 'real' magazine, in their eyes, was that other sixty percent, the part they filled with "news." But along about 1938, *Air Trails* came suddenly to the realization that *new products are news, too.*

In a rapidly-changing hobby, one fed largely by cottage industries, a new gadget could be introduced, or an old one upgraded, after every weekend flying session. Readers wanted to know about these advances, these overnight leaps in technology. But most manufacturers, because they were small, couldn't afford to buy the space to tell their stories.

The answer to this dilemma was the product review. When *Air Trails* discovered how well these free plugs worked for all concerned—readers, publishers, advertisers—they began to create endless variations on the theme. One of the most successful was the monthly engine review. This was later expanded to an annual roundup of motors that included full-size three view drawings of every engine being built—a marvelous resource for designers and dreamers alike.

Another form of free plug was the trade gossip column ("Don't Quote Me") in which new developments, and the occasional trial balloon, were 'leaked' to the public in advance of production. These ran for years in *Air Trails* under the byline 'The Traveling Salesman,' turned out by the omniscient Irving Polk, who knew everyone worth knowing in the trade.

Heady Times

We're talking late thirties now, and these were heady times for *Air Trails.* They had one foot in models and the other in full-scale aviation, and their ad revenues during this period began to climb straight up with no loss of airspeed. New engine manufacturers— and there seemed to be a couple of new ones every month—popped for full-page ads. Aviation schools like Spartan of Tulsa and Embry-Riddle in Miami touted their engineering and mechanic and drafting programs. Lucky Strike cigarettes monopolized the back cover, in color, while the muscular Mr. Charles Atlas peddled his pre-steroid body within, and an endless stream of kit and accessory makers provided the hundreds of 'popcorn' ads that filled every nook and cranny of every issue.

Free Kits

About this time—almost as if flaunting its wealth—*Air Trails* itself turned advertiser. It began a series of full-page ads in its nearest rival, *Model Airplane News,* offering a bonus kit with every *AT* subscription. (Bonus kits were another Street & Smith gimmick that the other mags could only imitate. Over ten thousand of Jim Cahill's Wakefield-winning *Clodhopper II's* went out in 1938, when subscriptions cost $1.50; by 1941 it was a Class A *Buzzard Bombshell*. Ten years later you could still get a 24" Sterling *Maverick* U-Control with a year's subscription, now up to $2.50.)

Four Hours by Air

In July of '38, the magazine flew (*flew!*) Gordon Light and Bill Winter to Detroit to cover the Nationals. The trip took Winter and Light just under four hours in a twin-engined Boeing 247, while a group of their New York flying buddies spent 36 hours (and two flat tires) covering the same hot, steamy ground in an open-windowed automobile. Sweet are the rewards of success!

All this time, the fictional Bill Barnes continued to dominate the *Air Trails* front pages, dogfighting it out with villains like the suave and wealthy Mordecai Murphy, "the Saver of Souls." But fiction was on the way out at *Air Trails.* By September of 1938 the mag's lone air novel was introduced with an apologetic note pointing out its educational and prophetic value. *[Bill Winter, in a 1991 letter: "I, personally, killed Bill Barnes to free* Air Trails.*"]*

'Air fact' was clearly the wave of the future, for a new war was brewing in Europe, and a dozen countries were building up their air forces. Reality, in 1939, was just about to overtake imagination.

Ten by Fourteen

In November of '39 *Air Trails* took another giant leap, this time to a *Life*-sized format. It was one of the few innovations that the other model mags never attempted to copy. The new 10" x 14" pages made the mag awkward to store, but photographs looked great.

(The change came just in time to present full-size root ribs for Maurice Schoenbrun's flounder-shaped *Rocketeer* cabin model.)

Two years later, in 1941, came yet another 'first.' *Air Trails* became the only model magazine to offer, by mail, full-sized plans for its construction projects. Plan prices started at a quarter, but soon dropped to a dime. The magazine itself still sold for 15¢.

This Fellow Adolph

Then came Pearl Harbor, and America, after twenty-seven months of pseudo-neutrality, finally took on its share of the European war. The highlight of that first war year, 1942, was a February article contrasting our government's lack of support for model building with that of other nations—particularly Nazi Germany. The article's opening line was a classic: "Say what you like about this fellow Adolph," it began, "he certainly has been one of the greatest boosters model aviation has ever had . . . ."

Modeling coverage, like modeling itself, suffered during the four-year conflict. War planes and war news overran the pages of *Air Trails,* and even though the bulk of the mag's wartime advertising was still model-oriented, the modeling section itself faded back into the far reaches of the book—back into those same endpages from which it had so recently emerged. The draft decimated the *AT* staff. Bill Winter, with more kids than even a New York draft board could count, moved into the editor's seat in '43. (He'd been *de facto* editor for years.)

But even Winter couldn't create news in a vacuum. Except for a few hardy pioneers in U-Control and a lot of hot air about rules and dethermalizers, not much happened among the Clan during the war.

Postwar Prosperity

1946, however, was a different story. In the months following V-J Day, advertising dollars—the lifeblood of every magazine—rained down once more upon the *Air Trails* roof. Most of the prewar manufacturers sprang back to life, while GIs flocked home to found new companies by the dozen. Wholesale houses got into shouting matches with one another, competing for the business of the hundreds of new hobby shops that were popping up all over America. And because *Air Trails* was *Air Trails,* and not *Model Airplane News,* even full-scale manufacturers—Piper, Aeronca, Culver—began shoveling money at the mag.

And the magazine blossomed. One of Winter's flying buddies, Walt Schroder, slipped in under the Winter wing as Model Editor. Charlie Grant, instead of returning to his old desk at *MAN,* took over the *Air Trails* 'Club Chatter' column, and was promptly dispatched to the Hotel Allis in Wichita, Kansas, to cover the '46 Nationals. Meanwhile, editor Winter began behaving strangely: he took to slipping off at odd hours for full scale flying lessons.

Sure enough, with the September '46 issue Bill Winter's name disappeared from the *Air Trails* masthead, later to resurface at *Flying,* a full-scale mag. Walt Schroder had bailed out a month earlier, to try his hand at building Mite diesels for a living. Both men continued to crank out freelance pieces for Street & Smith, but they were now at liberty to publish in *Flying Aces* and *MAN* as well—and they did.

Within months the reason for their defection became obvious. When the January 1947 *Air Trails* hit the newsstands, it was no longer *Air Trails.* With the suddenness of death, it had become something called *Air Trails and Science Frontiers.*

Science Frontiers?

Smokin' rockets, Flash! Street & Smith had come up with another one of their *marketing innovations*—and a real doozy this time. What in blazes was 'science frontiers'? (The cover shot—a close-up of the meteor-pocked surface of the moon, gave a hint.)

Air Trails had taken a giant leap into the future that left most of its regular readers a decade behind . . . and colder than outer space. In the year 1947, nobody in the aeromodeling world gave a sweet round damn about science frontiers, about rockets and moon landings and Willy Ley and Robert Goddard and Werner Von Braun—all that Buck Rogers stuff.

In 1947, *Air Trails* readers wanted to know about Jim Walker's new Remoto U-Reely controlline handle—about Ray Arden's 'incandescent' glow plug—about scale modeler Louis Casale's sleek, aluminum-bodied, ready-to-fly *Casalaire* ukie, made out in L.A. by the Tilson Brothers.

They wanted to read about barefoot Davy Slagle, the wonder boy of stunt, and J.C. "Madman" Yates, and their prewar heroes Goldberg and Struck, and the Brooklyn Sky Scrapers and the Cleveland Balsa Butchers and the Chicago Aeronuts. They wanted to know if the rumor coming out of Little Rock was really true: was John 'Kingfish' Sadler, that quiet, pipe-puffing proponent of low-wing free flight, *really* getting into U-Control speed?

Science frontiers, indeed!

One-Third, Two-Thirds, plus Tinsley

Beginning with that January issue, newsstand sales plummeted, and Street & Smith took the hint. By October, 'science frontiers' went away—disappeared quietly into the ozone—and the magazine shrank modestly back to its prewar 8.5" x 11" format. Sales recovered, and by the fall of 1948 *Air Trails* found itself slipping into its third decade of life with almost exactly the same mixture that had made it so successful during the late thirties: one-third full scale, two-thirds models, and a Frank Tinsley illustration on the cover.

A small, quiet man named Albert L. Lewis, co-founder and past president of the A.M.A. (and, incidentally, author of that immortal line about *this fellow Adolph*) was now flying left seat at *Air Trails,* a cockpit position he would retain, through bad times and worse, for the next eighteen years.

The price of everything from candy to Cadillacs had doubled during World War II. The postwar *Air Trails* now sold for a flat round quarter, and those 10¢ full-size plans of 1941 had jumped to 35¢ each—a discouraging amount of money to younger modelers. And Al Lewis cared about younger modelers.

For a few months after he took over, Lewis tried publishing two full-size plans per issue, printed back-to-back on a triple foldout page (Jim Walker's whip-control *Thunderjet* was one of the first.) It was a grand gesture, and the hobby was better for it. But the postoffice screamed when magazines fell open in transit, and the policy soon went away.

Different League

At this point—1948—both *Air Trails* and the sport of aero-modeling were at their social and economic high-water mark. The magazine was up to 134 pages, and pushing 200,000 circulation (more monthly readers, as Bill Winter pointed out in 1985, than all five of the mid-eighties model mags combined.) Science frontiers were long forgotten, and happy days had come again.

This brief postwar boom at *AT* is remembered fondly by retired AMA director John Worth, who was just beginning to write for the mags at that time. "In those days," John recalls, *"Air Trails* was THE model magazine to write for. It was in a different league from *MAN."* A feature article, with pencilled plans, might net you a $200 check—the buying-power equivalent of $800 to $1000 today. (Try getting more than $300 for that same article now!)

But was Street & Smith content to be rolling in this high clover? Oh hell no. Eighty years of publishing experience had convinced them that good times don't last. Science frontiers might have flopped, but they kept right on scratching about for other ways to exploit this floodtide.

Baker's Dozen

One answer was to revive and upgrade the *Air Trails Model Annual.* "Annuals" had been around since before the war. They were a publisher's dream—and an editor's nightmare. An annual added another full round of ads to the year's twelve-month cycle. Best of all, they squeezed a thirteenth magazine out of the same staff that had formerly been producing twelve.

Hoo-eee! More work for the same money! But the long-suffering Al Lewis hung in there, one of the few people left at *AT* who really gave a damn about all those toy planes that filled the back two-thirds of the magazine. (Cartoonist C.B. Colby, nominal editor before Winter elbowed him out in '43, *hated* model planes.)

The postwar *Air Trails Annuals* were a great success. With monthly magazine sales at an all-time high of 231,000, and the *Annuals* selling up to a quarter-million on the newsstands, *Air Trails* moved into the second half of the century at the very pinnacle of the aeromodeling heap.

Stick Forward and Locked

But Street & Smith was right: good times don't last. As the fifties wore on, the magazine's circulation figures first levelled out, then nosed over, and finally tucked into a near-vertical dive. In the face of the postwar baby boom—the biggest indigenous population spurt in U.S. history—*Air Trails* readership began plunging down, down, down.

Two factors were at work. First, the model airplane hobby—like aviation as a whole—had begun to lose its widespread appeal and public support. Casual newsstand browsers no longer reached automatically for any magazine with a flying machine on the cover. Second, television was starting to chip away at magazine readership—*all* magazine readership. (It took another twenty-five years for magazines to bounce back from the blow TV gave them during the fifties and sixties. An entire generation of Americans had to teach themselves how to read with one eye and watch the tube with the other.)

As early as 1953, *Air Trails'* newsstand sales began to reflect this downslide. Street & Smith—now 98 years old and with its assets tied 100% to the printed word—panicked. They began grasping at straws. They pushed *Air Trails* into a long series of dead-end paths: career counseling and bicycle repair and amateur photography and magic tricks—just about anything they thought might attract youthful readers.

The April 1954 issue was the beginning of the end. That was the month that *Air Trails* became *Air Trails Hobbies for Young Men.* The new title—as long and gangly and unfocused as the teenagers they were hoping to reach—didn't help a bit. Neither did shortening it the following year to the even more meaningless *Young Men,* and putting pictures of flathead Ford street rods on the cover.

The Best Policy?

This shotgun approach to youth interests simply failed. Two years later, in December of 1956, the title was changed once more, back to something that more closely reflected the magazine's readership and ad content, which had changed little in twenty years: *Young Men* became *American Modeler.*

But honesty, it turned out, was no better policy, and *"American Modeler"* went limping into the lean decade, the post-Sputnik sixties, at less than half its 1950 speed, Al Lewis still valiantly at the controls. It survived a takeover by rival publisher Condé Nast in 1962, and a change the following year to bi-monthly publication, an economy move that *Flying Models* had also been forced into. During these tenuous times, only *Model Airplane News* managed to remain monthly.

With every issue, *American Modeler* seemed to grow more sluggish, its cover art darker and more ominous. When, in 1963, a hungry new west-coast magazine called *R/C Modeler* rose up to take a bite of the shrinking aeromodeling pie, and, at the same time, the slotcar-racing fad sprang out of nowhere, it was a full twelve months before either of these events registered on the moribund *American Modeler*. At last it replied, almost inaudibly, with a new subtitle: "Cars—R/C—Planes," its cover mumbled.

The pulse was weak, the patient barely responding to stimuli.

Demons

And then, in mid-summer of 1966, just when death seemed immanent, one of those rare medical miracles occurred. The patient not only recovered—it leaped out of bed, put on its old business suit, and went back to work for another nine years! Some said it was an organ transplant, while others saw it as a clear case of possession by demons.

The known facts of the case are few: A model-minded gentleman named Ed Sweeney bought *American Modeler* from Condé Nast, lock, stock and liabilities, retired Al Lewis and put Bill Winter in his chair. At the same time John Worth, newly-appointed Executive Director of the ailing AMA, halted publication of *Model Aviation,* the Academy's thirty-year-old, on-again-off-again newsletter, and turned the job of publishing the Academy's news over to *American Modeler*. In exchange, Sweeney was allowed to integrate the AMA's 20,000-member subscription list with his own.

All this was done in the dark of night, without so much as a leaked rumor to the AMA's membership. The first clue anyone had was the cover of the July/August *American Modeler,* which appeared by magic in every member's mailbox. "Cars—R/C—Planes" was gone from the subtitle. In its place was the curiously familiar line, "The MODEL AVIATION Magazine."

Under the Table

Economically, it was a good move for both parties, as under-the-table deals ought to be. (Bernie Winston, of America's Hobby Center, claimed his *American Modeler* ad response instantly jumped 32%.) But the other model mags screamed bloody murder. Why wasn't the publication of AMA news put up for bid among them all? Why should they continue to support the Academy of Model Aeronautics, which was now in bed with one of their competitors?

Neither question was ever really answered to everyone's satisfaction, and John Worth, the man who guided the Academy from a deficit position in the early sixties to the largest sport aviation organization in the world before his retirement in 1990, remains to this day the arch-villain of the east in the minds of many longtime Clan members.

But the *Air Trails* story doesn't end there. A couple of years later *American Modeler* changed its name one more time, to *American Aircraft Modeler.* Then, in March of 1975, despite its lucrative AMA connection, it collapsed once again. This time it died on the spot—from simple mismanagement, if we can believe the autopsy.

The AMA, left without a voice, decided to revive its old newsletter in the form of a full-fledged, ad-supported monthly—the current *Model Aviation.* And if you think the other mags screamed when the AMA subsidized one of their competitors, what do you suppose they said when the AMA *became* one of their competitors?

Flying Aces, Flying Models

The current *Flying Models* was born in June of 1947, right in the middle of the postwar modeling renaissance. It arose from the ashes of two older magazines—at least that's the company myth—

and until 1953 it still carried the subtitle "Including Air World and Flying Aces" on its cover.

I have a soft spot for *Flying Models*. *FM* got into model airplanes about the same time I did. *FM* was pretty juvenile during the forties and fifties—and so was I. Of all the model mags, it wasted the least time on full-scale aircraft, and that suited my prejudices, too. Furthermore, it didn't seem to give a damn about its image—about what outsiders might think of it. Right from day one, *Flying Models* knew who it was and what it liked. And what it liked was sport model aircraft of all types—strictly fly-for-fun stuff.

FM has always looked (to anyone who pays attention to ad space) like it was just on the verge of bankruptcy. It never could afford to compete with *Air Trails* or even *MAN* for the latest and hottest contest designs. So it targeted the sport modeler—the guy who builds and flies and crashes just for grins. When controlline was king, *FM* published ukie flying saucers. When 1/2-A engines temporarily revived freeflight in the early fifties, it gave us FF flying wings and silly, deltoid-shaped space ships. In between, there were balloon-powered lifting bodies and simple catapult gliders and twin-fin rubber models with little heart-shaped rudders to give to your sweetie on Valentine's. Kid stuff.

Not the sort of magazine to take itself—or the hobby—too seriously. As a child, I liked that a lot. And so I always supposed that *FM's* predecessor, *Flying Aces,* was cut from pretty much the same cloth.

What a disappointment, then, to root through the AMA's Renaud Library and discover that *Flying Aces* was—right up to its death in 1946—predominantly a fullscale and fiction magazine, and not like *Flying Models* at all! About all the two mags had in common was cheap pulp paper and a firm conviction that their average reader was hopelessly adolescent in both body and mind.

Fiction Forever

The hard-nosed Charlie Grant had purged *Model Airplane News* of its fiction stories early in the thirties. *Air Trails*, under Bill Winter, abandoned potboilers just before the war. That left only

Flying Aces in the air-fiction business, and they never bailed out—they rode it all the way down.

If you loved those old *Flying Aces* stories in your youth, take my advice and don't try to reread them now. Like most juvenile fiction, they're pretty embarrassing to adult eyes. They're potboilers, pure and simple, and potboilers weren't meant to last. At 1¢ to 2¢ a word, "air novel" writers were into quantity, not quality—they ground that stuff out by the ream, and the editors poured it into their white space like swampwater.

For years the *Flying Aces* motto was "Three Aviation Magazines in One"—meaning air fiction, air fact, and modeling. But it was fiction that filled the bulk of every issue, and much of their "fact" was little more than thinly disguised fiction: speculations about which countries' air forces were likely to meet in battle next, or how the Nazis might go about attacking the Panama Canal.

"During the thirties, *Flying Aces* couldn't wait for another war to begin," lifetime modeler Terry Tombaugh once told me. "They were tired of re-fighting World War I." He said this with a shy grin, and I could hear the affection in his voice. There was obviously something in these yellowing pulp pages that I was missing—something that wasn't, after all these years, recoverable even *between* the lines, where all the best history is written.

Mystery Solved!

So I called Bill Northrop, founder of *Model Builder*—he had once declared *Flying Aces* to be "that greatest of all model magazines"—and asked him what was going on. And Bill cleared up the mystery for me with a simple confession: *it was air fiction that drew him into modeling, not vice-versa.* As a child, he was a voracious reader. He loved air stories, and read them wherever he found them. *Flying Aces* had more air stories than anyone else. (The editor at the time was fiction writer Arch Whitehouse, creator of 'Crash' Carringer.)

Then, said Bill, there were all those little airplane plans back in the endpages. After a while they began to look kinda interesting, so he built one or two. And that's how another lifetime modeler was created . . . .

Frank Zaic, semi-retired now and living in the San Fernando Valley, agrees. "The model plans were an extra gift," Zaic remembers; he too bought *Flying Aces* primarily for the stories. Phineas Pinkham made the magazine feel "more intimate," in Zaic's words, than Charlie Grant's *Model Airplane News,* with its earnest desire to teach, teach, teach.

More intimate. More human. These are the terms people use over and over to describe *Flying Aces.* Clan members have always been dreamers; now I began to understand that many of them dreamed in flesh and blood as well as spruce and muslin. And who was more flesh-and-blood than bumbling old Phineas Pinkham, that intrepid Ace of the Great War from Waterloo, Iowa?

Classics

For all its fiction orientation, however, *Flying Aces* still managed to publish its share of classic model designs. The magazine's star designer, before the war, was young Ben Shershaw: his *Cumulus, Cloud Cruiser, Champion, Cadet, Folly, Miss Exchange Club,* and *Pioneer* are all well-known gassies that first appeared in *FA.* Earl Stahl published most of his rubber scale designs there, as well as his *Hurricane, Gypsy* and *Hi Climber* sport models. Throughout the thirties, Lou Garami was a regular *FA* contributor, and names like Plecan, Weathers, Bassett, McCullough, DeAngelis, Effinger, Bowers and Schoenfeld appeared, too.

Despite these big-name contributors, though, *Flying Aces* became one of the first victims of the great economic shakeout of 1946. The magazine had put its money on war fiction, and nobody wanted to read about war in '46. The publishers finally realized this, and tried to turn *FA* into a fullscale mag, *Flying Age.* When that failed they created, briefly, the prototype of today's in-flight airline mags—a where-to-go, what-to-see publication called *Flying Age Traveler.* "We don't have to sell aviation anymore," the August 1946 issue proclaimed. "*Flying Age Traveler* will be everyone's magazine."

But the idea was twenty years too soon. In the winter of 1946-7 most Americans were still traveling by car and bus and train, and the publishers' dream of a "fashion, entertainment, humor" magazine for air travelers was hopelessly premature. *Traveler* died in the spring of '47, and the mag's meager assets were sold to a couple of New York crossword-puzzle publishers named Joe Hardie and Raymond Kelly.

The First FM

At that point, *Flying Models* was born. The first issue, dated June 1947, told you everything you needed to know about the philosophy of the new owners. And it was almost all good.

For starters, there were five construction articles in this premier issue: a gassie, two rubber jobs (an indoor and an outdoor), a solid-scale Fokker *Triplane* and a sport U-Control model. The gassie, featured on the cover, was Bernie Schoenfeld's *Lilliput*, a classic little polyhedral cabin model with lovely elliptical lines, .09 powered, with a rocket climb and an old-fashioned two-wheel landing gear. (One foot in the past, one in the future . . . exactly like the magazine itself.)

"With Model Builders" and "Logging the Motor Mart" were there, two regular columns, one chatty and one technical, that ran unchanged for decades (the former lasted into the slick-paper era of the seventies.) AMA Director Russ Nichols was given a page for Academy news, and every corner of the new mag was stuffed with hints and kinks, with drawings and photos and info on the latest (as well as the oldest) building and finishing tricks. Something, in short, for everyone.

Two slender threads tied the new *Flying Models* to the old *Flying Aces*. On page 34 of this first issue, an attempt was made to revive the defunct Flying Aces Club. And our old friend Phineas Pinkham appeared in a short fiction yarn starting on page 38. But both of these were back-of-the-book items, and neither survived the first year of publication.

Before that first year was over, in fact, the new mag was already attracting writers like Cal Smith, Bill Winter, Walt Schroder, Gordon Light, Bruce Wennerstrom, Bill Dean and Hank Cole. Then, in 1950, *FM* began its yearly practice of scooping the other mags by a full month with Nationals photo coverage. "Details next issue," they promised, but meanwhile, here were dozens of sharp black-and-white shots of the July Nats—the first glimpse most modelers would get of the annual gathering of the clan.

The prolific illustrator and model designer Cal Smith held the *FM* editor's position briefly during 1947-8, before it was taken over by old-time modeler Walter Holtze. Holtze guided the mag until 1957, then dropped back to managing editor under Bob Buragas (and, later, Don McGovern.)

Fixit

This was the 'Fixit Wright' era at *Flying Models*, when readers were instructed every month, via an Archie-and-Jughead style cartoon, on such modeling basics as how to install a bellcrank or retrieve a freeflight from a tree. It was Buragas who contributed some of the best story lines for the strip, which lasted a little over a decade.

A number of illustrators drew Fixit and Tailskid and Bunny over the years, including George Heil, Bruce Wennerstrom, Frank O'Conner, and late-fifties cover artist Gil Evans. Evans drew the sexiest Bunny of all—a long-legged, long-haired combination of Jayne Mansfield and the girl-next-door—and this was the Bunny who was still outsmarting and outflying the boys in May of 1958, when the series came to a sudden and unheralded end. (The June issue, out in early May, contained Jim Walker's obituary, but no sign of Fixit and friends. It was a bad spring for heroes—and heroines.)

Throughout the sixties, under Don McGovern's editorship, *FM* kept intact its Hardie-Kelly diversity and its fly-for-fun philosophy, even though Ray Kelly died in '61 and Joe Hardie in '67, and the magazine had passed, by decade's end, into the hands of railroad-mag publisher (and longtime modeler) Hal Carstens.

Slick

In 1971 *Flying Models* 'went slick', dropping their old pulp newsprint in favor of a whiter, tighter bond. Don Dewey's highly successful *R/C Modeler* had introduced slick paper in 1963, and by now—these were the hobby's leanest years, remember—all the other mags had pretty much quit thinking for themselves and begun simply imitating whatever *RCM* did.

267

Radio control was coming of age—just completing its long evolution from a tinkerer's delight to a packaged consumer item—and out in California *RCM* was surfing the crest of this new advertising wave. Freeflight and U-Control were in eclipse, boats and cars only slightly on the rise. The money and excitement was all in radio control, so *Flying Models*, like everyone else, veered in that direction.

But not completely. Even today, under its current editor, controlline expert Bob Hunt, *FM* still manages to publish a good mix of the modeling spectrum. Don't look for the old Hardie-Kelly ideal of five new plans a month, though—there just aren't that many original designers left among us any more.

Model Airplane News

Model Airplane News began with the January and February issues of 1929. These were the two 'false start' issues that have never been officially recognized as part of the magazine's history. And no wonder—they were pretty awful. Then came a blissful silence for four months, followed by the July issue, with its famous boy-launching-Curtiss Hawk cover painting, and this is the magazine that begins *MAN*'s official corporate history.

In the eyes of most Clan members, however, *Model Airplane News* didn't really get off the ground until December of 1931, when an Army-trained aeronautical engineer named Charles Grant captured the editor's chair. Before Grant, *MAN* wasn't so much edited as simply compiled. Filling a monthly magazine is never easy, but some of those pre-Grant issues were—to put it kindly—under-inspired.

Rambling fiction stories would fill half or more of every issue. Full-size plans for even the simplest models would be spread over ten to twelve pages, so that an entire page might have nothing on it but a few rib bays of one wing panel. The writing was often garbled. Here are the trimming instructions—complete and unabridged—for a DeHavilland *Moth* rubber model in the August 1930 issue:

*'When the balancing point has been found, work it
back and forth and set the wing 1/3 forward of it.'*

And lots of luck to you, flying fans!

Loftus-Price

MAN's editor in these pre-Grant years was one Captain H. J. Loftus-Price, reputed to be an English airman from the Great War. This was an era when aviation charlatans—aces from the European front who had never been east of Brooklyn—could be found in every corner bar. For this reason, many people have assumed that Loftus-Price was just another 'house' name, and not a real person at all. Not true: the man's picture appears in the August 1931 issue, standing just behind New York Mayor Jimmie Walker and another near-mythical character of the era, that future *fuehrer* of the Junior Birdmen, Lawrence Shaw.

MAN's resident guru of aeronautics at the time was a WW I Austrian engineer, one Professor T.N. de Bobrovsky, whose chief contribution to the hobby was to popularize the term *leading edge* for the then-current "entering edge." The professor's aerodynamics were sound, but his full-scale history was, not surprisingly, a bit Eurocentric. (He credits Henri Farman, for example, with the first 360° turn, forgetting that the Wrights were making forty-minute flights around the patch at Huffman Prairie *four years* before anyone else on the planet had learned how to bank an aeroplane without dying.)

Not surprisingly, Professor de Bobrovsky disappeared without a trace the minute Charlie Grant came aboard.

Gimmicks

Grant inherited two circulation-building gimmicks from Loftus-Price. The first was reflected in the magazine's full title at the time of the changeover: *Junior Mechanics and Model Airplane News.* The 'junior mechanics' referred to occasional shop projects that Loftus-Price would use to fill up some of that monthly white space: canoes, mouse traps, canvas wood carriers, Morris chairs for the den. Grant lost no time in dropping this junior mechanics foolishness: he had hired on to edit a *model airplane* magazine, not to write about Morris chairs.

269

The second gimmick was MAN's 'house' club, the American Sky Cadets. Charlie Grant had graduated to the editor's desk directly from the exalted position of New Hampshire State Commander of these same Sky Cadets. But that didn't stop him from chucking them overboard at the first opportunity. Grant just couldn't bring himself to grind out the sort of patriotic twaddle that the fictitious "Commander Carlson" was writing for the Air Adventurers Club over at *Air Trails*. White space was precious, and, to Charlie Grant's way of thinking, the world was much in need of solid technical information about flight.

Kotula

One of Grant's first moves was to hire a new illustrator, a young man just arrived in New York City from the wilds of the southwest—a fellow who claimed to have flown *Jennies* and studied art in Tulsa. Did the young man have a pilot's license? He didn't. Could he draw? He could. Within months he was promoted from illustrator to cover artist, a position he held at *Model Airplane News* for 37 years—until publisher Jay Cleveland retired in 1969.

The young man's name was Josef Kotula. He really *had* flown Jennies in Oklahoma, and proved it by soloing a *Cub* in '36, after just three and a half hours of dual. In his long illustrating career, Jo Kotula probably saw his name on more magazine covers than any other American artist except Norman Rockwell.

Slogans

MAN's slogan, in 1932, became "A Course in Aviation for Fifteen Cents a Month," reflecting the new editor's interest in full-scale as well as model aviation. (Grant continued full scale design work throughout his eleven years of *MAN* editorship. He held nineteen aircraft patents during his lifetime.) Despite the depression, circulation took a jump that year—a sign that the magazine's fullscale slant was appreciated. The following year the cover price rose confidently from 15¢ to 20¢, and its slogan became "The Only Magazine Devoted Exclusively to Experimental Aviation."

It was under Charlie Grant that *Model Airplane News* worked out the basic model-magazine formula for the thirties, the formula that *Air Trails* and *Flying Aces* both adopted as the decade progressed. It was a simple one. On the cover you put a 'real' airplane. Up front you packed in half a dozen articles on full scale aviation—some historical, some up-to-the-minute, some fiction. Then came the models: two, three, as many as five construction projects. Some contest reports. Some name-dropping. Some news of the Clan.

The full scale stuff up front was the bait that sold extra copies on the news stands. Few modelers objected to it; scale has always been part of the modeling picture. After the war, and after *Flying Aces* went belly-up, *MAN* cut back its fullscale coverage to one or two pieces a month. But it clung faithfully to those Kotula cover paintings of fullscale aircraft.

World War II was tough on *MAN*. Charlie Grant left in '43, and the mag was officially without an editor for the duration. Freelance writer Howard McEntee took on the job in October of '45, but revenues continued to fall, and while *Air Trails* was growing fat on the modeling renaissance of the late forties, *MAN* kept losing weight: by 1950 it was down to a lean 56 pages.

The Winter Season

Stability didn't return until the magazine hired Bill Winter as editor, in 1950. By then Winter had been freelancing for a couple of years, and was ready to return to harness—and a regular paycheck. All his old editing skills, learned at *Air Trails* under Street & Smith, came back in a flash: reader surveys, product reviews, a careful mix of full scale and model material. Plus plenty of plans.

Winter was, beyond question, the most professional editor in the modeling field. His personal biases seldom showed through. Rubber and gas, controlline and freeflight and radio all got their fair share of space. He had an unfailing eye for good design in every field. When, during Nats awards ceremonies, other editors would approach a winner about buying his design, they often found that Bill Winter had been there first—well before the contest began.

His monthly editorial, "MAN at Work," was usually worth, by itself, the price of the magazine. Few other writers could paint the big picture of our hobby the way Bill Winter could. (Few other writers could even see it.) For ten long years, from 1950 to 1960,

MAN grew and prospered on the energy of this one man. As late as 1966, *Model Airplane News* could still boast the top paid circulation of any American model mag.

When Winter quit to go back to freelancing in the summer of 1960, his old pal Walt Schroder took the reins, mumbling, "I'm always following Bill Winter"—and just in time to reap the publicity from the famous U-2 spy plane incident. Winter had published three views of this 'top secret' craft more than two years earlier, and when the story broke, *Model Airplane News* became front page copy all over America.

Schroder stuck to Winter's formula for the next two decades. Walt was neither a thinker nor a writer . . . more of a diarist . . . but his heart was in the right place: he loved the whole hobby, and respected its history even as he garbled it hopelessly in editorials.

But Schroder, along with publisher Jay Cleveland, were the last of the old guard. When, in 1969, Cleveland retired, time was already beginning to catch up with *Model Airplane News*. The magazine's principal owners, the DeFrancisco family, were patient. They kept Schroder aboard—even elevating him to the title of President and Publisher. But when Walt finally stepped down in late '78, it must have been a great relief. MAN was at last free to follow the market, which was by then almost 100% R/C-dominated.

Slowly, throughout the 1980s, the DeFranciscos began turning *MAN* into a clone of *R/C Modeler*. To do otherwise made no business sense. Let *Flying Models* and the AMA's *Model Aviation* ride herd on 'old fashioned' modeling: indoor and freeflight and controlline and all their confusing splinter groups. By the late 1980s, ninety percent of America's aeromodeling dollar was being spent by R/Cers; who could blame *Model Airplane News* for following the crowd?

R/C Modeler

To anyone with an eye for the bottom line, 1963 must have looked like one of the worst times in history to launch a new model airplane magazine. The industry was deep in the post-Sputnik doldrums; nothing was selling but plastics and slot cars and a few zip-bang rockets. Freeflight was 'dead' once again, R/C hadn't yet taken off, and even controlline—that mainstay of the hobby since World War II—seemed to be on its last legs.

Flying Models was down to fifty pages every other month, and *American Modeler*—that sad ghost of the old *Air Trails*—had been forced to go bi-monthly that very spring. Only an outsider to the hobby industry, an outsider and a hopeless optimist, would dream of going after a piece of such a shrinking pie.

Out in Sierra Madre, a small foothill town at the northeastern fringes of Los Angeles, lived just such a person. He was a lifer, a modeler-since-childhood who had just recently discovered the joys and sorrows of radio control. No big-name designer, no contest winner, this fellow—just your average-joe sport flier with a bottomless passion for the hobby.

His name was Donald Dewey, and his qualifications for magazine publishing included a couple of stints as editor of a club newsletter, and . . . well, so much for qualifications. Oh, yes: he was a good writer, and a fair typist, and he could spell. Also, he was likeable and surfer-boy handsome, with a breathtakingly photogenic wife named Sally—and good looks are no liability in American business. Also, he had a flying buddy and business partner named Chuck Waas, who was just as wild-eyed and optimistic as himself.

Last but not least, Don Dewey had, across the front of his house in Sierra Madre, a broad screened-in porch.

The first issue—October, 1963—of *R/C Modeler Magazine* was typed up and pasted together on that very porch. Forty pages, pulp paper, black-and-white throughout, with a splash of red across the cover that bled over onto the full-page ad on the back—an ad for a now-forgotten product called the "Justin Micro-Tie."

The Justin Micro-Tie was not a fashion statement, but a fairly bulky (1.5" x 4") printed circuit board designed to simplify the typical five-servo multi hookup of the day—eliminating, according to the ad, "up to six plugs and 44 solder connections." Besides the Justin ad, there was a two-page centerspread for C&S single-channel and reed multi radios, a page and a half for Kraft equipment, one full page for an eastern mailorder house called Lee's Hobby Industries and another for the Sig Manufacturing Company of Montezuma, Iowa. These were the major advertisers—and most of them had come aboard by barter rather than cash.

Cover price of this first issue was a penny a page: forty cents. (*FM* and *MAN* were still at 35¢, while *American Modeler*, with its bi-monhly issues now pushing 100 pages, had already made the jump to 50¢.) A modest seven thousand copies of this first issue were printed, with distribution through Sig authorized dealers across the country.

Formula for Success

So how do you slant a brand-new magazine to make it appeal to the maximum number of readers? Well, you can take some cues from your competition. For one thing, you want to avoid looking too regional. (*Flying Models'* R/C coverage, by 1963, often read like the club newsletter of the Long Island Drone Society.) And you want to avoid looking overly technical, too—the way *Grid Leaks* sometimes did. (Paul Runge's *Grid Leaks R/C Data Service*, a slim bi-monthly magazine then in its sixth year, was at that time America's only exclusively R/C publication.)

You take some cues from yourself. You're a sport flier, and you have a sneaking suspicion that what *you'd* like to see in a magazine is pretty much what most other sport fliers—meaning 95% of the R/C crowd—would like to see, too. So you play your hunches, and you design the mag pretty much to suit yourself.

You need heroes, of course—the current contest winners, the big names. In October of 1963, these included Phil Kraft, Cliff Weirick, Doug Spreng, and Jim Kirkland, among others. But you don't want these heroes dominating your magazine; you don't want to scare off the average flier with an experts-only look. If you're smart, you'll try to walk a tightrope between simplicity and complexity, between the legions of amateurs out in the field and the handful of super-experts at the top. If you're smart.

And Don Dewey was smart. For the lead construction feature in that first issue, he chose Phil Kraft's slightly outdated pattern biplane, the *Stagger-Bi*—hot but not the hottest, high tech but not intimidating—and paired it with a simple single-channel job by a relative unknown, *RCM* art director Barry Halsted.

Because his front porch was only an hour north of the '63 Nationals site at Los Alamitos, Dewey was able to scoop the other October mags with a complete rundown (not just early photos, a la *Flying Models*) of the Nats radio event. And then, for regional balance, a breezy phone interview with Pappy de Bolt, and a picture story on the July record trials in Dahlgren, Virginia, where Maynard Hill had just pushed the R/C altitude mark up to 13,328 feet.

Elsewhere in the issue, technical editor Hank Giunta showed readers how to clean up their messy installations without buying a Justin Micro-Tie, while a writer with a curiously familiar name— Frank Justin—reminisced casually about how he got started in R/C. The rest was almost pure product review, according to the now-ancient Street & Smith dictum that *new products are news, too.*

Setting the Tone

People liked what they saw, and Volume one, Number one sold well. Within three months *RCM*'s cover price was up to fifty cents, and a couple of new names had appeared among the contributors: writer-designer Ken Willard and photographer Dick Tichenor. Tichenor understood the simple but profound secret of model plane photography—*a beautiful female makes any plane interesting*—and Ken Willard, despite his thirty years of modeling experience, had a marvelous knack for writing straight across—not down—to beginners and hackers.

The tone for the new magazine was set.

Don Dewey knew his audience. In October 1963, 75% of America's R/C addicts were adult males with less than four years of radio control experience. Willard and Tichenor both spoke directly and naturally to these people. (Three decades later, the same statistics still hold. Small wonder that both of these men remained, for most of those three decades, solidly aboard the *RCM* boat.)

Slick

That same December issue that introduced Tichenor and Willard also introduced the first 'slick' paper to the model publishing world—a world whose mainstay, for forty years, had been old-fashioned yellow newsprint, known as pulp. Slick paper costs more than pulp, besides being heavier and more expensive to mail. Photos may reproduce slightly better on slick, but the glare makes it positively aggravating to read. Slick has only one real virtue: it's whiter than pulp, so it looks more sophisticated, more glamorous. It has *image*—and image, in America, will win out over substance every time. The eastern magazines resisted for a while, but *R/C Modeler* had clearly raised the ante. Eventually everyone went slick: *American Modeler* in '68, *MAN* in '70, *Flying Models* in '71.

Meanwhile, Don Dewey's brainchild was growing like Jack's beanstalk. Issue number four (January '64) jumped to 62 pages, and two months later the mag got its first full-color cover. Success attracts: soon Dewey had lured Ted "Channel Chatter" Strader away from *Flying Models*; next came columnist Jerry Kleinburg, a well-known Class 1 competitor from San Antonio. Ken Willard began his "Sunday Flier" column that September, and later in the fall a clever, multi-talented draftsman named Dick Kidd signed on as art editor (he would, over the years, become *de facto* editor-in-chief.)

In January of '66, after freelancing half a dozen articles for the mag, Dallas flier/designer Charles Cunningham began his "Cunningham on R/C" column. Like Willard, Chuck Cunningham had a gift for explaining the basics of the sport with a light touch—so much so that he's still doing it today. Since Willard had to drop out in 1989 for health reasons, "Cunningham on R/C" has become the oldest and longest running column in RCM's history.

After those first three issues, the R/C industry slowly, one by one, began to line up behind Dewey with its advertising: Royal Products of Denver . . . Stu Babcock . . . McNabb's Citizen-Ship Radio Corporation—and finally Polk's in New York, then Orbit and Min-X and Sterling Models of Philadelphia.

By the magazine's third anniversary—October '66—most of the big advertisers were aboard, and *RCM*'s success seemed assured: it was pushing 100 pages, and already calling itself "the largest and most widely read model aviation publication in the world." Behind the scenes, finances were still touch-and-go every month, and would remain so for some time to come. But the handsome blond sport flier from Sierra Madre had demonstrated beyond doubt that the market niche was there: America was ready for a good R/C-oriented magazine. And *RCM's* trajectory has been steadily upward ever since.

Model Builder

From a distance, starting a new magazine appears deceptively easy. From 3,000 miles, it looks like a snap. That's the distance from which Bill Northrop watched Don Dewey struggle through the first few years of *R/C Modeler*. Northrop had stepped into Ed Lorenz's shoes as R/C editor of *Model Airplane News* in late 1964, just a year after *RCM* began. Almost immediately Bill and Don struck up a phone friendship, and soon began sniping at one another in their columns. It was good harmless fun, and great publicity for both.

Then *RCM* began to mushroom, and *MAN* began to imitate it slavishly, and Bill Northrop couldn't stand it any longer: nothing would do but he move west and create a magazine of his own. Not a rival to *RCM*, mind you, but a traditional model airplane magazine of the sort we all grew up on—the kind of full-spectrum rag that was just then going broke everywhere you looked. The kind of magazine *RCM* was steadily and relentlessly replacing.

Idealists are a dime a dozen. But idealists willing to put their whole life behind their dream are more rare. In 1971, "Little Willie" (Dewey's nickname) Northrop did just that. Unaware of the railroad magazine of the same name, published from 1937 to 1941, he decided to call his new baby *The Model Builder*. (The *"The"* disappeared quietly in November of '73—nobody ever used it, anyway.)

Volume one number one, dated October 1971, was sweated together in the family room of the Northrop house on Del Ray Drive in Santa Ana. The masthead was padded with the names of two family cats—Prince and Charlie Brown—in addition to those of Bill and his wife Anita. It was a shoestring operation. Three thousand copies were printed, with most of them given away as samples.

Right from the start, *MB* had the flavor of a west coast *Flying Models* . . . for adults. It was strong on fly-for-fun, and—without ever looking old-fashioned—it was strong on nostalgia, too: in its first twenty years, *Model Builder* managed to resurrect and reprint virtually every important design (freeflight, R/C, controlline) from the thirties and forties.

This format attracted some of the cream of the old-time modelers, and the magazine's list of contributors swelled. ("Contributor" was an honest designation: for the first few years, even the regular columnists went unpaid.)

Model Builder was the first magazine to give a solid voice to both R/C soaring and the old timer movement in freeflight, as well as the first mag to give R/C helicopters a regular column (beginning in December of 1973.) One of soaring's best writers, Le Gray, came aboard in the third issue and stayed. Jack Transue started the "Plug Sparks" column in January of '73; in August John Pond took it over, and has run it faithfully ever since—only Bill Hannan's "Hangar" column is older.

Kraft, Top Flite, Heathkit, Sig, Pro-Line, K&B, Ace, Orbit—the earliest *MB* advertisers were mostly R/C-oriented, but Northrop persevered with his full-spectrum approach. Until 1978. That spring, Dick Tichenor of *R/C Modeler* defected briefly to the Northrop camp, and Walt Schroder of *MAN* 'retired' to *Model Builder* a few months later.

At this point the magazine made a brief, aggressive attack on Don Dewey's turf by becoming *R/C Model Builder*, with 76 up-front pages dedicated strictly to radio control. Four new R/C columnists signed in: Bob Underwood, Dave Brown, Hal deBolt, and Ron 'Quadra' Shettler—plus engine experts Dale Kirn, George Aldrich and Otto Bernhardt. (Dale had already been the controlline pinch hitter for years.) Scale draftsman Peter Westberg became a regular. Discount house advertising—long reviled in *MB* editorials as destructive to the grassroots hobby shop—were suddenly welcome.

It was a short-lived experiment. The bulk of *MB's* subscribers were old-time, broad-spectrum modelers—not the type who spend lavishly on mailorder radio gear. To try to reach the *RCM* crowd would be tantamount to starting all over again in the publishing business, something nobody would want to do twice. The discounters' ad response was poor, and slowly they drifted away. By the fall of 1980, the "R/C" had disappeared from the cover, Walt Schroder was packing for his move back to the east coast, the magazine was down to 100 or so well-balanced pages, and *Model Builder* had become *Model Builder* once more.

Ah, Bill! Who can blame you for wanting more than just satisfaction for your labors! The money really *is* greener on the radio side of the fence, and all of us who held our breaths during the "R/C" phase of *MB*—fully expecting freeflight and controlline and indoor to disappear from its pages forever—gave a great sigh of relief when the worst failed to happen.

Who can make a living selling bellcranks and dethermalizer fuse and microfilm solution? Who ever could?

And what other publisher, retiring (spring of '92) after two decades of nonstop deadline pressure, is still driving a twenty-year-old car, eh? (Awright, so it's a Stingray!)

You wrote—hands down—the best picture captions in the business (remember that shot of Hank Cole's homemade thermal detector: "Knowing how is nice, but knowing when is better.") Partly because you didn't hobble yourself by trying to fill two lines completely, the way your heroes had always done. But mostly because you knew the whole hobby, intimately. And cared.

Your baby's in the hands of a new publisher now—Mark Thiffault of Challenge Publications. If Mark manages to do even half the job you did, he'll be a hero to all of us.

We know you put in those twenty years mostly for the love of silk and dope and the smell of tolulene. And we know, too, that if model building is alive and well in the next century, it will be at least partly because of WCN and *Model Builder* magazine.

Thanks, Willie!

Roll Call: SHOPS

*Thousands have come and gone over the years,
and everybody has a favorite. Here are a few
to jog your memory:*

Brown's Hobby Center up by Van Cortlandt Park, NYC
Edwards Hobbies on East Cass in Tampa
Fischers Hobby Service, Louisville
Stanton's of Chicago and **Corr's** of Washington, DC
Haines Hobby House on South 6th in Reading, PA
Lincoln (NB) Hobby Shop, down on P Street
Buzz & Doug's Hobby Shop, Seattle
Crosby's Hobby Centre on Massachusetts Ave, Cambridge
Hoffy's Hobby House in Downey, CA
Tom Herbert's **Westchester Hobbies** in White Plains
Kirtland (Ohio) **Hardware and Hobby**
Steve Vargas Hobby Shop, New Brunswick, NJ
Rich's Hobbytowne on U.S. 46 in Parsippany
Bill Scott's **Hillcrest Hobbies** in San Diego
Red's Hobbycraft, Cleveland (Red Hillegas, Prop.)
Good's Hobby Shop on N. Main, Dayton
Bob Steele Hobby Center, Indianapolis
Ken Ballard's **ABC Hobbycraft**, 6th & Vine, Evansville
Joe's Hobby Center, Detroit
Pico Models in Culver City, CA
Gilbert's on Route 15 in Gettysburg
Ace Model Shop, Pasadena, CA
Ted Morrison's **Sky Devil Model Shop**, Oakland
TAMBE: The Airplane Model Builders Exchange, Brooklyn
Swaney's in Long Beach
The Hobby Counter, Johnny Clemens' shop in Dallas
Brooklyn Hobby Den, out on Fort Hamilton Parkway
Still's Hobby Haven in Beaumont, TX
Hobby Land on Main Street in Hackensack
Vic's Hobby Supply, Portland, OR
Frontier Hobbies in Buffalo

Chapter Eleven

SEE YOUR LOCAL DEALER

*Why the lack of hand-launch glider kits in hobby shops [when]
it's the most popular event at most contests? Jobbers . . . feel
they aren't worth handling.*

—Flying Models, *June 1959*

(Burbank, CA: 19 October '91) You get there early. You always get to a new shop early, and you wind up waiting outside the door, impatient as a kid. You're not a kid—far from it—but you forget that the minute you walk into the shadow of that ancient, L-shaped neon sign that says HOBBY SHOP.

It's quiet on this end of Victory Boulevard at nine-thirty on a Saturday morning, but you aren't here to watch the cars go by anyway. You're here to press your nose to the glass door and peer into the deep, cool shadows of the shop. Just like a kid.

Tony and Addie's Hobby Lobby, established 1952.

What catches your eye first are the hanging models—dozens of them, maybe a hundred. Like a flight of passenger pigeons, they blot out the shop's high ceiling, spilling down every wall to just above head-high. R/C, free flight, ukie, glider. Every shape and color and type, from 13" stick-and-tissue rubber jobs to massive radioplanes. Kit designs, magazine designs, originals. Layer upon layer upon layer—a whole lifetime of aeromodeling, hanging light and motionless, suspended in time.

The first glance is overwhelming, but gradually individual models begin to swim into focus. Isn't that a *Civy Boy* back there? (Paul Gilliam once lived here in the San Fernando Valley, flew with

281

the San Valeers.) And that four-engined Lockheed *Electra* in Western Air Lines paint—could it be Earl Carpenter's controlline job that won the '67 Los Alamitos Nats?

A couple of giant red monoplanes dominate the foreground—a matched pair of prewar French lightplanes, midwingers, open cockpit, lovely scalloped trailing edges. *Mostiques?* Yes! Farman *Mostiques*, each one over six feet in span, with full flying wires and huge ivory-colored Williams Brothers antique wheels and . . . my God, *look at that propeller!* The one on the left is *rubber* powered! A six-foot *rubber model!* Nobody builds six-foot rubber models since . . . what? 1935? Yet both of these planes look like new. Is this place in some kind of time warp, or what?

Stand Back and Look Close

Tony and Addie's Hobby Lobby: "T & A's," to the locals. Owned and operated by the longest-running mother-and-son flying circus in American modeling—Addie Mae and Tony Naccarato. Short and stout and overcharged and as much alike as a pair of dual spark plugs, the Naccaratos are a single spirit in two bodies: both of them totally dedicated to the shop, totally dedicated to things that fly (*"We do not carry model cars,"* their phone recording says emphatically) and totally dedicated to both the past and future of the hobby. (Together they sponsor the Blacksheep Flying Squadron, a club that, according to its newsletter, has soloed 600 kids in U-Control in a single year.)

T & A's is your classical 'shotgun' shop, narrow and deep and jammed with merchandise—a shrine to old-fashioned, full-spectrum model building, and one of the few hobby shops left in America that isn't totally dominated by radio control.

"We build and fly everything—indoor, freeflight, controlline, R/C," Tony likes to boast. Although it's obvious from the models on the ceiling that flying scale, and particularly electric flying scale, is dear to both their hearts. Tony and Addie (it's hard to talk about them separately: they design together, build together, fly together— two good friends who happen to be blood-related) have been pioneers in electric freeflight, electric controlline and electric R/C, both indoor and out. Those two quarter-scale *Mostiques*, for example,

282

are indoor radio models. The rubber-powered one weighs 26.5 ounces, the electric an ounce and a half less.

(Think about that for a minute: a silk-and-balsa quarter-scale R/C model at just over a pound and a half, ready to fly! If this is nostalgia, then it's *cutting edge* nostalgia—a prime example of the endless challenges that every branch of aeromodeling offers.)

Building Board

The shop opens promptly at ten, and on this particular Saturday, early business is light. Tony handles most of it alone, darting back and forth like a shooting-gallery target behind the long glass counter that runs down the left side of the store. His mom spends the morning hovering over a plywood door blank that serves as the shop's building board—and focal point. Almost everyone who comes in goes first to the board to see what Addie is up to now.

"Addie Naccarato is probably the best model builder in the world, living or dead, male or female," her son says proudly. "She has built *hundreds* of models." And it's true: by the time Tony was born, toward the end of World War II, his mom had already been turning out stick-and-tissue models—by Comet, Cleveland, Megow, Modelcraft, Peerless—for nearly a decade. Her older brothers would start them, then lose interest, and little Addie would step in to finish them up. Masterfully.

When Addie's dad noticed her talent, he began to encourage her independently of the boys. This was mid-Depression, and twenty-five cents was big money, but somehow Daddy always seemed to find enough change to cover the cost of his daughter's next kit.

Her favorite haunt, during her teenage days, was a place called Tony's Hobby Shop, in downtown Los Angeles. Its owner was an energetic and air-minded young fellow, handsome and curly-haired (and single, as luck would have it) whose name was Naccarato . . . .

Some marriages may be made in heaven, but others are made in model airplane shops. Addie and Tony tied the knot in 1942. There's a photo of the two of them in a '43 *Air Trails*, cranking away on a ukie speed model. In the picture, Addie is great with child.

When that child was born, and grew up to be just as avid a designer-builder-flier as his parents, the Naccarato family was complete. Throughout the 1950s, the three of them practically lived at Sepulveda Basin, L.A.'s best-known flying field, and an easy fifteen-minute drive out Burbank Boulevard from the family's new shop on Victory.

As the '43 *Air Trails* photo suggests, the elder Naccaratos—Addie and 'Big' Tony—were among the earliest pioneers of U-Control in the L.A. basin. They became personal friends of Jim Walker; their son still speaks of Walker as you would a favorite uncle. (An uncle whose idea of a gift was a three-foot-square box full of dime gliders and *Interceptors* and *Hornets* and *Firebabies*—'factory reject' kits with hardly a blemish on them, culled out of the American Junior production line by the hand of a perfectionist.)

When Walker died unexpectedly in 1958—he had been called home to Portland by company lawyers during a Los Angeles trade show—the Naccaratos simply couldn't believe that their friend and idol wouldn't be coming back. They mourned him like a family member. They stored his famous R/C lawnmower for nearly a year, in no hurry to return this symbol of Walker's creative spirit to the family and business that—in their eyes—had contributed far more than the Cox lawsuit to Jim's ill health and last, fatal stroke.

Big Tony followed Jim in 1980, but the spirit of both men lives on in T & A's. U-Control is alive and well here. Everything in the shop reflects Big Tony's touch, and mother and son refer to both of these fallen giants casually, almost as if they'd just stepped out for coffee together.

Fits and Starts

Like everyone else who wanders in, I'm drawn to Addie's building board. Today's project is a 100" scale pusher flying wing—the old Hill *Pterodactyl* from the thirties—electric, of course—for the annual Northrop flying wing contest that's only two weeks off. Addie confesses to a special love for flying wings. One of her earliest wings was an original 1/2-A combat design, back in the days of the Wasp and Thermal Hopper.

Tony has penciled rough plans for the *Pterodactyl* on brown wrapping paper, and I watch the big ship take shape as the day passes.

Like most modelers, Addie works in fits and starts, standing motionless for minutes while she studies the structure or the plan, then moving swiftly into a cutting-fitting-gluing cycle. The drawings are full size, but the detail is slim, little more than scale outlines, with a suggested bulkhead or two. Addie spends much of her time doing what modelers do best: problem solving, visualizing, designing in air. Her hands, when she finally picks up a tool, work in sure, swift strokes—the hands of a craftsman. She's done all this before.

As she works she whistles to herself, partly as a way of fending off kibitzers. She is seldom without an audience, and, because she's Addie Naccarato and her picture's been in a hundred magazines, people can't resist trying to draw her out, pull her attention away from the building board—often with stupid *see-me* questions.

Addie Naccarato has reached the age when she doesn't suffer fools gladly. Without ever being impolite, she refers such questions to her son. "Propellers?" she'll say, without looking up. "Better ask Tony. He's the prop expert." A thumb jerked over her shoulder directs the questioner toward the retail counter.

And Tony—tee-shirted, neatly trimmed beard, gentle voice, looking for all the world like a sixties shrink—is precisely the person to ask. Infinitely patient, he spends most of his day's energy not selling but educating. For both Naccaratos, moving merchandise—pecking out receipts on the small cash register that keeps the store alive—appears to be a sort of sideline, at best.

Just now Tony is scrutinizing the bare bones of a little Piper *Vagabond*, built from a Sterling kit. The builder, standing anxiously in front of the counter, is a woman in her mid twenties, collegiate looking, neatly dressed and groomed. The *Vagabond* is her first model, and it's meticulously done.

". . . that's why I was looking at your wing so carefully," Tony is saying. "To see if it's warped. That's what I learned from flying indoor—even the smallest warp in a wing can cause trouble . . . ." Educate, educate, educate; and always gently, tactfully. Pass on the secrets of a lifetime (three lifetimes, really: dad, mom, son) to everybody who walks in, everybody who cares enough to ask.

Directly behind Tony, towering above him like an altar, is an immense wooden cabinet, labeled 'engine parts.' A hundred and twenty drawers, each of them stuffed to the hilt with that same casual orderliness you see on every shelf. Above the altar, a soldier course of kits marches away toward the front windows. T & A's looks like the kind of shop where you could walk in and ask for a set of points for a Brown Junior . . . and get them.

It won't hurt to try.

"Tony," I say, after he's sent the *Vagabond* builder on her way with high praise and a roll of yellow tissue, "I've got this old Veco .29 I'd like to fly some vintage stunt with, but it's missing the prop drive washer. Don't suppose you'd have anything to fit it?"

"Let me look around," Tony answers, without visible surprise. "Is it thick and tapered, or thin and flat?"

Two minutes later a thin, flat Veco drive washer is added to a growing stack of esoteric goodies (diesel fuel, nitrate dope, a silly-putty DT for handlaunch gliders) that I'm piling up on the far end of the counter.

Stay much longer and I may not have money enough in the bank to buy my way out of this place.

The specialized hobby shop like T & A's came into its own—began its spread from major cities to the suburbs and small towns—after World War II. Metropolitan areas like Los Angeles, of course, had a good selection of shops all through the prewar decade. When Big Tony opened his first store downtown in 1936, he was going head-to-head with a number of older, well-established businesses. Principal among them was Barney and Peg Snyder's Modelcraft, on 54th Street. The Snyders started business in 1932, and by '36 had already branched out, as so many shops did in the thirties, into kit manufacture, as a way of supplementing their income. (Hobby dealers had a lot more time on their hands before sales taxes and workmen's comp and computers—and an idle mind almost invariably leads a modeler into kitmaking.)

Department Stores

But the urban hobby shops of the thirties had more competition than just each other. Some of the biggest model-plane retailers in those days were the major department stores. And not only the ones that sponsored famous clubs—Kresge's and Bamberger's in Newark; Stix, Baer & Fuller in St. Louis; Jordan Marsh in Boston—but almost every large downtown drygoods store: Foley's in Houston, Bloomingdale's in New York, Mandel Brothers in Chicago, Strawbridge & Clothier in Philadelphia . . . the list is endless.

In those long-gone days before diversity and specialization, when every kid wanted a model plane kit, it didn't take much moxie to staff a hobby department. (Got a sick clerk? Bring in some body from shoes.) The simple, brightly-packaged rubber and solid models of the thirties practically sold themselves, and even a shoe salesman knew what you needed to build 'em: glue, pins, a razor blade.

Then came engines, huge and expensive and tricky to operate. Nice fat profit in engines, but you had to hire an expert to sell the things. (And to buy them, as well—not every brand was a winner, and a store could get stung.) By WW II, department stores had begun backing away from the model airplane hobby: too complex, too much stock, too little turnover. Selling shoes was simpler.

This left the specialized hobby shop pretty much in the saddle, by 1950. Hence the great blossoming of shops (fulltime, part time, short time) during the postwar decade. Model supplies were suddenly available in every neighborhood, every crossroads town of two or more drugstores. A happy situation for the mid-century modeler—and much too good to last.

Discounters

What killed the little neighborhood hobby shops of the postwar era—besides the general decline in aviation interest during the 1950s—was mailorder discounting. Discounting began innocently enough. Not long after the war, a couple of big New York mailorder houses, America's Hobby Center and the Mercury Model Airplane Company of Brooklyn, started advertising complete flying outfits—plane, engine, accessories—at prices considerably lower than the cost of the individual items bought separately.

It wasn't an original idea. Back in 1938, Major Moseley had offered his *California Chief* kit ($7.90) plus a $12.50 Baby Cyclone engine for the combined price of $15.75 postpaid. But the *Chief* and the Baby Cyke were both mail-order-only items, unavailable except direct from the manufacturer.

AHC and Mercury were doing something different. They were discounting *other manufacturer's stuff*—buying at wholesale, selling at something less than suggested retail.

As solitary pioneers, the two of them did only minimal harm to the hobby dealers' already declining business. But the precedent was set. When radio control began its rise to power during the sixties, dozens of firms jumped into the mailorder discount field, robbing the local, full-service dealers like Tony and Addie of a percentage of their big-ticket sales. (Mailorder discounters tend to handle only expensive, high-turnover items.)

Hobby dealers, unable to make a living selling only accessories, went broke left and right. As a consequence, the retail hobby situation today has returned to almost exactly where it was in 1935. Only major metro areas can support a well-stocked, well-rounded shop like Tony and Addie's. In smaller towns, and especially in rural areas, mailorder has once more become the chief source of hobby supplies. Without big-ticket items—engines and radios and ready-to-flys—a small dealer simply can't survive, even on what seems, at first glance, like a generous markup.

The Discount Structure

The hobby industry's discount structure, in its classical form, goes something like this: The manufacturer of a $10.00 item sells it in large lots to a wholesaler for a 55% discount, meaning $4.50 per item. The wholesaler, or "jobber," after warehousing these lots as briefly as possible, breaks them into smaller lots—'job lots'—and ships them out to dealers at a 40% discount, meaning $6.00 each. So the retailer stands to make a gross profit of $4.00 on each $10.00 item—far more than either the jobber or the manufacturer made.

An enviable position, it would seem.

But even without competition from mailorder houses, all is not roses for the retailer. To earn his 40%, he has to deal directly with the customer and all his idiosyncrasies. He has to keep his store open at convenient hours, six to seven days a week; answer endless questions; suffer his stock to be pawed over by multitudes and replace, out of his own pocket, broken and pilfered items; provide facilities for the lame and halt, and insurance for the merely clumsy; cheerfully buy back any item a customer suddenly decides he doesn't want; cover bad checks; collect and record taxes for city, state and federal governments (and pay additional taxes for the privilege); run periodic sales to eliminate, at cost or less, items that haven't moved within a reasonable time; and hope, when all these expenses are met, that something remains of that 40% to feed his kids.

Nobody, to my knowledge, has ever gotten rich doing this.

If you happen to live within driving distance of a good, full-service hobby dealer, a dealer willing to help you find a part for that Veco .29—a dealer who's ever *heard* of a Veco .29, for that matter—you're lucky. *Support that dealer every time you get a chance.* When you're out test-gliding in the park and strangers show an interest in your model, give them that dealer's business card. As often as you can, buy from him, even if it costs you an extra five to fifteen percent.

I live near a city of half a million, a military center with an unusually large aeromodeling population. It barely supports two good hobby shops. When its population was under 200,000 it supported four, sometimes five shops at once. This is the trend all over America, and it doesn't bode well.

When the last local dealer goes under, the hobby/sport/obsession of aeromodeling—with a history as long and colorful as the twentieth century itself—will go under, too.

Do what you can, my friend, to keep that from happening.

Roll Call: Clubs

Wherever two or three are gathered together in the name of modeling, there a club is born. And this has been going on since at least 1910. Over the years, a few have become famous— IMAC, the *Balsa Butchers*, the *Sky Scrapers*, the *Thermal Thumbers*, the *Aeronuts*, the *Brainbusters*—but hundreds of others have come and gone with less fanfare. Here are just a few:

Monroe (MI) *Knights of the Dope Bucket* - Jamaica (NY) *Prop Spinners* - *Sons of Brooklyn* - *Hangar # 13* (Beloit WI) - Downers Grove *Thermal Hunters* - Augusta (ME) *Flying Maniacs* - Baltimore *Aero-Craftsmen* - Green Mountain (VT) *Modeleers* - Ames (IA) *Prop Busters* - Minneapolis *Thermal Sniffers* - Selma (AL) *Prop Twisters* - *Helldivers* of Sioux City - Burbank (CA) *Model Club* - *Cowtown Sahibs* and *Cowtown Circle Burners* (Ft. Worth) - San Diego *Aeroneers* and *Airliners* - *San Valeers* and *Valley Hawks* - Kokomo *Flying Wildcats* - *NY Society of Model Engineers* - *Thunderbirds Club* of NJ - Reading (PA) *Aero Modelers* - *Screamin Demons* (Long Island) - *Central Gas Model Plane Society* - New York *Aeronuts* - *TAMBE* (Brooklyn) - the *Camden (AK) Daredevils* - *Tulsa Model Aeronautical Engineers* - Bristol (CT) *Balsa Busters* - the *VFW Model Airplane Club* of Clarksburg, WV - *Chicagoland R/C Modelers* - *Tampa Trim Tabs* - *First All Speed Team* (L.A.) - Lodi (CA) *Knuckle-Busters* - Hollywood *Flying Tigers* - Yonkers *Glo-Devils* - North American (Rockwell) *Flightmasters* - *New England Wakefield Group* - Galveston (TX) *Gulls* - San Francisco *Vultures* - *Omahawks* - *Greater Detroit Soaring and Hiking Society* - Detroit *Sky Guys* - Dayton *Buzzin Buzzards* - Helena (MT) *Flying Glue Pots* - Chicago *Balsa Wasps* - Elmira *Flying Sparks* - Butler (PA) *Flying Dutchmen* - Reno *Sagehoppers* - Shelby (OH) *Balsa Buzzards* - Minneapolis *Dope Fiends* - Chula Vista *Flying Goats* - Sea Cliff (NY) *Prop Splitters* - West Palm Beach *Spin-Dizzies* - Muncie *Gas Hawks* - Detroit *Balsa Bugs* - Johnson City (TN) *Hilltoppers* - *Alaska Model Association* (Anchorage) - *Prop Jockeys* of Vero Beach, FL - Corvallis *Comets* - *Republic Aviation Model Society* (RAMS of Long Island) - Delaware (OH) *Model Maulers* - Amarillo *Planesmen* - Sarasota (FL) *Flamingos* - Brazil (IN) *Ground Pounders* - Bethesda *Clobber Club* - Philadelphia *Flying Tomcats* - Greenville (SC) *Plane Nuts* - Houston *Two Cycle Terrors* . . . and *The Lost Controllers* of Wilmington, Delaware

Chapter 12

HEROES

He says he doesn't take modeling seriously, considers it purely as a hobby. But we've found out that the modeling hobby continues to take more and more of your time, until it's difficult to find time for anything else.

—*Air Trails*, December 1937

Doing it for a living takes much of the pleasure out of model building.
—Duke Fox, Fox Mfg. Co.

There are dozens of routes to hero status among the Clan. You can fly well and persistently and forever, like Los Angeles Wakefielder Bob White, who has won (and lost) a string of contests longer than most of us can remember. You can design one good model that other people win contests with for years (like Paul Gilliam and his *Civy Boy*—or Phil Kraft and his *Ugly Stik*, easily the most imitated R/C model in history.) You can win the high-point trophy five times at the Nationals, like Woody Blanchard did in the fifties (the same Woody Blanchard who once put up *ten straight maxes* to qualify for an FAI event that never took place.) Or you can spend a quarter-century chasing a single trophy, as 'Georgia' George Perryman did the Mulvihill.

You can publish a ton of sport designs in the mags; that worked for people like Paul DelGatto, Roy Clough, Owen Kampen, Ted Strader, Bill Evans, Dee Mathews. You can write a column or edit a magazine, or perform heroic deeds for the AMA. You can get your picture on a magazine cover under the tongue-in-cheek headline "Iowa

Farmer Builds Remote-Control Model," the way Iowa farmer (and then current AMA President) Claude McCullough once did.

If worse comes to worst, you can even become a manufacturer.

People who stick with the hobby long enough often wind up doing more than one of these things. In the course of eighty years, there have been hundreds of such folk. Every one of them have been heroes—local, regional, national. And we modelers are no different from normal people: we need our heroes. All we can get.

No way am I going to squeeze eight decades of these people into a list this size, in a book this size. You know it and I know it, and even the Pope knows it. Still, the hour is late, and we ought to have a roll-call of our heroes—before any more of them kick the bucket.

With that in mind, let's get going:

Lieutenant (USNR) **H.W.** "John" **Alden** was almost singlehandedly responsible for the NAA's 'Junior Clause,' which gave modeling its national leadership in the dark days between the death of the old Airplane Model League (1933) and the maturing, around 1939, of the present AMA. Charlie Grant mistrusted Alden because he once tried to cop Charlie's job at *Model Airplane News*. But Alden was totally dedicated to modeling; he charged on just long enough to help found the AMA in '36. Then his health failed and he dropped out of the picture.

Alvin Anderson (1918-1990) was a Chicago flying buddy of Goldberg's, and the man CG credited with inventing the pylon. (When the *Zipper* first hit the market, Anderson was listed as co-designer.) A full-scale prop maker, 'Alvie' is best remembered today for his 1937 *Anderson Pylon*, a contemporary of the *Valkyrie*. Check out the *Pylon*: this guy loved BIG models.

Mel Anderson (1902-1986) was born in Minneapolis, but moved to LA at age six so he could become one of the Famous Engine Manufacturers of Southern California. (Atwood, Brodbeck, Bunch, Cameron, Cox, Hassad, Holland, Johnson, Ohlsson—and who have I missed?) Anderson began pursuing the single-cylinder dream in 1932. He's credited with introducing both the front rotary valve and the needle valve into modeling. In 1938 he set a record of two hours, one minute, 54 seconds at Long Beach, flying a seven-pounder powered by a Baby Cyke. This was a *free flight*, gentlemen. All of the various Spitfires were his, of course, including half a million .049s produced between 1949 and 1953.

Everett N. Angus of Oaklyn, NJ was a textile engineer by trade, a former AMA president, and one of those fanatical supporters of modeling before mid-century. During the war, Angus was almost singlehandedly responsible for preventing a ban on all model flying, when the country was full of myopic paranoids who mistook even pigeons for German bombers.

Ray Arden (d. 1965) designed the cranky little prewar Atom .09, the curse of Class A. But after the war he more than redeemed himself with the impeccable Arden .19 and its half-size brother, the .09—engines that introduced the ball-joint conrod that made Leroy Cox rich enough to fight Jim Walker's patent and win.

Arden is best known, of course, for relieving the world of the miseries of spark ignition. He showed up at the Minneapolis Nats in '47 with his first "hot plugs" and a special fuel mix containing nitromethane to keep them glowing. And thank God for it! Ray Arden's glow plug, G.E.'s cheap transistor and Top Flite's Monokote have been the three most important advances in postwar modeling. Everything else is pure cosmetics.

Bill Atwood (d. 1978) was probably the most prolific of the LA engine designers. After doing the *Baby Cyke* for Major Moseley, Atwood went on his own with the *Hi-Speed,* the *Phantom,* the *Bullet* and the endless *Champion* series that concluded with the postwar *Glo Devil.* By the late thirties he had so many engines on the market that he was competing with himself! Some were sold out his front door on East Gage Street, others out a side door with a totally different address. All the best 1/2-A glow engines were his: the *Wasp* and the *Shriek* and Cox's entire *Tee-Dee* line, from the .010 up to the hottest .15's. Even those miserable little *Wen-Macs* were Bill Atwood designs.

As a kid, Atwood was a fierce competitor. He won a trip to Memphis for that first Playground Nationals back in '27, where he flew a clock-spring model in the 'any-power-except-rubber' event, taking an uncontested first with an official flight (whoopee!) of 5.2 seconds. The next year he won every event in the *LA Examiner* contest. During the early thirties he was California State Champ four different times. It was a lot of work, but Bill was young then, and he loved it.

Sid Axlerod (d.1981) moved into the vacancy left by Goldberg when he bailed out of Top Flite in '54 to start Carl Goldberg Models. Axlerod and Mike Schlessinger gave the world Super Monokote, the first successful mylar film covering. When Top Flite introduced the first Monokote in the spring of 1966, Ken Willard said, "Don't get me wrong; it's not going to replace all the standard covering materials." But it did.

293

Russ Barrera (1917-1979) was a true lifer, a clan member since the days of Lindbergh. Anyone who missed his Russ-Craft Model Museum in San Marcos, CA missed an exhibit far richer, at the time, than the AMA's. After Russ died, most of his collection was bundled into an 18-wheeler and shipped east to be integrated into the headquarters collection at Reston. The trailer sat around too long, leaked, and some irreplaceable, one-of-a-kind models were ruined. But then, who cares about the past?

Maxwell Bassett of Philadelphia (b. 1916) was unquestionably the father of American gas modeling. Bassett did to the rubber model exactly what Henry Ford did to the horse: put it out to pasture, pushed it out of the mainstream, relegated it to the status of a minority sport. Which is just what controlline did to free flight after WW II, and R/C did to everything else a couple of decades later.

Bassett showed up at the St. Louis Nats in 1935 with a small-finned, parasol version of his *Miss Philly* design, which pleased Charlie "Low CLA" Grant no end. Later in the year, he turned a cabin model loose at Camden, New Jersey and followed it by air across three very small states, which garnered him tons of publicity both in and out of the hobby—and played right into the hands of the anti-gas faction at the time. Bassett's swan song was the '37 Nats, where he topped a 53-minute Goldberg OOS by a solid twenty minutes, won $212 in cash and prizes, and got his model back. He was smart enough to quit modeling at this point.

William Bennett of the Circus Circus casino group is the man behind the Las Vegas Tournament of Champions, an annual R/C pattern event that has given our humble pastime hell's own amount of prestige—probably 10% of what it could use—and allowed Americans to see firsthand the flying of at least one absolute master, Hanno Prettner of Austria.

Joe Bilgri (b.1919) is a heavily disguised Texan from northern California, one of the people who pumped new life into indoor flying after it hit bottom in the mid-fifties. Joe lived in LA before the war, but was too bright to do so afterwards.

Dick Black (d. 1967) of the Ann Arbor Airfoilers was a lover of freeflight flying scale. He became co-founder (along with Carl Fries) of the National Free Flight Society. Dick wrote MAN's "VTO" column until his death, when the job was taken over by Dave Linstrum.

Vernon Boehle (pronounced, but not spelled, "Bailey") of Indianapolis was so successful with his early-thirties tractor rubber designs that Gordon Light, writing in *Air Trails* in January of 1937, credited him with singlehandedly killing the twin pusher. Certain it is that Boehle owned the brand-new Brown Junior that flew off to Canada on Goldberg's *Valkyrie* at the '37 Nats. Vern's best known model is the Boehle *Giant*, a fifteen-footer built specifically to win the Texaco event, which it never did.

Colonel **Hurst Bowers** is a master scale modeler and a true gentleman from a place he calls Vah-JIN-yah. His earliest modeling memory is of a balsa glider kit, which his mom helped him cut out with a pair of sharp sewing scissors—a trick he still uses today on thin sheetwood parts. Col. Bowers is curator of AMA's huge modeling museum. I spent days there, just gawking. When I asked him what would happen to it all after the last child of the Air Age died, he replied, "Well, I don't care about that. I've had a grand time putting it all together!" This wonderful, existential answer would have put him on the hero list even if he wasn't also responsible for most of Flyline Models' lovely little rubber and gas scale kits.

John Broadbeck is the B of K&B, manufacturer of the postwar line of *Torpedo* engines (no relation to Atwood's prewar *'Hi-Speed Torpedo.'*) Broadbeck and Lud Kading introduced the first 1/2-A engines in the late forties. The story goes that Mel Anderson made a run of miniature glow plugs for them, and when they came back too soon for a second run, Anderson decided the 1/2-A market must be bigger than he thought, and went to work on the *Baby Spitfire*. As early as 1957 Broadbeck was campaigning for an 'Old Timers' event at the Nats, for modelers who had flown prior to 1940.

Walter L. Brock (1884-1964) was the pole star of the Illinois Model Aero Club during the late teens and twenties, a time in which IMAC itself was the pole star of the American modeling movement.

Bill Brown (b. 1911) was one of the Philadelphia Model Airplane Association's earliest members. He came from a family that didn't need Lindbergh to make them air-minded: his grandad owned a *Jenny*. Brown created the most famous commercial model engine of the thirties, the *Brown Junior*. Only the GHQ outsold it.

Bill Brown was one of the first people to see the luck factor developing in free flight. In the spring of '36 he donated a trophy to a big IGMAA meet for *the highest average of three flights*. That meant you had to get your model back at least twice, and called for a radically different flying strategy than was then prevalent in the east, where the single longest flight (chased by timers in automobiles) always won.

Like Ford with his Model T, Brown refused to update the *Junior* as years went by, so that by 1939 it died a natural death—along with the *Brownie*, which was an unsuccessful attempt to compete with Irv Ohlsson's popular 23.

In later years, Brown returned to his first love, compressed air. He was responsible for the *Campus CO_2* engines of the forties, as well as a line of really small puffers in the seventies. These last he builds right in his home workshop, much as he did the earliest *Brown Juniors.*

Don Brown began as a free flighter, lost his first R/C model in 1952, won intermediate at the '57 Nats with a galloping ghost rig, then flew his way onto the '61 and '63 international teams. He finished fifth in the world in '63 with an early version of his Dee Bee *Quadruplex,* one of the first digital proportional rigs.

Willis C. Brown was a lifer from Boston, one of the founders of the Jordan Marsh - Boston *Traveler* "Junior Aviation League" of the late twenties. Brown served as president of the AMA from 1936 to 1938, and continued to write for the mags into the early 1960s.

Johnny Clemens (1913-1991) worked for Comet in the late thirties as a road salesman in the south, including Texas—where he settled in 1940 to open The Hobby Counter on Greenville Avenue in Dallas. It's still open. Johnny held his first AMA post in '40, directed the Dallas Nats in '50, and then became the longest-suffering AMA president (1971-78) to date. Back in the forties he was known for his beautifully-built ukies.

Myrtle Coad. As 'Mom' Robbers, she and her first husband founded the Oakland Cloud Dusters in 1937. During WW II she continued sending the club newsletter, *Propwash*, to every member overseas. In 1948, Mom took the women's championship at both the All-Western Open and the Olathe Nats. That same year she became Executive Secretary to the newly-formed Western Associated Modelers—"the keeper of the records, distributor of the newsletter, guardian of the rules and by-laws"—a thankless task she performed for over a quarter of a century.

Hal "Pappy" deBolt's single greatest contribution to modeling was the application, during the early fifties, of controlline building techniques (some would say "*Buzzard Bombshell* building techniques") to R/C. Before deBolt, R/Cers built with sticks; afterwards they used sheetwood and block balsa, and their models lasted longer.

As a designer, deBolt is the clan's greatest anomaly. When he comes up with a new plane, it's invariably a good one; but when he tries to tell you what makes it fly, it sounds like he lives on another planet. DeBolt is one of the very few Renaissance men of the hobby, having made it to the top in all three fields—free flight, U-control and radio. And who can argue with that?

Joe Elgin worked for the Pachasa brothers (Cleveland Models) for only one year, 1939-40. But in that year he designed some of the prettiest model airplanes ever kitted, including the entire *Playboy* series, the *Condor* gliders and all of the 'Brave Nations' rubber models.

Duke Fox (1919-1991) had a father who encouraged his modeling interests by giving him a Baby ROG kit in the late twenties—after which he won "about forty" Junior Birdmen first-place bracelets in San Francisco contests. "That old colonel whose job it was to run the Birdman clubs for the *Enquirer* didn't get paid unless he ran a contest a week," Duke recalled, "so every weekend my dad took me to the city to fly."

Fox tried valiantly (and unsuccessfully) to rescue the Berkeley line when it went under in 1960. But what he'll be remembered for is the Fox .35, the best of the "small" engines that killed the .60-powered 'barn-door' stunt movement of the mid-forties.

Like most successful business people in the hobby, Duke made the bulk of his money in other fields. In a typical year—1966—Fox Manufacturing made (in addition to a full line of engines and accessories) gas caps for tractors, wheel nuts for hot rods, spindle shafts for cotton pickers and release buttons for Vietnam-bound bombs.

Paul Gilliam (d. 1976) designed his first *Civy Boy* in '46—a beautiful, dangerous airplane, and one of the earliest 'pencil bombers.' Based, like every pylon FF, on Goldberg's *Zipper* layout, the Civy Boy was extreme: it had a long tail and a 50% stab and a balance point right on the trailing edge of the wing—a hair-trigger force arrangement that, when it worked, was spectacular, and when it didn't was even more so.

Walt Good (b. 1916) is America's "Mr. R/C." When the first Nats radio contest was held, back in '37, Walt was there, with equipment he and his brother Bill designed—equipment that Beacon Electronics was still selling fifteen years later.

Walt was responsible for the 'two-tone pulse width' system, one of the first multi-channel proportional radios, introduced in '56. He carried the AMA's ball—successfully—in every one of their early matches with the FCC. A physicist, he's retired now and living in Florida, where he can fly all he wants. And nobody deserves it more.

Charles Hampson Grant (1894-1987) fell in love with things that fly at age fourteen, in 1908. In less than a year he had designed his own single-stick pusher model, which came within ten feet of Percy Pierce's "world" record distance of 431 feet. His mother, a landscape painter, encouraged his aviation interest. His dad didn't. The old man was a thoroughly humorless Victorian-era banker who was dead certain that flying machines of any size were manifestations of satan—and he never missed an opportunity to say so.

297

Nevertheless, Grant went to Princeton engineering school to study the devil's work, and then joined the Army Air Service during World War I. The Army shipped him to Dayton, where he served for a time under Colonel Virginius Clark, of the Clark Y airfoil.

Grant was a tireless creator, in both full scale and modeling. In 1919 he invented, for a Dayton toy manufacturer, the first automated prop-carving machine. With it, one man and a helper could crank out 1000 propellers a day. The device was a full eight years ahead of history; nobody really needed a thousand props a day until the Lindbergh summer of 1927.

In the early twenties Grant founded a boys' camp in Vermont— ostensibly to build character, but actually to promote model aviation. A couple of the campers who came under his spell were Howard McEntee, who grew up to be the pied piper of fifties R/C, and Joe Kovel of the *K-G Gassie*. Many new rubber designs flowed from this boys-camp experience, including a series of stick and fuselage models that had one unusual characteristic for the time: even a beginner could make them fly.

In 1928 Grant decided to kit some of these boys-camp models. But this was the time of maximum Lindbergh madness, and he couldn't keep up with the demand, so he turned production over to the Kingsbury Toy Company of New Hampshire. For them he designed, in two styles and four sizes, a model called the *Grant Silver Arrow*.

The fat times rolled on, and Kingsbury sold over 200,000 *Silver Arrows* before the Depression finally plowed them under in 1930. Too bad—their *Arrows*, like most of the other Kingsbury toys, were moderately priced. The far better-known *Silver Ace*, a Spirit of St. Louis look-alike that came out of Chicago and didn't fly half as well, sold for as much as $15—twice what a Kingsbury *Arrow* cost.

And yet even the Arrow, at $7.50, seems like highway robbery today. Twenty-five dollars a week was considered good wages at the time, and new Fords were selling for under $500. But this was the tail-end of the Roaring Twenties, when greed was king. A couple of years later, after the bottom fell out and wages dropped to $10 a week, rubber model prices sank to well under a dollar bill, where they remained for more than two decades.

When the Kingsbury kingdom collapsed, the *Silver Arrow*'s designer began to cast about for a new career.

Charlie Grant spoke and thought clearly, but wrote English like it was a second language. (One of his 1928 ads sounds like 1950's Japanese English: *"This Challenger Scout makes very flat glide and beautiful easy landing."*) Nevertheless, *MAN* hired him as editor in late 1931. It was a good choice. By then Grant had a pretty fair idea of how model aerodynamics differed from full scale—something that could be said of very few people at the time.

From his editor's seat, Grant led the clan through the traumatic changeover from rubber to gas. It wasn't easy. When too many people dragged their feet, refusing to give up gummibands, Grant played his ace card. He began an endless series of *MAN* articles on rubber motor performance—articles that were so boring and so full of gratuitous mathematics that they drove almost every serious designer in America straight to gas. (These articles, later published as chapters in Grant's book *Model Aircraft Design,* were undoubtedly what 1938 Wakefield team member Henry Stiglmeier had in mind when he said, "Precise calculations constitute another procedure in the design of a model airplane on which one can waste much time.")

As *MAN* editor, Grant encouraged modelers all over the world to submit photos of their latest ships to his "Air Ways" and "Gas Lines" columns. Then he'd print the photos, and anonymously critique each design. In this way he was able to repeat the basic principles of model aerodynamics over and over, month after month, until these principles became so well understood that an entire generation of model builders assumed this body of knowledge was genetic.

Hardly a month went by without a mini-lecture on one of his pet theories. His favorite was the "Law of Rotational Stability." Out of it grew the endless debates about the holiness of the Center of Lateral Area, or CLA. Proper placement of the CLA was supposed to prevent spiral dives. Charlie Grant invented the CLA, and not everybody thanked him for it.

With gas replacing rubber during the mid-thirties, the spiral dive had become the nemesis of free flight. Longitudinal stability was something people could deal with (*move the wing back when she stalls, move it forward when she dives.*) But lateral stability was something else. The spiral dive— its causes and cures—was a total mystery. Sometimes your perfectly docile free flight, veteran of dozens of successful hops, would suddenly go berserk and spin in. Was it a wind gust? A bad launch? A loose fin? A curse from on high?

Once a gassie tightened up into one of these death spirals, it seldom recovered—even if the motor quit before impact.

According to Grant, the cure was simple. In order to balance the projected side area of wing and rudder, you needed to design your fuselage with lots of area below the "longitudinal axis of rotation," an imaginary line about which models are supposed to rotate when they decide to roll over and die. This imaginary line, or axis, runs by definition through the model's Center of Gravity. Ideally, it should run right down the crankshaft of the engine, as well. Line up the CG, the CLA and the thrust line, said Grant, and your troubles are over.

You could carry this CLA thing to extremes, of course. Then you wound up with a *Wedgy* or a *Zombie*, a couple of late thirties freeflights with fuselages shaped like Boston Red Sox pennants. But you didn't have to go that far. Just lay out a nice, conservative model according to Grant's dictums, and what you're likely to wind up with is a high thrust line parasol.

Grant *liked* high thrust line parasols. They looked like some of the full-scale lightplanes of the era—the Corben *Ace,* say, or the Pietenpol *Air Camper.* They looked like his own *K-G Gassie.* In short, they looked like *airplanes.* Charlie Grant never outgrew the need for models—serious models—to look like full-scale airplanes.

The Law of Rotational Stability. It was a good and useful theory. It led an entire generation of modelers across the deep and treacherous chasm between rubber and gas. If it did nothing else, it taught them that the vertical fins on rubber models were far too big for gas models, and ought to be cut down.

There was only one real problem with Grant's Law of Rotational Stability, and it didn't show up until the summer of 1938. It was called the *Zipper.* The *Zipper* was a totally new type of freeflight, designed by a former indoor flier named Goldberg. It had a very low thrust line (dangerous!) and a very high CLA (unadvisable!) and yet it climbed faster and floated longer and handled more power than anything before it. On a thirty second engine run, the Zipper beat everything else hands down.

Comet—Goldberg's employer, and the company that kitted both the Zipper and its little brother the *Mercury*—didn't let Charlie off the hook easily. Not even in his own magazine. In a December 1939 ad, Comet declared:

If they want to create something as good or better than the Zipper,
they must forget old theories and concentrate on new ones.

What old theories? Whose old theories? Comet didn't say. But in 1939 there was only one old theorist.

After freeflight 'went pylon,' after it became strictly a power game, cutting its ties with full-scale planes forever, Grant lost much of his enthusiasm for it. He slipped quietly out of the model scene during World War II, and when he returned, he returned to the basics: stick-fuselage rubber jobs that taught kids the hows and whys of aerodynamics. Despite the fact that fullscale aviation had treated him indifferently, Grant never lost his belief in the value of an aviation education for America's youth. And he never lost—right up until his death in 1987—his love for simple things that ride the invisible air.

By the time Grant died the hobby had changed utterly, and only the hard core of lifers still recognized his name. It was time for him to go. He had lost some of his crustiness, and was even heard, once or twice, to joke about his CLA theories. ("I got them to thinking, didn't I?" he'd say with a sly grin.) To people who didn't know Grant well—to people who remembered him only as the short, fiery amateur boxer who once coldcocked a mouthy spectator at a *MAN*-sponsored contest—this seemed like an erosion of character.

As usual, it took Bill Winter to sum up, in a single sentence, Grant's contribution to our sport. "Model planes didn't fly," Winter said, "until Charlie told 'em to use bigger stabilizers."

Tony Grish was one of the Grish family of St. John, Indiana, producers of the most beautiful propellers of the fifties, the Tornado Plasticotes. Tony—along with brother Stan and golden-haired sister Theresa—was a hotshot competitor, especially in U-Control speed. (When Theresa married Orioles centerfielder Al Pilarczyk in the late fifties and quit flying, it just about broke everybody's heart.) Stan and Tony had been prewar freeflighters, responsible for a hundred or so ignition engines called the Tarzan .60. The brothers tinkered with plastic props as early as 1938, but it was orders from NACA-Langley during the war that put them solidly in the propeller business.

Bob Holland won the National Championship at the first Navy Nats (Olathe, 1948.) In '57, Holland's .049 *Hornet* hit 21,000 RPM on a Kaysun 5-1/4 x 3 plastic prop; "Sounds like other half-As on a flywheel!" people said. The *Hornet*, successor to the *Wasp*, was a great engine—still is—but that didn't keep the ever-expanding Cox line from crowding Holland and everybody else out of the small-engine business during the post-Sputnik doldrums of the early sixties.

Hi Johnson designed the semi-scale Spitfire stunter that Dennis Alford flew (with a Johnson .32 in the nose) at the '59 Nats—the model Bill Dean called "the best looking stunt entry of the contest." He also designed a full line of Kenhi ukies, to match, model for model, Veco's 'Indian' line (*Papoose, Squaw, Chief, Brave, Warrior.*) And also the worst-selling model airplane kit in history, a pretty cabin R/C called the Kenhi *Buzzard* (250 manufactured, 200 sent to the incinerator when Kenhi folded.)

Hi was a genuine aero engineer—graduated from Cal Poly during the Depression—but he chose to stay with his first love, models, throughout most of his life. He worked for Gil Henry at Veco after the war; became the working half of Kenhi Models; and later owned Dynamic and Hi Johnson Models outright. Hi almost died back in the forties, in the Northrop flying wing crash that killed Richard DuPont. Fullscale finally claimed him when he pulled the wings off a sailplane in 1981. I hated that; Hi Johnson was both loveable and modest, two rare commodities in the San Fernando Valley.

Dale Kirn, the father of 1/2-A proto speed, won Senior flying scale at both the '49 and '50 Nats, and anyone who saw him handle that beautiful B-25 in the Dallas wind knew he earned the trophy. In 1956 he toured the country demonstrating Monoline for Victor Stanzel, flying 1/2-A models with aplomb on a *fifty-foot* line. It was nifty, and ten years earlier it might have set the sport-flying world afire; but controlline, like the rest of modeling, was already on the wane by '56.

Ed Lidgard is a rubber modeler par excellence, designer the Comet *Sparky*, which everyone, even my wife, has built. Ed can wind more power into a rubber motor than anyone else alive. Watching his models climb is simply *frightening*—there's no other word for it.

Gordon Light (b. 1915) won the American-sponsored 1932 Wakefield event with a flight of 25:53, but the contest was afterward declared unofficial by the Brits on a technicality. The next year his model, proxy-flown in England by rubber expert J.E. Pelly-Fry, outflew everything else, but was trimmed for circles, while the rules perversely required a *straight flight* for qualifying. (Pelly-Fry declared that Light had been cheated twice in a row.) The following year, however, Light won beyond question.

None of this ever appeared in Light's numerous magazine columns—"The Model Workshop" and "Dope Can" in the prewar *Air Trails*, and "With Model Builders" in the early *Flying Models*—all of which were thoughtful and even-handed and invariably light-hearted.

Howard "Everything Under Control" **McEntee** lead a whole generation of beginning R/Cers through the treacherous fifties. He made his living chiefly by freelancing, writing every day about the things he loved most—primarily ham radio and model airplanes—and thus turning his hobbies into his life work. Toward the end he regretted this. "I don't have a hobby any more," he mourned.

Claude McCullough was an avid free flighter who took up U-Control after seeing Walker demonstrate his *Fireball* at the '41 Nats. For some reason, this led him into R/C. For years he refused to build R/C models that looked like anything anyone ever saw before. Then the scale bug bit, and he still hasn't recovered.

Walt Mooney (1926-1990) was, in the words of his friend and flying buddy Bill Hannan, "probably the most productive designer of model airplanes in the United States, if not the world." Half-A sport and scale was his focus in the fifties, but he's best known for the dozens of 'peanut scale' (13" span) models he published—one per month—in *Model Builder*.

Frank Nekimken was one of the founders of the Chicago Aeronuts, and a partner with Gerry Ritzenhaler in producing those beautiful Ritz gas props of the thirties (some of which were folders!) Frank was high up in the Chicago Parks Department before the war, and sparkplugged the '40 and '41 Chicago Nats. Later he worked his way into American Legion headquarters in Indianapolis, and, *lo!* the Legion became a great postwar sponsor of aeromodeling.

Gerry Nelson, whose father designed the full-scale *Hummingbird* glider with the retractable engine, has been ahead of the curve in every R/C field he tackles. Jim Walker dreamed of Goodyear races in '49, but in the late fifties Gerry actually made them happen. In the sixties he helped found the U.S. soaring movement, then marketed a fiberglass sailplane that was twenty years ahead of its time. Now he's selling all-metal power models, so you can bet that the future lies that way.

Russ Nichols took over the AMA 'temporarily' when Al Lewis was drafted in '42. With some assistance, mostly from Carl Wheeley and Billie Fritchey, he kept it alive until '63, when Worth took over. Thank you, Russ!

Joe Ott (1900-1986) got his start as model editor for *Popular Aviation* during the early thirties. In partnership with the Whitman Publishing Company and yo-yo king Donald Duncan, he began a kitting business, and by 1936 he was turning out 30,000 kits a day. He supported the magazines throughout the war with huge ads for scale warbirds built with "Ott-O-Former" and "Ott-O-Tube" construction, but the postwar doldrums put him out of business.

Nathan and Irwin Polk are a pair of 'demon modelers' of the thirties who virtually put the east coast on the modeling map. Irv started the Bamberger Aero Club in Newark, then turned it over to Nat so he could go to work for Lawrence Shaw to create the Junior Birdmen. In '35 they both quit to found Polk's Modelcraft Hobbies in NYC, America's second-oldest mail order shop. After that, they started the Metro Model League of New York, organized the first national trade show for model supplies, founded the Eastern States Championships, directed at least four Nationals, helped get the

AMA off the ground and then (in the late fifties) steered the Hobby Industry Association into supporting the Air Youth Championship program. Whenever a Nats was near collapse, the Polks saved it; whenever a team needed support, they were there. More heroes like Irv and Nat we could use.

Dan Pruss and his fellow Chicagoans in the S.O.A.R. club showed America how an R/C sailplane contest ought to go. From 1971 to 1976, the annual SOAR Nationals was THE glider bash on this continent. Soaring events at the AMA Nats (and even the much-touted LSF Tournaments) all took a back seat to SOAR, and SOAR's energy and leadership began with Dan. I never understood how that bunch of guys could be talked into busting tail for a week in the hot sun, year after year—until I was on an FAI team with Dan. I'm by nature a loner; I despise team spirit and groupthink and all cooperative action whatsoever. But I would have followed Dan Pruss to hell and back. He was a man.

Edward T. Packard, "The Modeler's Friend Since 1919," is the founder of Cleveland Model and Supply. He had a huge line of true-scale rubber models on the market by 1930, at which time he mounted a double-sized version of Cleveland's 22" *Travel Air Mystery Ship* on top of a four-cylinder Austin Bantam—the car itself was a kind of 3/4 scale copy of a Model A Tudor Sedan—and drove it (very slowly) around the country with a sign on the side that said *"Have You a Hobby? Why Not Build Model Airplanes?"* If you read the old mags, you'll find that Ed's name was Pachasa until the mid-fifties, when Packard Motors went defunct and he decided to carry on the grand tradition.

Bob Palmer is one of those unbeatable Los Angeles stuntmen of the late forties, a contemporary and flying buddy of 'Madman' Yates. In '48 Palmer injured his hand and had to knock off flying for awhile. When he got back in the circle, he found that the pull of an Orwick .65 was too painful, so he began designing .29 to .35 sized stunters. For the next thirty years, stunt fliers all over America followed his trend.

Percy Pierce built a series of twin pushers that began, about 1909, to smack the far wall (200' away) at the 66th Street Armory in NYC. This was the signal for the New York Aero Club to move outdoors. The move was to Oakwood Heights airport on Staten Island, where Pierce's friend and flying buddy Cecil Peoli met one Captain Baldwin, of airship fame. Baldwin taught Peoli to fly, took him to Europe as an exhibition pilot, and got him killed the following year in a *Red Devil* biplane. Pierce himself kept both feet on the ground, became model editor of *Aeronautics* and then general editor of *Fly*, and lived to the ripe old year of 1962.

John "Kingfish" Sadler was a middle-aged Arkansas businessman who, until 1934, considered himself the world's greatest fisherman. Then he bought a Cleveland profile rubber kit—and built it, just for a lark. Within a year he was winning local contests, and his fishing suffered. Low wingers fascinated Sadler: first rubber, then gas. His Dennymite-powered *Pacemaker* was published too late (January '40 *Air Trails*) to make a name for itself on the contest field—by then the fast-climbing pylon types owned the skies. After the war Sadler took up ukie speed, where he went to the top once again. Then R/C beckoned . . . .

Walt Schroder (1906-1990) married at forty and spent his honeymoon at a modeling trade show. He edited *MAN* from 1960 to 1979; before that he was associated with the production of the prewar Bantam engines and the postwar Mite diesels. His best-known designs are the *Jersey Javelin* freeflight, the *Dreamer* twin-boom ukie, and the *Windy Joe* R/C trainer—but what he'd prefer to be remembered for is his part in helping Bill Bennett organize the Tournament of Champions.

Armour Selley began flying models in 1909. He was a natural, and as soon as he made a name for himself he went into the model-supplies business in Brooklyn. After Lindy he began to advertise an excellent line of stick models, including a 30" tractor he called the *Gull*—as well as the *Heron* and the *Albatross*, a couple of class-act twin pushers.

In the early thirties, no doubt in response to what Mark Smith once called "the futility of the kitting business," Selley made a play for the mass market—the toy market—with a line of prefab flying scale kits molded from something he called "Selley-tex," a kind of cheesecloth impregnated with plaster of paris. Selly-tex killed his reputation. Duke Fox remembered those kits vividly: they stank. I never saw one, but I'll take Duke's word any day.

Leon Shulman is another of those magic guys from Brooklyn who can make anything fly. He spent the first part of his life designing and chasing freeflights (*Wedgy, Sky-scraper, Zomby, Banshee, Zoomer*), and the second part directing R/C contests all over the east. In between, he created the magnificent Drone diesel, and a ukie called the *Secret Weapon*, and also won rudder-only at the '57 Nats. Oh, yes—he had a hand in Top Flite's *J-3 Cub*, too. And he ain't done yet.

S. Calhoun Smith (1915-1964) designed every sort of model, and built them so lovingly they couldn't help but fly. Illustrations, cover art, editing— Cal did it all at one time or another, including a short stint as boss of *Flying Models* (1947-8.) He seldom competed, though he did win the first-ever Navy Carrier event, at the '50 Dallas Nats. But it was his R/C designs that keep him alive: the *Nieuport Bipe*, *Monocoupe*, *Wonderwings*, *Droop Snoot*, *Jersey Lightnin*—plus his lovely little *Blunderbus* sport free flight.

Bob Stalick flew his first gassie, a Berkeley *Bootstraps* with a Baby Spitfire, in the back field of his Oregon farm. It covered less than 100 feet before colliding with a barbed-wire fence, but he was hooked on models for life. He still flies freeflight—may never be cured.

Earl Stahl began modeling in the late twenties, when, in his words, "everyone was hacking out a *Spirit of St. Louis*." He made his name as a rubber scale designer during the thirties, then came out of retirement briefly with a lovely little .02-powered *Emeraude* lightplane in the April, 1960 *MAN*. Low wingers are Stahl's forte´.

Ted Strader makes my personal hero list for two reasons. First, he was a prolific designer of Sputnik-era freeflights and small radioplanes—*Snoopy*, *South Wind 10*, *Duet*, *Whirlwind*, *Gypsy*, *Miss L*, *Strutz Aircrate*, *Mister E*—just when I needed him. Second, he wrote (for the *Strutz*, October-November '61 *Flying Models*) the greatest launch-photo caption in R/C history: *"Off we go,"* it reads, *"into the turbulent, signal-jammed, vile grey yonder."* That was single channel in a nutshell.

Henry Struck is one of those rare all-around designers. Beginning with a combination rubber/gas job in the short-lived *Model Aircraft Builder* of 1936, he published over eighty—yep, 80!—models. Best known are his Berkeley kits: the *New Ruler* and *American Ace* and *Bootstraps*, the *Flying Cloud* Wakefield, the *Sinbad* gliders, the *Sea Cat* flying boat and all those 1/2-A scale jobs. My personal favorite: a 42" FF bipe called the *Skybuggy*.

Sal Taibi (b. 1920) was standing at a bandsaw cutting balsa for 'Berkeley' Bill Effinger in 1939; today he does the same thing for his son Mike—so what's new? In between, he designed more contest-winning freeflights—*Powerhouse*, *Pacer*, *Brooklyn Dodger*, *Spacer*, *Starduster*, to name a few—than anyone else, Goldberg included. The war made him a machinist and a Langley Field Brainbuster; the peace turned him into a Californian. Even today, you can judge the quality of a FF contest by Sal Taibi. If he's there, it's a good one.

Jim Walker (1904-1958) made his living from freeflight and controlline, and managed to keep R/C for a hobby—if a man of his energy could be said to have a hobby. (Doctors once told Jim to take up golf, but he was soon playing day and night and winning too many tournaments for his own good.)

Because he died three years after Cox broke the U-Control patents, some people like to say the lawsuit killed him. As well say Sputnik—launched five months before his death—killed him. When the air age was over, there was no reason for Jim Walker to go on living.

Carl Goldberg, who saw Jim come and go, and was no slouch of a character judge, had this to say of him: "He was much greater than most people realized."

Ken Willard's *CAVU* free flight design dates to the late 1930s. By the time he began his "Sunday Flier" column in *R/C Modeler* (September 1964) he had already published well over twenty models—most of them FF and small R/C—and seen at least ten of them kitted. He had also invented Babcock's 'kick-up' elevator, won Intermediate at the '59 Nats, pioneered indoor R/C, and flown a radio model from the mainland to Catalina Island.

Most designers have only one original shape in their head. Ken has two: a boxy, homely landplane and a boxy, pretty seaplane. Plus his *Top Dawg* midwinger. Sure, he puts the same wings and stabs on everything—but he's still miles ahead of most of us in originality.

Bill Winter (b. 1912) has two loves, modeling and fullscale flying, in that order. He's a born editor in both fields. He knows instinctively that an editor is Head Cheerleader, and that cheerleaders sometimes run out of steam. When that would happen in one field, Bill would switch to the other.

The problem was, the two fields weren't mutually supportive. Model mags have always carried fullscale material, but the fullscale mags, after WW II, quit reciprocating. So whenever Bill was editing a model mag, he could keep his hand in fullscale; but when he was doing fullscale, he'd get lonesome for models. This worked to our benefit, because he wound up spending most of his time with us.

No one else in all of modeling history has had Bill Winter's eye for the big picture. He's our chief philosopher-historian, and when he retired from regular writing the hobby lost an irreplaceable voice.

John Worth (b. 1924) took over as Executive Director of an ailing AMA in 1964. Within four years he had beefed up the organization's liability program and given it a public voice—*American Aircraft Modeler*. Result: membership started to climb, and the number of chartered clubs jumped from 120 to 450. He retired in '91, having created the modern AMA. There are periods in the life of every democracy when it needs a dictator at the top. John was a good one.

C.O. Wright (1896-1980) of Topeka was the sixth president of the AMA; he built models before serving in WW I, then returned to the hobby in the thirties and never dropped out again. C.O. loved helicopters and delicate freeflight scale jobs, and he wasn't afraid to fly them in the wind—Bill

Hannan quotes him as saying, "If you can build 'em in the first place, you can always repair them."

Frank Zaic (b. 1912) is the technical historian of American aeromodeling. His ten *Yearbooks*, beginning in '33 and covering most of the years up to 1965, were pure labors of love, full of up-to-the-minute theory and meticulous three-views. (Frank is, among other things, a qualified patent draftsman.) Every one of those *Yearbooks* is still in print—forming a marvelous record of model aircraft evolution through the pre- and postwar years.

Ω

Well, there you are! I've run out of book long before I ran out of modelers. So here, with apologies, are some of the rest of the Clan—good people all, who should have made it into the main text, but didn't:

Art Adamisin (and most of his family: Archie I and II, Alan, David, Dennis and Marie), Jack Albrecht, Fred Angel, Randy Archer, Bud Atkinson, Clyde Austin, Ernie Babcock, Bill Baker, Cezar Banks, Rogers Barton, Plenny Bates, Kit Bays, Pete Bechtel, Bob Benjamin, Leon Bennett, Royal Benson, Phil Bernhart, Jesse Bieberman, Walt Billett, J. Broadfield Billings, Bill Blanchard, Bill Bogart, Dick Branster, Joe Bridi, Dario Brishigella, Hardy Broderson, John Brown, Don Burnham, Bill and Charlie Cannon, Ken Cashion, Mike Charles, Frank Chastler, Bill Chenault, Stan Chilton, Scott Christensen, Hobie Clay, Vern Clements, Herb Clukey, Hal Cover, Louis Culler, Dixie Cutrone, Frank and Joe Dallaire, Ted Davey, Bob Dodgson, Al Doig, Alex and John Drobschoff, Bill Dunwoody, Dick Ealy, Ralph Fidance, Larry Fogel, Bill Forrey, David Fortuna, Rae Fritz, Frank Garcher, Jerry Gause, Walt and Ray Ghio, Bill and Annie Giesking, Sherman Gillespie, Lew Gitlow, Harold Goldclank, Phil Granderson, Mike Granieri, Jim Gray, Mike Gretz, Jim Grier, Ted Grzesczak, John Gunsalles, Cecil Haga, Bob Haight, Jack Hamilton, Dick Hanson, Carl Hatrak, Bob Hatschek, Clarence Haught, Dave Haught, Mike Hazel, Jack Headley, Ray Heit, Al Hellman, Steve Helms, Harry Higley, Gil Horstman, Wendell and Ray Hostetler, Tom Hutchinson, Bob Isaacson, Tony Italiano, Ed Izzo, Roger Jaffe, Don Jehlick, Art Johnson, Caldwell Johnson, Dick Johnson, Helmer

Johnson, Ken Johnson, Jim and Larry Jolly, Doug Joyce, Matt Kania, Dave Katagiri, Herb Kelly, Bill Kessler, Aubrey Kochman, Vern Kreibel, Larry Kruse, Jed Kusik, Hubert Lacey, Bill Langenberg, Bob Larsh, Tom Laurie, Clarence Lee, Fred Lehmberg, Al Lidberg, Paul Lindberg, Bob Lien, Rich Lopez, Jack Luken, Dan Lutz, Frank Macy, Christy Magrath, Lou Mahieu, Roy Marquardt, John 'Doc' Martin, Billy Maxwell, Jack McCracken, Tom McClaughlin, Paul McIlrath, Bill Melton, John Merrill, Bob Meuser, Laddie Mikulasko, Bob Miller, Richard Miller, Dick Modlr, Conley P. Moody, Royall Moore, Eddie Morgan, Owen Morris, Tom Mountjoy, Walt Moucha, Fritz Mueller, Harry Murphy, Will Nakashima, Bill Noonan, Bob Novack, Dick Odle, John Oldenkamp, Vern Oldershaw, Bob Oslan, Paul Palanek, Bill Pardue, Les Pardue, Bob Parker, Dan Parsons, Dave Peltz, John Perry, Robin Pharis, W. Hewlitt Phillips, Mitch Poling, Fernando Ramos, Ocie Randall, Fred Randell, Jef Raskin, Dave Rees, Fred Reese, George Reich, Harold Reinhart, Larry Renger, Doris and Bob Rich, Stu Richmond, Dave Roeblen, Bill Roseberry, Roger Roth, Skip Ruff, Howard Rush, Daniel Lee Rutheford, Dan Santich, Dick Sarpolus, Paul Schaaf, Walt Schoonard, Bill Seidler, Dave Shadel, Keith Shaw, Jack Sheeks, Danny Sheelds, Phil Shew, Hazel Sigafoose, Paul Simon, Dick Sladeck, Bob Sliff, Ed Slobod, Tip Smiley, Charlie Smith, Russell Snyder, Pete Sotich, Wayne Spears, Glen Spickler, Don Srull, Jack Stafford, Tom Stark, Hobie Steele, George Steiner, Herb Stockton, Herk Stokely, Dave Stott, Bert Streigler, Dick Struhl, Art Suhr, Cliff Tacie, Barney Taft, Fudo Takagi, John Tatone, Jim Taylor, H.A. Thomas, Chuck Tracy, Al Tuttle, Bill Tyler, Bob Upton, Ron Van Putte, Dan Veronica, Charlie Vivell, Joe Wagner, Herb Wahl, Barnaby Wainfan, Paul Walker, Bucky Walter, Buzz Waltz, Bill Warner, Hans Weiss, Ted White, Nelson Whitman, Bob and Dolly Wischer, Harry Williamson, George Wilson, Chuck Wood, Ernie and Randy Wrisley, Ray Wriston, Dave Youngblood, Doris and Ed Yulke, Don Zipoy, Nick Ziroli.

index